CHASING PERFECT

CHASING PERFECT

THE WILL TO WIN

IN BASKETBALL

AND LIFE

BOB HURLEY

WITH DANIEL PAISNER

CROWN
ARCHETYPE
NEW YORK

Copyright © 2013 by Bob Hurley

All rights reserved.
Published in the United States by Crown Archetype,
an imprint of the Crown Publishing Group,
a division of Random House, Inc., New York.
www.crownpublishing.com

Crown Archetype with colophon is a trademark of Random House, Inc.

Library of Congress Cataloging-in-Publication data is available
upon request.

ISBN 978-0-307-98687-0
eISBN 978-0-307-98688-7

Printed in the United States of America

*Photograph on page 121 is courtesy of Peter Mecca. All other photographs are
courtesy of St. Anthony High School and the Hurley family.*

Jacket design by Michael Nagin
Jacket photography by Frank Longhitano

10 9 8 7 6 5 4 3 2 1

First Edition

To

SISTER MARY ALAN,

whose selflessness and dedication to the students of
St. Anthony High School inspired me in the years
we worked together.

CONTENTS

PERFECTION IS
NOT ATTAINABLE,
BUT IF WE CHASE
PERFECTION
WE CAN CATCH
EXCELLENCE.

—Vince Lombardi

HARD WORK

Monday, November 21, 2011

Unofficial first day of the season. In Jersey, like in most states, there are rules that tell us how often we can practice, and when. Used to be we could practice this week, leading up to Thanksgiving, but now we have to wait until the first Monday after the holiday. Now we can only work on our fitness, which is okay by me.

My teams, we're almost always the best-conditioned team on the floor. That's been my big thing. I've learned it's the one part of the game you can control as a high school basketball coach. You can have a bunch of big men one year, a bunch of sharp-shooting point guards the next year, or maybe it happens that a stud power forward gets tossed from the team for disciplinary reasons. But fitness is a constant. It doesn't change, one year to the next.

You can count on it.

I want my guys to be able to run the other team into the ground. Always. I want them to out-last, out-hustle, out-think their opponents, up and down the court. But these things only happen if your guys are in shape, if they're prepared. End of the game, I want to see the players on the other team gassed, hands on their hips, gasping for air. I want my guys to see it too. I want them to look for those moments, late, when they box out their man and he doesn't fight back. When they see their opponents bending over during a time-out. I want them to learn to spot all those little tells that might give us even the tiniest edge—psychological, physical—so we can turn it to advantage. I want them to learn to sniff out even the slightest whiff of weakness, so we can bury the other team when it counts. Doesn't mean we're always the fastest team. Doesn't mean we're always the most talented team. But we'll be in the best shape.

We don't get tired. And one of the main reasons we don't get tired, past couple years, has been Omar Jones, our team trainer. He knocks the tired from our guys before the season even starts. Like right now.

Omar's a St. Anthony alum, a former college football player. Now he's back at his high school alma mater, teaching health and phys ed, and he's got a lot of creative ideas on how to train these kids on a nothing budget, with bare-bones facilities. He works with them all year, and what I love about Omar is how he puts himself through the same paces. He's young, built like a football player, still in tremendous shape, and my guys respect that he's in there lifting right alongside them. Running. Doing crunches, squats, push-ups. Whatever Omar asks them to do, he's doing it himself, and the players really respond to that. They respect it. Same way I used to run the floor with my players when I was first starting out, when I could still keep up with them. It puts it out there that what we're asking them to do is no more than we'd do ourselves. That it's what the game deserves.

In the off-season, we encourage our players to work out on their own—running, mostly. Lifting, occasionally. Summers, it's hard to keep them to a real schedule, because everyone's off in a hundred directions. A lot of my guys will play on our summer team, but a few of them won't, so we try to give them a routine they can all follow. This way, they're all starting from the same place. Last week of August, Omar will get them back into the gym, lifting on Tuesdays and Thursdays. Then, before the season, we'll switch to Mondays, Wednesdays, and Fridays. Between workouts, they're supposed to run. And rest. That's a big part of what we expect from these kids. Some coaches, they only know how to push their players. They want them to be hard chargers at all times, in every way, but we expect them to listen to their bodies. To know that if we're running hard in practice once the season begins, they need to go home and put their feet up. They need to know what their bodies can take.

Today, though, we've hit a snag. A pipe burst over the weekend in our weight room, so we have to improvise. Already, we're improvising, because our weight room is just a converted storage area, off the school cafeteria. We cleaned it out a couple years ago, painted it, turned it into a makeshift auxiliary gym, with benches and free weights and pull-up bars. Nothing fancy. What the kids call "old school," which pretty much describes St. Anthony itself. Really, there's a lot you won't find in our weight room. No elliptical machines. No treadmills. No Nautilus equipment. No frills. Just a bunch of resistance bands and boxes for step-up drills, some floor mats, and whatever else Omar has been able to cobble together to allow him to do his thing, only now he has to get our guys to drag the equipment from the storage/weight room to the school cafeteria, which also doubles as the school's central meeting space, auditorium, main hallway, and locker area.

At some schools, space is so tight, administrators have to find multiple uses for all their facilities. At a tiny school like St. Anthony High School, with only 230 or so students, no gym, no grounds, no budget, we use every available inch of space, over and over. Even our bathrooms are pressed into multipurpose duty, doubling as locker rooms for our gym classes and athletic teams.

The shortage of space hits you full in the face at the end of the school day, on the changeover. Most of the kids are headed home or to some after-school activity, but our guys grab their gear, which they've stuffed into their lockers along with their books, and wait for the cafeteria/hub/hallway area to clear out. They chat with their friends, flirt with the girls on the cheerleading squad, maybe duck into the boys' bathroom to switch out of their school clothes. It takes awhile. The kids with no good place to go are in no particular hurry; the kids who play ball are happy to be distracted, because they know what's waiting for them once practice starts. Eventually, the square basement room thins, and it's just the guys on the team, waiting on me to tell them what to do.

Yeah, it's a little strange, the way we manage to compete at the highest levels of high school basketball despite such spartan, basic conditions. We're at a disadvantage, clearly, but somehow we've turned our have-not circumstances into a kind of edge. The contrast can be startling to our juniors and seniors. Every year we've got guys being recruited by some of the biggest, most storied programs in the country, with awesome facilities. These kids go off on their official visits, and they're wowed by gyms the size of football fields, by the fiberglass backboards, by the first-class locker and training rooms, the state-of-the-art equipment. Basically, by the way top college players are pampered and coddled.

But, really, it's not that strange at all. Our guys have gotten used to the St. Anthony deal. Even our upperclassmen, they consider our bare-bones facilities a point of pride, a badge of honor. Gives our team a kind of us-against-the-world mentality. We've taken a negative and turned it into a positive. How? Well,

just about every team we play has its own gym, a
real locker room, a real training room, so it's become
a great motivator for us. My guys, they never trash-
talk our own place. It's always clean, painted, and it's
the best we have. We do the best with it. But they'll
absolutely go to another team's gym and poke holes
in it, find something to diss. Like, they can step into a
weight room and see that the equipment is still brand-
new, like it's never been used. Like, you can step to the
rim and see there's dust on the backboards, because
they've hardly been touched. They see stuff like that,
and they're all over it.

Where we play, at the METS Charter School on
Ninth Street in Jersey City, a couple blocks from
St. Anthony, you'll see fingerprints all over the
backboards from the way my guys attack the boards.
The prints run all the way to the top of the box above
the rim. The guy who runs the facility for the city,
Bob Fosetta, Windexes the backboards every year just
before the state tournament, so it's like we're starting
with a clean slate, but you'd be amazed how many
gyms we've been in where there's a thick coating of
dust over the hoop. Tells us right away that team isn't
ready.

Like I said, it's our juniors and seniors who notice
the contrast most of all. On this year's team, we've
got senior Kyle Anderson, one of the top high school
players in the country, a six-eight swing-type player

who can handle the ball like Magic Johnson and
dominate down low. He just decided to go to UCLA.
We've got our center, Jimmy Hall, another senior,
headed off to Hofstra, and our other big man, Jerome
Frink, just back from a trip to Florida International,
where he's being recruited by former Knicks head coach
Isiah Thomas, where alumni and boosters have been
pouring a ton of money into the program. Josh Brown,
a junior, has signed a letter of intent to play at Temple
University, another first-rate basketball program. So
these kids have seen how the other half lives. They
know what we're missing.

And it's not just the recruiting visits that mark
the contrast. It's the games on our own schedule.
A lot of these kids played for us on last year's team,
as sophomores and juniors, when we won the state
championship at the RAC—the Rutgers University
Athletic Center—in front of five thousand people. Or,
when we went on to win the Tournament of Champions
at the Izod Center, in the Meadowlands, former home
of the New Jersey Nets. So they've played in some
big-time facilities.

Up and down our bench, it's much the same: we've
got Rashad Andrews, coming back from that team;
a six-five wingman from Queens, he's penciled in as
one of my starters. And Chris Regus, a talented guard
who played with us as a sophomore, along with the
promising Hallice Cooke, a terrific outside shooter who

figures to fill a lot of big minutes for us as a junior. So most of our guys have seen and tasted what it's like to play ball on a grand stage.

When we're in season, the way it works is we'll walk over to the charter school, where we rent gym time. It's where we play our home games too, but it's not our gym to do with as we please. We've got to watch the clock. We've got to make sure our freshman and junior varsity teams get their practices in, get their games in. We've got to make sure our girls' team gets the floor. When one session ends, there's another group waiting, so there's no time to goof off or procrastinate or even to get in any extra shooting work or run some new plays. Every minute matters.

But today we're in our own building—in the cafeteria, yeah, but at least we're on our own clock. The burst pipe means Omar has to get our guys to push all the cafeteria tables to the side and then haul in the weights and bands and heavy balls from the storage room. It's a workout in itself, but our guys don't seem to mind. They go at it hard. They pair off to toss the heavy ball back and forth, to spot each other while they press, to stretch. They get their heart rates going by running tiny laps around the small cafeteria. It's almost funny to watch, these big, lanky kids, some of them stretching to six feet, seven inches tall, six-eight, six-nine, going all out in such a cramped, tight space.

After twenty, thirty minutes, they're drenched in sweat, bone-tired, spent, but Omar's not done with them.

He's just getting started.

Just so happens that on this day we're being visited by two youth coaches from the Philippines. This alone isn't so unusual. Happens all the time that coaches stop by to check out what we're doing—foreign coaches, especially. They take a tour of the States, they try to see a professional game, a college game, a top-level high school game. What they really want to do is check out the practices, only it's not so easy on the professional and collegiate levels. Those practices are usually closed. But we're always getting calls from coaches who want to watch us practice, and we open our doors pretty wide.

First ten, fifteen years I coached, I had no idea this was even possible. Never even occurred to me to drop in on another team's practice session, although I wish it had. You can pick up a lot of drills, a lot of different approaches. It can be enormously helpful for a young coach, and so I'm usually happy to help out—only here, now, I must admit I'm a little embarrassed I don't have more to show these guys. They've come all this way, and all they get to see is a bunch of kids high-stepping around a multipurpose high school basement, using each other for resistance, motivation, support. Doing step-up drills on rickety cafeteria chairs. Bunching up for a team huddle, hands in, while Omar gets them to shout out "Hard work!" on the count of three—our rallying cry from last season.

It must seem absurd, from the perspective of these coaches from the Philippines, but to us it's the most natural thing in the world. It keeps us grounded. Plus, it's closer to what we're used to than the cathedrals of basketball you'll find at UCLA or Temple, or even at some of the richer parochial schools in our state. It's closer to who we are, I guess you could say. We're like the amateur boxers who train at some of the older gyms in Jersey City—places like Bufano's, where the sweat hangs in the air like it's been there forever and the seams in the mat in the ring are held together by tape.

So you'd think our players might be a little put out by the nothing-special surroundings, but that's not the case at all. In fact, I think it's just the opposite. I think they've come to embrace the history of St. Anthony basketball. The whole aura. The ways we have to practice, it's more in keeping with how they grew up. A lot of them come from one-parent households; they're scrambling, scraping to get by. They've been playing in tiny recreational gyms since they were kids. Outside, in the parks, with rusted-over backboards and chain-link nets . . . or no nets at all.

They're at home with how we play, because it's how they've always played. It's who they are.

PREGAME

What Winning Means

GOOD IS NOT ENOUGH IF BETTER IS POSSIBLE.
—*Unknown*

ONE LOSS IS GOOD FOR THE SOUL. TOO MANY
LOSSES IS NOT GOOD FOR THE COACH.
—*Knute Rockne*

This is a book about winning.

Mostly, it's a book about finding ways to win consistently, over time, but it's also about the constant search for winning moments in every part of our lives. It's about finding the right mix of purpose and preparation in all of our pursuits, so that we can call on just enough of each to help us accomplish our goals. And underneath all these things, it's also about how I came to build a life and a career coaching high school basketball in a tiny, rundown, underfunded parochial school in the toughest part of a tough city, with no gymnasium, no training facilities, and no real shot at any kind of long-haul success.

In sports, winning is usually measured at the end of a series, a tournament, a season. The idea is to push yourself as far as you can, to reach as high as you can, to play as fast and hard and smart as you can, to come away with whatever's on the line. A loss or a hiccup of some kind on the way to a championship is to be expected; in some cases, coaches even go looking for struggle along the way, so they can use it to motivate their players or redouble their focus.

In basketball, seasons are won or lost in practice. If you're fit, focused, and prepared, good things will happen. Games are won or lost with each possession. If you take care of the ball, find the open man, attack the boards, you'll put yourself in position to win, as long as you find a way to keep your opponent from doing the same things. In a high school game, there are hundreds of tiny battles that decide the outcome. Each battle is important. Each matchup, each switch on defense, each blocked shot . . . they all add up. Every move matters. Even the moves your players make off the court factor in. Each and every player, up and down the bench. The moves he makes in the classroom, the moves he makes at home, the ways he interacts with his friends.

A lot of high school coaches, they leave their players alone away from the gym, but I try to get in their heads. I try to instill a work ethic, a sense of pride, and hope it spills onto the floor during games. It's mostly about basketball, but it all ties in. I get on them about school, about family, about work if they happen to have a part-time job. Basically, I look to make the most of every opportunity. To practice hard, so we can play even harder. To remind my guys that the way they play on both sides of the ball is key, every possession. Stop the other team from scoring, and you'll win that one battle. Create good shots on your end of the floor, and you'll win that battle too. It's basic math: find a way to win more possessions than the other guy, and you'll win the game. Make positive choices away from the court and you're more likely to make positive choices in the run of play. Take care of your relationships—with your teammates, your coaches, your teachers, your parents—and your relationships will take care of you.

In every other sport, the idea is essentially the same. Put together enough good drives, possessions, touches, at-bats, rallies, whatever, and you're in strong shape. Allow the other team to win the bulk of these tiny battles, and you're weak, exposed. Doesn't get any more bottom line than that, and when I started out as a player, and even as a coach, this was the way I approached each game. Didn't matter if we were in a pickup game on the playground, or in a rec league game, or in a revenge-type game against a bitter collegiate rival. Over hundreds and hundreds of games, the idea was to help our guys put together more "good" possessions than the other guys. Didn't matter if we edged out the other team by a single basket, a single point, as long as we found a way to win the game.

So that was always the goal—to play well enough to win, even if it meant playing *just* well enough to win. After all, who really cares if you win on a last-second shot or going away? Who really cares if you're trailing at the end of the third quarter but find a way to battle back and come out on top? A win is a win.

Over a long season, the same principle applied. It was okay to lose a game or two, or even seven or eight, as long as you won more than you lost, and more than the other teams in your bracket, division, league, region. Don't get me wrong: I hate to lose. Always have, always will. But you could find a way to absorb each loss and maybe even learn from it. Over the long slog of a season, a couple losses here and there didn't much matter. If you could make it to the postseason or the elimination rounds of a championship tournament, it only mattered that you put yourself in position to win. It only mattered that you were playing well and that all of your players were coming together and working as a team. Like the 2011 New York Giants, on their way to Super Bowl XLVI. As I write this, it feels like the entire New York metropolitan area is still buzzing with the Giants' big win, but hardly anybody seems to care or even remember that the Giants were a mediocre 7–7 with just two weeks to go in the regular season. They'd gotten off to a promising start, and then lost a bunch of games, and in early December their won-loss record showed that they were as good as they were bad. At the time, few people in and around football thought they had anything but a long-shot chance to make it to the postseason, let alone the Super Bowl. But they won their final two games of the regular season, squeaked into the playoffs, and somehow managed to pick up steam along the way. Each week they got better, stronger, tougher to beat. And against those long-shot odds, they made it all the way to the Super Bowl, where it no longer mattered that they'd been 7–7. They belonged on that field in Indianapolis, on football's biggest stage, just as much as their opponents, the New England Patriots, belonged on that same field. Didn't matter how either team got there, just that they were there, and you could even make the point that the Giants were better prepared for the Super Bowl than the Patriots, simply because of everything they had to go through just to get there. It's like Tom Coughlin and his coaching staff had taken all of the team's midseason and late-season struggles and used them to motivate their players. To get them thinking they were a better team on the back of what they'd endured.

The idea, by every measure, is to come out ahead. That's all. Doesn't sound like much, but it's everything. And that's always been the way of it—in sports, at work, in life. To do just a little bit more, a little bit better. To make it to the next round. It's like that old joke about a group of guys, sitting around a campfire, talking about which one of them could outrun a bear. They went around the group, and all agreed that not a single one of them was faster than the full-grown bears who roamed those woods. But one guy in the group wasn't too worried about this. He liked his chances, in the unlikely event that a bear might show up and start chasing them. He turned to his buddies and said, "I don't have to be faster than the bear. I just have to be faster than all of you."

This was true enough. All this one guy had to do was outrun the guy next to him, and he'd make it to the next round; if another bear showed up the next day, our guy just had to outrun whoever was left. Again, it doesn't much matter if you come out ahead by a mile or a hair, just as long as you're ahead of the other guys in the pack running for their lives, same as you. And so, for the longest time, this was how I played and coached. As long as my team could find a way to get and keep ahead of the other team on the floor, the other teams competing with us in the standings, the other teams chasing the same title, we were doing okay. All we had to do was stay ahead of the field and worry about the bear later.

But then something happened to change my approach. I can't say for sure how or why it happened, but it happened. I didn't go looking for it, didn't even see it coming, but there it was. One day, middle of my first season as head coach of the boys' varsity basketball team at St. Anthony, losing even just one game seemed to suddenly matter. The slightest misstep seemed to suddenly matter. Winning big, instead of just winning at all, seemed to suddenly matter. Dominating, from wire to wire. Making a statement with every possession. Playing all out, all the time, without letup . . . these things seemed to matter more than ever before. To me. To my players. To a culture of St. Anthony basketball that seemed to spring up around our program. Without really realizing it, without really meaning for it to happen in just this way, our view of the game took on new shape, and I don't think it started with me. I don't think it started with my players either. There was just something in the air, in and around St. Anthony, left us feeling like we couldn't afford to lose. At all. Ever.

I don't know that this was a good thing or a bad thing, but I had to pay attention to it. I had to find a way to understand this shift and put it to work for us, to make sure we didn't start playing tight, tentative. Like we were afraid to lose instead of hungry to win.

Looking back, I can trace this shift in approach to the 1971–72 season, my last year as head coach of the junior varsity. We were undefeated that year, 20–0, and the talk among my players, away from the gym, was about not screwing up. The tone of all this talk was more about playing it safe than about putting it all out there. Nobody wanted to be on the floor for our first loss, which would happen eventually, of course. Nobody wanted to be the one responsible for making a bad pass at a crucial moment that might cost us the game, or a bad decision that could turn the momentum the other way, or even a stupid mistake off the court that kept him from suiting up and doing his part to help the team. There was a pressure to *not* lose, to *not* screw up, which was not at all what I wanted. That type of attitude can get a team into all kinds of trouble, and a coach who creates that type of pressure-packed atmosphere is setting his players up for a big fall.

But, like I said, it seemed to happen on its own.

The following year, I moved up to coach the varsity, along with a lot of my junior varsity players, and we carried that win-at-all-costs, win-at-all-times, pressure-packed mind-set with us. At the same time, we left the seeds of that type of thinking behind, so the younger kids who were rising up to the junior varsity for the first time began to think that way too. Remember, we had that long winning streak going, so the younger players now felt responsible for that, and all the weight that came with it. It fed on itself and became a part of our culture—again, not because it was something I'd drilled into my players, but because it had somehow found them, me, us. Soon, it reached all the way down to our freshman players, and even to the little kids in town who hoped to one day play for the St. Anthony Friars, where winning was now first and foremost and above all.

Jump ahead forty years, and you'll still find that mind-set in our hallways at school. You'll still hear little kids on the Jersey City playgrounds, in our summer leagues and youth programs, talking about what it means to play for St. Anthony. You'll still get it from those kids on my first few varsity teams, now pushing sixty, who move about our gym during home games like local legends, because they never lost and they set a kind of gold standard for the way the St. Anthony Friars should play. (They're grandparents, some of them, and here I am, still thinking of them as kids.) You'll feel it in the air and all around as our players get together each year on the Friday after Thanksgiving, which back then always marked our first official practice of the season. Only now, all this time later, I think I've finally figured out how to harness that approach and leave my players thinking that they *deserve* to win each and every game instead of just *expecting* to win each and every game. There's a difference. There's a difference in the way your players carry themselves when they deserve to win. When they prepare to win. When they stop going through the motions and hoping for the best and start doing everything in their power to ensure that they're the best.

This book is about that difference. It's about finding the will to win and putting it into play, and knowing that in order to achieve excellence you must first decide to pursue excellence. Success is not something that happens to you, I sometimes tell my players. *You* happen to *it*. That's an old line, not original to me, but it's worth repeating. (By the way, a lot of the quotes and aphorisms I share with my players are not original to me, but they're worth repeating—so I repeat them into the ground.) Nobody sets out to pitch a perfect game, or bowl 300, or drive a golf ball from the back tees for a hole-in-one. No team ever sets out to record a perfect season. But these things happen from time to time, and each time they do you'll find an athlete or a group of athletes who have fully prepared for these things to happen.

They've been preparing for them all along.

1.

A Sense of Where You're Going

LIFE IS A UNITED EFFORT OF MANY.
—*John Wooden*

I TELL KIDS TO PURSUE THEIR BASKETBALL DREAMS, BUT
I TELL THEM TO NOT LET THAT BE THEIR ONLY DREAM.
—*Kareem Abdul-Jabbar*

I don't have a first basketball memory. There was always basket-ball, going back as far as I know. Where I grew up, in Jersey City, it was our whole world. Wasn't just basketball. We played all kinds of ball, but basketball was what stuck, what mattered. Now that I think back on it, there was always a basketball nearby. In my hands. On my bed. Under the kitchen table. That's one of the great things about basketball. Doesn't take much to work on your game. Football, baseball, you need someone else to play with, even if it's just someone to throw to. But with basketball, all you need is to grab your ball and play. Don't even need a hoop. Just a ball and a little bit of imagination.

I played a ton of street basketball as a kid. Soon as I was big enough to reach the basket, I found a way to get into the game—and there was always a game. On some courts, there'd be better, bigger games than on others, and our thing was to always find the best game. Sometimes that meant waiting a good long while until our turn came around, and when that happened you can bet we didn't want to lose. The rule of the streets where I grew up was the same as anywhere else: if you won, you kept playing; if you lost, you'd have to slink back in line and wait your turn all over again. So, yeah, we played to win. And it wasn't just about winning. You had to do it against real competition. You had to push yourself. Otherwise, what was the point?

The first real game I ever played was against the Jersey City Boys' Club, when our St. Paul's CYO team came to play against the Boys' Club house team. To me, it was like suiting up in Madison Square Garden. It was December 1960. I remember the year because it was just before high school. I was thirteen years old, and it's like it was yesterday. I can still hear the referee's whistle. I don't think I ever played in a game with a referee before this one, and just about every time I heard that whistle it was for me. Why? Because I didn't know the three-second rule. Most of the courts I played on didn't even have a three-second lane—just a faded-over hash mark for a foul line—so how the hell was I supposed to know you couldn't clog the lane and wait for something good to happen? Some games, when we had a height advantage, this was our whole damn strategy, and here I was learning on the fly that it was a violation. My coach kept yelling at me, "Three seconds! Three seconds!" At first, I didn't know what he was talking about, but I figured it out soon enough. I was a quick study—but not so quick the ref didn't string me up a bunch of times. Third or fourth whistle, I stopped counting, but then I got the hang of it.

Okay, Hurley. Can't park yourself in the paint. Gotta keep moving. . . .

There was a lot I didn't know, going into that first grammar school season. Oh man, I was awful . . . but I got better as I went along. Our coach was a guy named Charlie Shaughnessy, and I liked him a whole lot. He was a young guy from the neighborhood, just out of college, and he couldn't have been nicer or more patient with us. I wasn't the only one who didn't know the real rules of the game, but Charlie broke it down and made it something we could get our heads around. He had a kind demeanor, and he was fun to be around, but at the same time he had our full attention. He commanded respect, and we were happy to give it to him.

By the end of the season he could see I was a player—or at least that I was serious about being a player. Wasn't there yet, but I guess I was on my way. He could see the game meant something to me, so he took me aside after our final game and gave it to me straight. He said, "Hurley, if you want to make the freshman team, you've got to work on your left hand."

I was planning to go to St. Peter's Prep, which had a very strong basketball program. Charlie knew that I was hoping to play ball there, and he knew what it would take, so I appreciated the advice. I didn't hear it as a knock on my game, just a way I could lift myself up and take my game to the next level. Something to work on over the summer, to get ready for the season, and it really rang in my head.

This goes back to what I always loved about the game of basketball, because I could take those words from a guy like Charlie Shaughnessy and do something about them. I could take my ball and go to the park or the rec gyms and just play, nonstop. I could dribble that ball up and down the street with my left hand all day long. I could sit with it on the couch in the living room and pass it back and forth between my hands, just to get a good, consistent feel, an easy handle. The only thing that could stop me was . . . well, *me*. If I wanted it, all I had to do was reach for it, commit to it. And it's not like I was going it alone. Finally, after all those years playing ball and not really knowing what I was doing, I had a coach give me some direction—and I took that direction and ran with it. I spent every single day of that summer playing ball, working on my left hand—usually in the playground on my street, or in the courtyard behind St. Paul's, where there was a constant game going. I'd grab my ball and head out to this or that court, dribbling the whole way there, always with my left hand. If you ran into me that summer, chances ran good to great I had a ball in my hands. Every day I played at least three hours. Sometimes a whole lot more. The only days I missed were when we went away for a week to Long Beach Island, for a family vacation on the Jersey shore, but even then I took my ball and found a place to play, and the whole time Charlie's words were ringing in my head: "You've got to work on your left hand."

So that's what I did. I worked and worked and worked. I did everything I could imagine to strengthen my left hand, to make it as comfortable on the ball as my right hand, my natural hand. It got to where I couldn't tell one from the other. They were just on different sides. Whatever it was I needed to do on the court— dribble, shoot, pass—I could do it just as well with my left hand as my right, and I showed up at St. Peter's for our preseason workouts thinking I'd put myself in good position to catch the coach's attention. It's not like he was about to marvel at my height. In ninth grade, I was only about five-four. That's nothing for a basketball player—nothing to get you noticed anyway. That's why Charlie put it in my head to work on my left hand, because when you're five-four you've got to be strong on the dribble, from both sides. You've got to be able to handle the ball in a way the coach can notice and appreciate. There were a hundred kids trying out for that freshman team, so if I went in there and announced my limitations, I'd get cut.

During tryouts, the freshman coach came up to me and paid me the biggest compliment I'd ever hear as a player. His name was Damian Halligan, and he'd found something to like in my game enough to seek me out. He came over to me and said, "You a righty or a lefty?"

Those words were like magic, and it was the first time I realized the impact a coach could have on a player. Over the years the situation would flip and I'd be on the other side of the conversation, but here I was on the receiving end. Before this, I didn't really have a clue what it meant to coach a kid, other than to set plays or make defensive assignments or bark out instructions from the sidelines. But here I'd taken the advice of a man I liked and admired and resolved to act on it. Here I'd gone from a kid who loved basketball, same as I loved every other sport, to a kid with purpose and motivation to make myself a player. Not just a kid who played, but a *player,* and it was all on the back of Charlie Shaughnessy's push. He knew I looked up to him. He knew I'd listen to what he had to say.

And I did. Thank God, I did.

But then I went and grew that push into something else. Something bigger. It didn't happen right away, but it got me thinking about the game in a whole new way. It got me to set aside all those other sports and concentrate on basketball. And most important, it got me to appreciate the positive influence a good coach could bring to a young player. Like I said, I was a late grower, but it wasn't just in terms of height. I was late to mature as a player, basically because I was late to taking the game seriously, to taking *myself* seriously, and it's only now I'm realizing that the kids I've enjoyed working with the most over the years have been the ones who were most like me. The ones who came late to the game. The ones who are open enough to believe you when you tell them their bodies will catch up to them, or that if they work on something it'll change their game. And I can say this to them with authority, from a place of experience, because that's how it was with me. You can have all the natural ability in the world, but if you don't know what to do with it you're nowhere. If you're not willing to work at it, you're nowhere.

When it comes down to it, every time, I'll take the hardworking, dedicated, motivated kid who's managed through sweat and effort to string together some good grades, even though he might struggle or freeze up on his SATs, over the kid with the perfect SAT scores and the spotty transcript. I'm a big fan of the person who grinds it out every day over the person with all kinds of God-given talent who can't keep it together or harness his natural ability because he doesn't have the drive or the discipline. Without drive or discipline, where the hell are you? You're nowhere.

Basketball's like anything else. You get back what you put into it. Only, with basketball, with five guys working toward the same goal, what you get back can be everything.

You have to realize, up until that first season playing for Charlie Shaughnessy when I was thirteen years old, I had no real hopes or goals or dreams. I was just a kid playing ball. If I'd thought about it at all, I would have probably said I wanted to be a baseball player, but only because baseball came a bit easier back then. Only because it didn't much matter if I was on the short side, like it did on the court. But I wasn't really thinking along these lines just yet. Wasn't in any kind of hurry. The world I grew up in was very simple. My father was a cop. My mother was a nurse. I didn't know what my life would look like in five years, ten years, twenty years . . . whenever. I liked school, but I liked sports even more, and now, with this one push from Charlie, I was turning from baseball to basketball. I was starting to see that with a little bit of focus and direction I could change the direction of my life—at least a little bit. At least for now.

Four years later, I was still in Jersey City, still at St. Peter's, only now I was at St. Peter's College. St. Peter's Prep was downtown, but St. Peter's College was up in Journal Square. They're both Jesuit schools, but they're only loosely affiliated, so it's not like you graduate from one and everyone assumes you'll go to the other. They're two distinct institutions, and at the time St. Peter's College had one of the best basketball programs in the area, so it felt to me like a good next move.

I was the oldest of four siblings, so I wasn't too thrilled about the idea of moving away from home. Folks who know me will tell you I'm a family-oriented guy, so I guess you could say I didn't want to miss out. Jersey City was just fine with me, and when the St. Peter's coach let me know I'd have a shot to make his team, I set my sights there. It was a long shot, mind you, but it was a shot, and I figured I'd take it, and in my head it was like I was thirteen all over again, working my left hand to match my right.

Freshman year, I went into the season in the best shape of my life. I was "dialed in." That's a phrase you hear now all the time, but back then we were just "good and ready." I ended up averaging almost twenty points a game for the freshman team, which was a big number, but then the realities of college basketball began to set in. This was key, because I didn't have a basketball scholarship. I went to St. Peter's on what was known as a New Jersey State Scholarship, which meant that after that one season I'd be competing for a spot on the varsity with a bunch of other guards with full athletic scholarships. The coach would have to cut one of those guys to make room for me, so that was the long-shot part of the deal. I didn't know it just yet, but that wasn't about to happen, even with my twenty points a game. I was banging my head against the wall, with no hope of busting through to the other side.

Plus, that St. Peter's team was the best team the school ever had. That team would go on to beat Duke in the National Invitation Tournament, back when the NIT was a big-time tournament. A lot of folks don't remember this, but in those days it seemed like the National Collegiate Athletic Association tournament changed its format every couple years. It went from eight teams to sixteen teams to anywhere from twenty-two to twenty-five teams. That's where the NCAA tournament was when I started paying attention. Prior to 1975, only one team per conference was invited to the tournament, which meant that if you were the second-place team in the Atlantic Coast Conference (ACC) one year, like Duke was that year, you weren't going to any Big Dance. (And by the way, if you'd called it a Big Dance in those days, people would have looked at you funny.) All those years, when UCLA was the team to beat in the Pac-10, USC had some great teams that were shut out of the tournament, so a lot of those strong teams ended up playing in the NIT.

So that's the kind of team I was trying to make—a guard-heavy team that would go on to knock off a Top Ten–type program like Duke in a big-time postseason tournament.

Man, I couldn't crack that team for trying.

All that summer of 1966, heading into my sophomore year, I worked my tail off. It was around that time that I read that great John McPhee book about Bill Bradley, *A Sense of Where You Are*. It felt to me like everyone I knew was reading that book—to this day, it's still one of the best, most thoughtful books ever written about the game, but at the time it was a great big deal because Bill

Bradley was a great big deal. If you were a kid from Jersey, playing ball, you looked up to Bill Bradley. He'd just graduated from Princeton, where he'd been one of the top players in the country, and it was such a thrill to watch him play. His game was all about hard work and dedication and out-thinking your opponent. He wasn't especially tall or fast or quick, but he was a lights-out shooter with an uncanny ability to put himself in the right place at the right time. Whatever was going on out there on the court, the game seemed to come to him—and to a short white kid struggling to latch on to a good college team, he was just about the perfect role model.

There was a paragraph in that Bradley book that really registered. I still think about it whenever a game goes a certain way. The author, who'd also gone to Princeton, was talking about a no-look, over-the-shoulder shot that had become one of Bradley's trademarks. He'd copied it from Oscar Robertson and Jerry West, the book said. Bradley explained that after you'd played the game as long as he had, after you'd logged enough time on the court, you didn't need to look at the basket. He said, "You develop a sense of where you are." That's where the author got the title.

I thought about Bradley's approach a whole lot that summer, trying to work myself onto that St. Peter's team. I thought about all the hours I'd put in, on all those courts, all around Jersey City, developing my own sense of where I was on a basketball court. And the thing of it was, no matter how many times I might have flipped the ball over my shoulder with my back to the basket, it would have only gone in every once in a while, only because of sheer dumb luck. I wasn't Bill Bradley. I wasn't that kind of player. The game didn't always come to me, much as I might have wanted it to. I was more of an eyes-open, looking-ahead kind of player, which was fine. You've got to play to your strengths, right? And one of my strengths was being able to see the floor, and watch the game develop, and find a way to fit myself into it that would help my team.

A sense of where I was? I guess, but with me it was more about playing with a sense of where I was headed—and the phrase applied to my time on the court and my life outside the gym as well. I was starting to think about what I might do for a career, just as I was beginning to realize that if a spot on the St. Peter's varsity wasn't even certain, a spot on an NBA roster was probably out of reach. So I had to think of something else. Didn't necessarily mean I had the first idea what that something else might be, only that I had to start thinking about it.

Meanwhile, there was my sophomore season to worry about, and there was a real turning-point moment for me in preseason, during a scrimmage against a team from the Eastern League, which in those days was just a notch below the NBA. At that time, the NBA only had ten teams, and the ABA was still a year away, so the caliber of these Eastern League players was good enough to make it to the pros today, and somehow we managed to play these guys tough. Somehow I was able to hang in there for a quarter and make an impression.

This was just before the St. Peter's coaches were making their final cuts, and going into the game I talked to our assistant coach, Mark Binstein, who'd always been very supportive. He didn't exactly have the ear of the head coach, Don Kennedy, but he knew what Coach Kennedy was looking for. Mark took me aside and said, "The way to impress the coach is to go out there and be aggressive. He sees you playing hard, he sees that you can do certain things out there, he's gonna keep that in mind."

Here again, I took a coach's advice and ran with it. I ended up scoring ten points in just one quarter—but that wasn't enough.

I wasn't dominant, or anything, even though I'd certainly managed to put my stamp on the game against first-rate players who
just a year or two later would have been playing some kind of
pro ball. Truth was, I don't know that there was anything I could
have done out there on the floor that day that would have earned
me a spot on that St. Peter's team because there was just no room
for me. I should have seen it coming, and now that it was here, I
should have done something about it, but all I could do was set my
disappointment aside and move on.

What I should have done was transfer. You see a kind of log-
jam blocking your path, and if you can't get past it, you look for
another opportunity. Happens all the time these days. A player
reaches a certain point, in a certain program, and he sees there
are a bunch of guards ahead of him on a coach's depth chart, so
he finds a situation where a coach might be looking for someone
to play point. It's not about going to a better school and a bigger
program, or a lesser school and a smaller program. It's about fit-
ting yourself in, finding a place to play. But nobody thought that
way back then. Nobody was advising me the way I try to do now
for my players. You want to see young players in a positive place
where they can make a contribution and find an opportunity to
improve, but players didn't have coaches and mentors looking out
for them the way they do today.

So what did I do? Well, I kept playing, wherever I could. I
found leagues, games . . . anything to keep me in shape. It was
frustrating not being a part of a competitive program, but I never
lost my love of the game or my desire to play it at the highest levels
available to me. I was drawn to the basketball court, for whatever reason. I felt at home there, most like myself, and at some
point in the middle of all these games and scrimmages and rec
league schedules I started to think about coaching. In some ways

I'd always thought about it, in a back-of-my-mind sort of way, but now I put it front and center. The year before, during my freshman season, my brother Brian had asked me to help coach his youth team. The head coach, Mr. Newcomb, was a fireman, and he couldn't get to practice one day, so Brian asked if I'd run the session so they wouldn't have to cancel. I was happy to do it, and the kids knew me from the neighborhood and seemed to like having me around, so whenever Mr. Newcomb couldn't make it, I'd fill in for him. That's all it was at first. I wasn't there in any kind of official capacity; I was just helping out. After a while, I started showing up at games. I knew a lot of the kids already because they were my brother's friends, but they were thirteen years old, and they knew I was a college player, so they thought I had something to teach them.

Now that I'd been cut from St. Peter's, I started thinking more and more about coaching, and somewhere in the middle of all this thinking and figuring I got an opportunity to coach the freshman team at St. Anthony High School. It was just a part-time gig—heck, I was still in college!—and I hadn't exactly gone looking for it, but I grabbed it before the folks at St. Anthony had a chance to change their minds.

First game I ever coached was in December 1967, against Don Bosco. Now, a lot of people around the country have heard the name Don Bosco because of the powerful Don Bosco Prep football program in Ramsey, New Jersey. This was a different school—Don Bosco Tech in Paterson, New Jersey. The basketball program at Don Bosco Tech wasn't quite at the powerhouse level of the Don Bosco Prep football program, but they always had good, competitive teams. Going up against them, it felt like the start of something. I remember stepping to our bench just before tip-off and looking at my kids. A part of me couldn't believe that they were now looking to me to jump-start their school basketball careers. I was just a kid myself, still fresh from my disappointment at not making the St. Peter's team, but as I looked up and down the bench at my players I felt a kind of calling. A sense of where I was headed, to bend Bill Bradley's phrase. The other thing I remember is that there were a ton of kids—twenty-two, to be exact. The rule at the school was that I couldn't cut anybody from the parish. We barely had enough uniforms to go around, but I ended up keeping to that philosophy over the years. Even when it wasn't the school's rule, I made it my rule. I never wanted to cut a kid, because I remembered what it was to be cut. I didn't ever want to be the guy who kept a kid from his dreams, from his development. And this wasn't just because I was a soft touch. It's because you can never really know how a kid will turn out when he's fourteen years old. Or when he's sixteen, eighteen . . . even into his early twenties. You don't know how their bodies will fill out, what kind of work ethic they'll develop, what kind of young men they're about to become.

And so you keep them around. Doesn't mean they'll all get minutes, but everyone will get the same shot in practice. They'll work the same drills, get the same looks.

So there I was, all of twenty years old, looking up and down the bench at these twenty-two kids—who of course were checking me out as well. And as my five starters went out to center court for the tip, I sat down and thought, *Okay, Hurley. This ain't half-bad.*

HARD WORK

I'm itching to get going on the season.

This nutty new schedule, I don't think I'll ever get used to it. For a long time we were in a nice routine, opening up practice the day after Thanksgiving—a double session that Friday, a double session that Saturday, and then on Sunday we'd break for a coaches' clinic we always run, "Coaches Versus Cancer." I'd get my guys to help out, to run drills, but it was basically just a light workout. Then we'd practice the whole next week and play our first scrimmage the following Friday.

That was our routine for a bunch of years, but now the state has taken that Thanksgiving weekend from us. Now we can't really run the floor with our guys until the Monday after Thanksgiving, which puts us about a week behind. It's only a couple days, but we miss out on those double sessions, on the clinic, so it's a big deal. A lot of teams, they're in the same spot, but the prep schools follow a different schedule, so it's tough for us to hit the ground running once the season's under way. Those are the teams we tend to play early on. Plus, when we travel to our big holiday tournament—in Boston this year, at the Shooting Touch Shootout—the teams we're facing will have been playing under a whole other set of rules. They could have as many as ten or twelve games under their belts, while we might have just two or three.

It's like you're playing at half-strength for a while, like you're playing catch-up.

One of the ways I've tried to compensate is to set up our preseason scrimmages against tougher teams. Used to be, we'd feel our way into the regular season against some halfway decent local competition, but all of a sudden we're facing teams who've had an extra week or two of practice, who've got their game legs, so I want my guys to be ready. I want to layer in scrimmages that'll be tougher and tougher—on paper anyway.

This year I happened to run into Mergin Sina, who coaches the varsity at Gill St. Bernard's, a private day school in Somerset County. We were out at Paterson Kennedy, competing in the fall league, and Mergin and I got to talking. I was bitching and moaning about our shortened preseason practice schedule, and a week or so after Thanksgiving, when we happened to run into each other again, we continued the conversation. Mergin was having some of the same concerns, so he offered to give us a game in his gym. He's opening up his season at a big national tournament in Florida, and he wants to be ready. We're opening up on Friday, December 16, against a small charter school in Trenton, Emily Fisher, and of course we want to be ready too, so we looked at our calendars and hit on this date.

We've already played a couple scrimmages, and

we looked mostly okay. This stage of the season, you don't even look at your opponents; you keep your focus on your guys, on what you're trying to do. Still, Gill St. Bernard's is one of the top teams in the state. This will be a step up, a chance for us to push our guys a little bit. I know Mergin's squad will give us a good game, which is just what we need to kick-off our season. The idea is to ease into your schedule. You work your way up the ladder, one rung at a time, and I think Gill St. Bernard's will be a good reach for us, a good way for us to see where we are. They've always had a strong program, and it's looking like they'll be one of the teams to beat in the south—along with St. Patrick, Trenton Catholic, Roselle Catholic, Cardinal McCarrick . . . the usual powers in the region.

I know it's going to be a good test for us, only our guys aren't exactly up to it. Jerome Frink, one of our two returning starters from last year, is out with the flu, so I try to slot in Jimmy Hall, who's been in and out of my doghouse almost from the day he joined our program, and Kentrell Brooks, a lanky, six-eight junior, but we don't move the ball all that well with either one of these kids in the big man role.

We're getting our first real look at Kentrell, who came to us last year from Christ the King in Queens. He's a bright, coachable kid, commutes to us all the way from the Bronx, so you know he's a dedicated player. That's usually how it goes. The kids who

come a long way to school, just for the chance to play
at St. Anthony, they tend to be my most motivated
players. They're giving up a lot just to be here. The
only knock on Kentrell's game is his size. He's rail-
thin—only about 170 pounds, which is next to nothing
on his giant frame. Clearly, his best basketball is ahead
of him, when he puts some meat on his bones, but for
now we're hoping we can toughen him up, and even
if we're not in for some of his best basketball just yet,
hopefully we'll get some pretty darn good basketball
out of him along the way.

Not today, though. And it's not just Kentrell—the
entire team is off. We're flat, stagnant. There's no
cohesion. We're not connecting on our passes. Our
shots don't fall. Defensively, we manage to keep the
other team in check, but we can't get anything going on
the offensive end, and it starts to worry me. Not a lot,
but some.

This stage of the season, while the team is still
taking shape, there's a lot that starts to worry me.
Doesn't take much.

Kentrell played some meaningful minutes for us in
the summer and fall. In fact, he started a lot of games,
after Jimmy Hall and Rashad Andrews got themselves
suspended. I don't think it's fair to Jimmy or Rashad
to share the details of their suspensions, but it's public
knowledge that they missed most of our summer, and
here at Gill St. Bernard's anyone in the gym can see

Rashad Andrews is not with us. Anyone who follows St. Anthony basketball knows we're counting on him to be a starter for us, but almost as soon as he finished with his summer suspension he went and made some other trouble—which I also won't go into. However, the upshot of this second misstep is that I decided to suspend him for the first thirteen games of the season, which feels like an eternity right about now.

It's early yet, and the idea of these scrimmages is to feel your way, to work on what needs working on, but at the same time you play to win. You play the game like it matters, because it does. You call time-outs to stop a momentum run. You pull out your guys when they make a bonehead play. You go to your bench when one of your starters gets into foul trouble. You draw up a new inbounds play if you think you need to switch things up.

At some point late in the game we're down six or eight points, and I lean over to Ben Gamble, my assistant coach. I've got a lot of assistant coaches, but Ben's my main guy, been with me for over ten years. Ben used to play for me too, back when I was first starting out. He helps me out with a lot of our pregame scouting, our preparation, our strategy.

Ben's thing is to look at video. He likes to see the run of play. Me, I try to take in a bigger picture. I eyeball everybody, everything. I pay attention to how a team warms up before a game, at halftime. I watch the bench. I consider all the little things, all the little tells. I look at body language. Ben will cover the basics, but I'll stand back and see how the other team's point guard interacts with his coach. This is the kid who's supposed to run the team on the floor, so I want to see him communicate with the guy who runs the team on the bench. Does the coach have his arm around his star player when they talk before the game? Does the kid respond positively, respectfully, to what the coach has to say? Is there a dialogue between the coach and his players? Or is it more of a dictatorship-type deal?

One of our team mottoes, this year as in years past, is "Victory loves preparation." We wear the phrase on our maroon warm-up shirts. We put it on signs. We repeat it in practice. Really, we can't stress the point enough, and Ben's the guy who handles a lot of that prep. He gets our kids thinking through what they can expect in any given situation, against any given opponent. But the preparation doesn't stop once we take the floor to start the game. There's all kinds of information that keeps coming our way—during the warm-up, during the game itself—so we never stop scouting until the clock winds down.

Typically, Ben will sit in the seat immediately to my right on the bench. I like to have him nearby during the game in case there's something I want to say, something I need to hear.

Like right about now.

"Might be a long season," I say, our guys on the short end of a seven- or eight-point margin as the final buzzer sounds.

"Got some things to work on," Ben agrees. "But we'll be okay."

2.

Warming Up

PLAY HARD, PLAY SMART, PLAY TOGETHER.
—St. Anthony Friars team motto, origin unknown

WHAT TO DO WITH A MISTAKE: RECOGNIZE IT,
ADMIT IT, LEARN FROM IT, FORGET IT.
—Dean Smith

I'm the oldest of four children. My sister, Sheila, is three years younger than me, and she was followed by my brother Brian two years later, and my brother Tim four years after that.

My father, Bob Sr., wasn't always a cop. When he came back from World War II, he worked for a time in the pressroom at the *Observer* newspaper in Hoboken, until the paper merged with the *Jersey Journal* in 1951 and he was out of a job. So he took the civil service test and went to work for the police department.

My mother, Eleanor, was a nurse. She always worked, back as far as I can remember, mostly part-time. She wanted to make sure someone was around for us kids, and with a nine-year difference between the oldest and the youngest, there was always a baby at home, so she did what she could to match her schedule to ours. For a long time she worked as the nurse at our local ice skating rink, which meant we all grew up on ice skates. I went skating every day after school, until I could start playing football in eighth grade. That was like our day care. For two hours each afternoon, we'd circle the rink, around and around, over and over. Eventually, you'd develop a whole lot of leg strength, but it got boring, going around in circles all the time. There was no ball, no way to keep score. It was pretty monotonous. After a while you just didn't want to go in the same direction as everyone else, so you'd turn and go back against the grain. Or you'd set up a roller derby–type game with your friends, and you'd all hold hands and whip the last one in line up the boards. We'd found all these different ways to amuse ourselves, to make a game out of it, which meant we ended up spending a lot of time in the penalty box. They had guards on ice skates patrolling the rink, trying to keep order. We weren't making trouble so much as letting off steam. The guards were always going to my mother, complaining about my behavior, and she was always telling me I had to set a better example for my sister and brothers.

Saturday mornings we'd hit the rink again, usually from nine to noon. After that I'd go home and listen to Notre Dame football on the radio with my father. That was his thing, because his brother, my uncle Dan, was a priest who taught at Notre Dame. My father was more of a baseball fan than a football fan. He absolutely loved baseball. He pitched on a semipro team in town. He was a terrific all-around athlete, and baseball was probably his best sport. But Notre Dame football was a big deal in our house, and then when they started putting the games on television, it was an even bigger deal. Everything stopped when there was a game on television. We raced home from whatever we were doing to watch. To the day he died, literally, my father kept tabs on the Fighting Irish. If he couldn't watch the game himself, he'd call me or my brothers on the phone to see how it went.

Sundays we'd usually go out for a drive as a family. We'd pile into the car and head west, on the Belleville Pike, to North Arlington. There was a hot dog place we all loved called Egan's, so that was one of our frequent stops. There was also an ice cream place out on Route 46 called O'Dowd's, which was always a great treat because they had real homemade ice cream, with great sundaes and a classic double-dip cone. It wasn't just an ice cream shop—it was a giant dairy operation. There was a lot to see and do, and I remember those Sunday drives as a special time in our family. I hated the driving part, though. I used to get carsick, so I had to weigh the benefits of an ice cream sundae and getting out in the country against getting nauseous in the backseat.

If I had to summarize my childhood and look for themes that maybe contributed to my career as a coach, I'd point to my parents' work ethic as the biggest takeaway. We didn't have a lot as kids. We didn't go away on fancy vacations or drive a fancy car. We had just enough, but not a whole lot more—and what we did have was hard-earned. My parents were always working two or three jobs to help cover our bills, but they never shrunk from that responsibility. I never heard them grouse or moan about having to go to work. It was just something they had to take on in order to provide for our household, and they did it in such a way that one of them was almost always around to look after us kids. Sometimes this meant bringing us with them to work, like how we used to follow my mother to the ice skating rink, but family was a priority. Education was a priority. Faith, too. We were a churchgoing family, only we didn't always go at the same time, as a family. In our parish, there was a kids' service early on Sundays, and the adults went later on in the afternoon, so we split up. But going was important. Work was important. Putting our best and fullest effort into everything we did . . . probably most important of all.

When I was about eight years old, we moved into an Italian neighborhood in Jersey City. I didn't know it was an Italian neighborhood at the time, but looking back I realized that up and down the street our neighbors and all of my friends had Italian last names. We Hurleys were Irish, on both sides, but when you're a kid this kind of thing doesn't come up. It didn't really matter where you were from. It only mattered that you were there—and in my crowd, that you could play ball. I only mention it because our next-door neighbors, the Iorios, had a son named Sam who had a basketball scholarship to go to Villanova, where he played with Bill Melchionni, who went on to win an NBA championship with the 76ers and an ABA championship with the Nets. And then, next door to the Iorios, there was my buddy Paul Lenzo, who was my age, and the proximity and influence of these two families probably had as much to do with my basketball development as anything else.

Paul's dad put a basket up on the garage, with a plywood backboard, and we used to play there all the time. It ended up, he had to put chicken wire over the windows facing the court, because the ball kept breaking the glass. You take enough shots, you send enough balls bouncing this way and that way, you're bound to break a couple windows, right? That was my first taste of basketball. Mr. Lenzo invited me to come by and shoot whenever I wanted, even if Paul wasn't around, and I took him up on it. For years afterward, Mr. Lenzo used to joke that he should never have made the offer, because I was there all the time. Even when the other kids lost interest, I would show up to play. Even when the sun went down and everyone else raced home for dinner, I would stay out there and shoot. The hoop was set up in such a way that there was a ledge in the right corner of the court, which fell into the yard of the house next door. I spent so much time in that corner, I developed a killer fadeaway jump shot, falling onto the grass with my release.

A couple years later we started going up to the next corner, where there was a little park on Linden Avenue, and we played there. We grew our games from one-on-one to two-on-two half-court, to three-on-three. With each man, the game took on a new dimension. We might have played full-court, but there was only one basket. At the other end of the court, there was a hole in the concrete where the basketball pole used to be, but the city never got around to replacing it, so that kind of put a cap on our game.

As we got older we found a park with a full court, and our games got more and more competitive. We played to win, which to us was the same thing as playing for fun. We also played touch football, stickball, box ball, punchball . . . as long as it had some kind of ball and some way to keep score.

My father didn't know a whole lot about basketball. Baseball, that was his sport. He used to take us down to Roosevelt Stadium to have a catch—me and my brother Brian. After a while Timmy would join in too. Sometimes my father would bring a Wiffle ball bat. If there were other kids around, he'd bring them along and we'd make a game of it. This was our routine a couple nights a week, but then I started spending more and more time playing basketball, and he didn't really have a way to help me with that. It's not that he wasn't supportive—just a little out of his element. I was in uncharted waters, in terms of my family, but that was okay, because you could go it alone on a basketball court. You could find a way to amuse yourself or work on your game even if no one else was around. Even if your father couldn't teach you how to shoot or pass or execute a pick-and-roll.

Here's what I learned from the game of basketball early on: if you kept at it, you got better. If you kept firing up those fadeaway shots from the corner of Paul Lenzo's court, they'd start to fall more often than not. If something was difficult at first, you could make it easier if you worked at it; you could figure it out as you went along.

I did fairly well in school. Not at first, but soon enough. In third grade, I moved from St. Patrick's grammar school to St. Paul's, which was a difficult adjustment. St. Paul's was a much more rigorous school, and in the beginning I struggled to keep up. If it hadn't been for the nun teaching my class, Sister Anita Claire, I don't think I would have gotten by. She was tough. I can't remember how many times I got slapped on the head, or had my ears pulled, or got my knuckles whacked with a ruler, but eventually I got the message. I had no choice but to catch up and pay attention to my work because I was so afraid of Sister Anita Claire—not because her slaps or whacks were truly painful, but because they were embarrassing. I hated being called out like that in front of the rest of the class, so I pushed myself to learn.

I did well enough at St. Paul's to get accepted to St. Peter's Prep, which was the best school in the area. At the time I didn't care that it was such a good school, only that it had the best sports teams. That's where my priorities were back then, and I took full advantage. I played football, basketball, baseball. I changed with the seasons. My interest in sports even spilled over into my first part-time job. My mother had started working at Bamberger's department store in Newark as the in-house nurse. She got me a job in the sporting goods department, which I thought was just the greatest setup in the world. I had to wear a jacket and tie, and I had to take the number 9 bus to Communipaw Avenue, near where we lived, and then switch to the 108 or the 1 to Newark—well over an hour each way. But I didn't mind the commute or the dress code, because I got to sample all the new equipment. And I had an employee discount, which I used to buy gloves, bats, balls . . . everything under the sun. I'd buy them for my friends or my brothers, or I'd pick up a bunch of old equipment from the warehouse. There was even a basketball hoop hanging in the store, and when things were slow I could clear out a little area and work on my shot. So all in all, it was an ideal job.

While I was in high school I don't think I gave any real thought to what I might do for a career. If I thought about it at all, I might have imagined myself playing professional basketball—that's how laser-focused I was on my game. But somewhere in there, in the back of my mind, I started to think I might like to be a teacher. A history teacher probably. For that, I credit a teacher I had during my sophomore year named Richard Hollander. He was one of those rare, dynamic teachers who really made an impression. He made the material just jump off the page. Whatever book he had us reading, he had stories for each chapter, so the history really came alive in the classroom, and it left me feeling like this was something I could do. Or at least, something I wanted to do, because I never in a million years thought I could do it as well as Mr. Hollander. In any case, he left me with a real love of reading and history, and for the first time I allowed myself to think of a life beyond sports, beyond basketball.

That would come later—only not exactly in the ways Mr. Hollander had me thinking.

I still had my sights set on a collegiate basketball career, which, as I've already detailed, didn't exactly go as planned. And out of that I managed to parlay my love of the game into a couple volunteer coaching gigs, which ultimately led me to my first job at

St. Anthony, coaching the freshman team. It was the fall of 1967. I was twenty years old.

This was around the time I met my wife, Chris. I was going into my sophomore year at St. Peter's, just getting used to the idea that a playing career wasn't in the cards for me. Chris was going into her senior year in high school. I thought she was just about the prettiest girl I'd ever seen. She lived in the next parish, on the south side of the city. There was such a big percentage of Catholics living in Jersey City back then that this was how we defined our neighborhoods. When you met someone, you never asked what street they lived on or what part of town they were from. You asked them their parish. I was from St. Paul's. Chris was from Sacred Heart. When I was growing up, our parish district covered a huge area. By the time my youngest brother was in grammar school, they had divided the district into two parishes—St. Paul's and Our Lady of Mercy—but in my day our classrooms were overflowing with kids. There were over two hundred kids in my graduating class in grammar school, crammed into just three classrooms. Looking back, it's amazing to think we learned anything at all, with just one nun assigned to each class, responsible for every subject, but by the time I started at St. Peter's Prep I was as prepared as any other kid. I had a solid foundation.

Chris and I hit it off right away. We'd had a lot of the same experiences growing up. We'd come from the same place—different parishes, but essentially the same place. We both had deep roots in Jersey City and wanted to make our lives there. Plus, we were in love, and it wasn't long before we decided to get married. We waited until I finished school. I was twenty-three years old; Chris was twenty-one.

Chris thought she was marrying a teacher. Heck, *I* thought she was marrying a teacher. That's all I'd ever wanted to be, other than a ballplayer. So that's what I was working toward, only I wasn't making a whole lot of forward progress. Very quickly, coaching had become a real passion. I was finding that I had a talent for it, and my teams were doing well, but there was no money in coaching. I think I made a $200 stipend my first year as the freshman coach at St. Anthony—if it was any more than that, it wasn't a whole lot more. I didn't really know what I was doing when I first started out as a coach. I knew how to play, that's all. I knew how to win. And I was good at connecting with my players and finding ways to motivate them. But I didn't really pay attention to fundamentals, to strategy. That would come later too.

A part of me thought it would have been nice to teach at St. Anthony once I finished college, because I made a real connection to the place, to the faculty, to the students, but they weren't hiring, so I started working as a substitute teacher in the Jersey City school system. I was lucky enough to hire on as a pool sub at Dickinson High School, which was almost like being a full-time teacher. You didn't get all the benefits that came with a full-time job, but the work was steady. I was a part of a permanent pool of substitutes for the entire school district, and Dickinson had over 3,500 students, so there was always an opening that needed to be filled. Occasionally, you'd show up and they wouldn't need you in the high school, so they'd send you to one of the grammar schools in the district.

It was a decent arrangement—not quite as secure as a full-time teaching job, but a lot better than a straight substitute teaching gig, where they'd either call you or not, depending on the day. The only drag was that you couldn't really teach. As a substitute, you're more like a traffic cop than an educator—you're a disciplinarian, really. You spend most of your time giving out cut slips, breaking up fights, trying to keep the incorrigible kids from getting under your skin. In my case, because I was so young, the students kept testing me. A lot of teachers, they can stand in front of a classroom with a certain authority, but I didn't have that when I first started out. I was too close in age, too close to that time in my own life, so I think the kids kind of sniffed that out and gave me a hard time. Plus, when you only have a group of kids for a day, there's not a,whole lot you can do with them, other than work your way through the regular teacher's lesson plan or maybe go over the assignments. Sometimes, though, you'd get a more open-ended placement—meaning you'd know in advance that a certain teacher would be out for a couple days, or even a week or more, so then you'd be able to get to know the kids a little bit, maybe do some interesting things with the material.

More and more, during basketball season, I found myself watching the clock and counting down the hours until practice, because that was the time I could really feel like I was teaching these kids, like I had something to offer that might make a difference. It was like being stuck, running in place, but then at the end of the day I'd be cut loose. It was frustrating, and I talked to my father about it from time to time, about how it felt during the school day like I wasn't making the kind of contribution I wanted to be making, so he tried to get me to think of a different career, maybe something to do with law enforcement. Chris thought this was a good idea too. She could see I was frustrated with the way things were going on the teaching front, so she encouraged me to let my father help me on this, to try something new. It worked out that there were opportunities opening up in probation in the Hudson County court system, so my father made a couple calls and helped me get a job as a provisional. This meant that I could take the civil service test and then work part-time as a provisional for a year or so until I could get hired off the list on a full-time basis. So that's what I did. In between, I supplemented my income by grabbing whatever odd jobs I could squeeze into my busy schedule, whatever I could find to fill the time and start putting together a stake for our young family. I even taught gym for a stretch at St. Anthony.

This went on for a year or so, but I didn't mind the long, uncertain hours because I knew at the other end there'd be a career in probation. I just had to put in my time and twiddle my thumbs until my name came up on the civil service list, and I'd be all set. And in the meantime, I had my coaching gig, which was turning out to be my real focus. No, it wasn't a way to make a living, but it was certainly a calling, and one of the great side benefits to a career in probation was that it would leave my afternoons and evenings free during basketball season. The hours were a lot like teachers' hours, so there was a good fit. I was assigned to my old neighborhood, so I knew the streets like I knew my own name. Turned out I even knew some of the guys I had on probation. Guys I'd gone to school with. Guys I'd played ball with. In fact, I used to play softball and two-handed touch in a couple bar leagues in town, but because a lot of my teammates were in the system it was becoming a conflict of interest. Still, I told myself, this was all part of the job, all part of growing up. I'd had a lot of fun, playing ball all over the city, but it was time to set some of that aside and do whatever I needed to do to get off to a good start at work, to make the right impression, to leave a mark.

My arrival at St. Anthony coincided with the school's first big successes on the basketball court. My first year as freshman coach, the varsity won its first state championship, under coach John Ryan, the guy who hired me. The following year, 1968–69, they won it again. It was like the dawn of a new era. When I was growing up, St. Peter's Prep was probably the best basketball team in Jersey City. There were about a dozen high schools in the city at the time, and we all played each other. St. Anthony had always had a competitive team, but we knew them as a small Catholic school that tended to play in the middle of the pack. They were decent, but not great. They'd had some good individual players, but because it was such a tiny school, they never had the depth of talent you'd find at some of the other schools. At St. Peter's Prep, for example, we had over 1,000 boys in the student body; at St. Anthony, there were just over 150, so it was tough for them to compete.

In a typical high school program, it's the varsity coach who sets the tone. He's keeping tabs on whatever's going on with the junior varsity, and if there's a budget and a demand for a freshman team, he's got his hands in there too. Whatever style he likes to play, whether he's a defensive coach or a run-and-gun type of coach, it's usually reflected in the younger teams, because the idea is you're developing players who will one day step up to the varsity and play in that coach's system. So as a freshman coach, you don't really get to call the shots. You coach the game of course. You make all the substitutions and work the refs and create the matchups, but your main job is to feed and fuel the varsity team, long-term. At St. Anthony, the way John Ryan ran the program, the freshman and junior varsity coaches were assistant coaches on the varsity team as well, so I had to be at all those practices, all those games, in addition to our freshman schedule. And I had to groom my guys and prepare them to step up and play for Coach Ryan somewhere down the road. So there was a lot going on, a lot of different agendas to follow.

In those days we bounced around a lot of local gyms. Remember, St. Anthony High School didn't have its own gym, so we grabbed whatever gym time we could, wherever we could. For a long time we practiced at White Eagle Hall, the bingo hall at St. Anthony Parish downtown. I used to love our workouts at White Eagle because the gym was smaller than a regulation court, and there was almost no out-of-bounds territory before you ran into one of the side walls, so our practices there were intense. Our guys would beat each other up pretty good in that gym, which I always thought was an advantage; it forced us to play tough and smart. Our players loved it too, only I don't think they loved it so much in the middle of any one scrimmage. Really, those games were cut-throat, brutal, but they kept coming back after graduation. It became a real rite of passage after they went away to play college ball: they'd come home from school on break and run with us at White Eagle. They looked forward to it, my former players all said—but when they were playing for me, I don't think anyone looked forward to it. There was too much at stake. They weren't playing just to play. They were fighting for my attention, fighting for minutes. Just fighting.

We also used the Sacred Heart gym, where my wife, Chris, used to go to school, and the court at the Number 5 school, which was even smaller than the White Eagle gym. Depending on where we were practicing, our guys had to sometimes hop a bus after school—not a school bus, mind you, but a regular Jersey City bus out to Greenville—just to get to practice. Or we'd pile the kids into our own cars and ferry them back and forth. So there was a lot of coordinating, a lot of hustling, just to manage the schedules of all three boys' teams, and a lot of that fell to the head coach. He'd let me know where we were practicing and when.

In all the years I've been coaching at St. Anthony, I don't think we've played another school that didn't have its own gym. Even the schools that have bad gyms have a gym. We've played in some crappy places over the years, but my kids have never walked onto a floor and complained about the conditions. It's like it's been programmed into them to appreciate the opportunity to play on any floor, to make whatever adjustments they need to make in their game, to compensate. In some of these gyms, like the Number 30 school in town, the ceiling is so low, you can't really take an outside shot from the top of the key. The short kids tend to do well on that kind of floor, because they can still shoot. The tall kids, they put up a shot and the ball will hit the climbing ropes, which goes down as a turnover.

Once, we played at a tournament in Florida and had to scramble for a place to practice. Somehow we wound up playing at a local Catholic school with indoor/outdoor carpeting instead of a regular gym floor. We'd played on tile floors, on cement floors, on linoleum floors . . . but never on indoor/outdoor carpet. The court was lined like a basketball court, only with chalk instead of paint or tape, so my guys were a little off their game. (We managed to win that one tournament, though, after practicing on that surface, so maybe our guys had an extra bounce in their step, fresh legs, from all that time on the carpet.)

After two years, John Ryan moved me up to coach the junior varsity, and our games became a little more meaningful, our practices a little more competitive. The kids on my team were a little bit older, a little bit bigger, a little bit better. Basically, they were one year closer to being varsity players, so I tried to ratchet up the intensity in our practices and in my style during games. For the most part, this worked out pretty well, but every once in a while my emotions took over—at least, a little bit; at least, at first. I was a bit of a hothead, I guess you could say. Even today I can flash my temper on the bench during the game, but I like to think I can control my hotheadedness. At least I think to try, but back then I wasn't always in control. I was still young, still finding my way as a coach, still learning how to develop these young players so that winning didn't always matter as much as growing their game. But I hated to lose. Happily, we didn't lose all that much—just two games my first JV season, but I think one of those losses came back to bite me. We were up by twenty points in a game against St. Peter's New Brunswick, in their gym, and then the game got away from us. All of a sudden we couldn't hit our shots, and St. Peter's couldn't miss, so they eventually took the lead. They ended up winning the game, and I'm afraid I went a little berserk. In the locker room after the game, I put my hand through a blackboard. I hit it pretty hard—so hard our school had to pay to replace it. In my defense, I was upset about the loss—but, really, that's no defense when you're supposed to be coaching kids and setting a good example for them. You're supposed to keep a measure of control. The only good piece to my little tantrum was that it happened behind closed doors, in a locker room, but of course word got out. There were damages—beyond the cost of replacing the blackboard.

John Ryan ended up having a big influence on me as a coach. He took me under his wing, started sending me out to coaching clinics, gave me a push. I began spending a lot of time with him and some of the older coaches. I always tell people it was John and his crew who taught me how to drink beer properly. After practices, we'd usually go out to Richie & Pat's Tavern, or Dahoney's, or Gillick's. There were a bunch of Jersey City taverns they liked to frequent, and we'd sit down and have our beers and talk about our team. Before long, we'd lay out a bunch of loose change on the bar and start diagramming plays with the coins. Or someone would pull out a napkin and start drawing plays on that.

I'd never know how long we'd be out. Sometimes it was just

for a beer or two. Sometimes we stayed out for a couple hours. On those nights I'd go searching to find a pay phone so I could call Chris and tell her I'd be late. I'd say, "It's one of those nights. We're doing the Xs and Os. I don't know when I'm gonna get out of here."

Up until this time I'd been coaching with my gut. I knew the game from playing it, not from studying it, talking about it, or breaking it down. I knew what it took to win, but not what it took to put your team in a strong position to win, game after game. It took hanging out with John Ryan and his assistant coaches to get me to really analyze my approach, to understand the Xs and Os aspect of the game. It forced me to develop my own philosophy, my own style. It was like learning to play chess. It was one thing to know the basic rules, to understand which pieces can move in which way, to just *play*, but it was a whole other level to develop a winning strategy, to anticipate and try to counter your opponent's moves, to know when to be aggressive, when to defend. All of that.

The comment about learning to drink beer properly has nothing to do with the number of beers we'd put away on these long nights out. It has to do with the contrast to how I used to drink beers with my friends. A lot of times, all through college, we'd wind up on some street corner or other, standing outside in the cold, drinking our beers. We were just kids. But here I was, drinking beers like a refined gentleman, discussing important matters (like basketball!) in respected establishments. I'd gone from drinking beers with boys to drinking beers with men, and I took it in as a kind of rite of passage.

The reason I think this blackboard incident came back to bite me was because John Ryan ended up leaving St. Anthony at the end of that season. We didn't repeat as state champions, after back-to-back titles, but he got an offer to become the assistant coach at Manhattan College, and he grabbed at it. Naturally, as the current JV coach, I thought I was ready for the varsity job, so I put in for it, but a lot of the administrators didn't think I was ready. They thought I had a volatile personality. Looking back, they were probably right, but I didn't see it that way at the time. There was one priest in particular, Father Walter Walewski, who didn't like me at all, probably because we were too alike. I was a young alpha male, and he was an old alpha male. Trouble was, for me, Father Walewski ended up becoming the chief administrator of the high school, so it didn't exactly help my coaching career that I kept butting heads with him.

I never knew for certain if that blackboard incident cost me the varsity job, but it certainly didn't help. And it certainly didn't make me feel very good when the school offered the job to Bill Brooks, who'd been an assistant coach at Seton Hall. Bill was teaching in the Union City school system and thought it made sense to coach at the high school level, so he became the new St. Anthony coach. Luckily, he didn't bring in a new staff, which meant I could stay on as the junior varsity coach, even though it kind of rankled that I'd been passed over for the varsity job. I thought I was ready for it. I thought I'd proven myself. But I wasn't, and I hadn't. Father Walewski and I didn't always agree, but over time I was able to agree with him on this. I was a little too young, a little too brash—less qualified than a guy like Bill Brooks, who'd been an assistant at the big-time college level.

After all, I still had to learn my Xs and Os.

3.

1973–1974: MR. HURLEY

**THE IDEA IS NOT TO BLOCK EVERY SHOT. THE
IDEA IS TO MAKE YOUR OPPONENT BELIEVE
THAT YOU MIGHT BLOCK EVERY SHOT.**
—Bill Russell

THERE IS WINNING AND THERE IS MISERY.
—Bill Parcells

I was a coach first. These days I'm a whole bunch of things. I'm
an educator, a mentor, a motivator, a college adviser, a fund-
raiser. But coaching came first. My job was to win ball games.
That's why I was hired. The emphasis wasn't so much on helping these kids get into college, or turning their lives around, or

instilling the values of hard work and discipline. That was all a part of it, but these things weren't exactly a priority. That all came later. Soon enough, but later.

I wanted to win. First and foremost. I wanted to win because I was competitive. I wanted to win because I wanted to keep my job. I wanted to win because these kids deserved to win. They didn't always want it for themselves as much as I wanted it for them, but that was part of my job too—to get them to want it, to understand what winning meant, why it mattered.

Why did winning matter? Why does it matter still, after all these years? After all, winning in a vacuum is a small reward. But winning in context is huge. Why? Because winning is an outgrowth, a by-product, an emblem. It's a reflection of your hard work, which at the end of the day is supposed to be its own reward, right?

It doesn't always work out that a team or a competitor who puts in the most effort, who prepares the hardest, will come out on top. But over time, more often than not, that's how it goes—and how it goes on a high school basketball court is usually tied to how it goes *off* the court as well. By that I mean, if you work at it, prepare, keep your focus, maintain your composure, and do everything in your grasp to get and keep ahead in the game, you'll usually do okay in school as well.

So, absolutely, winning is important. It's like a carrot at the end of a stick. It gives us something to shoot for. A goal. A purpose. And it tells us exactly what we need to be doing if we mean to get better—if we hope to succeed, on and off the court.

Those first couple years at St. Anthony, those first couple teams, a lot of my players came from involved, success-oriented families. That was the baseline. Maybe these kids had older brothers or parents who'd gone to college. Maybe they had a parent with a good civil service job, or a steady union paycheck, who wanted a little something more for their children. Almost all of them came from two-parent homes. Education was important. Basketball was a kind of sideline for most of my players, what they used to call an extracurricular activity. That's how it had been for generations—in Jersey City and all over the country. It wasn't the kind of front-and-center, all-consuming priority it's become now. It wasn't a ticket up and out of a bad situation. It was just something to do to fill the time between school and dinner. A way to keep some of these kids in shape and out of trouble. A positive outlet for all of that bottled-up teenage energy.

Good things, all.

I had a lot of two- and three-sport athletes back then, which I guess is what you'd expect at a small school like St. Anthony. That doesn't mean we didn't have some solid players. We did; in fact, there was a lot of pure basketball talent on my first teams. It's just that there was no way my fellow coaches could fill out their football or baseball rosters without dipping into the same talent pool, because, hey, it's not like the pool was all that deep to begin with. We had a bunch of good athletes at the school, and they played everything; when one season was done, they moved on to the next.

Once I was passed over for the varsity coaching job vacated by John Ryan, I stayed on for another two seasons as junior varsity coach under Bill Brooks. I'd felt slighted at first, but I was determined to get past it. I wanted to do a great job and set aside any concerns that St. Anthony might have had about my maturity or my ability to lead the program, because in the back of my mind I started to think maybe Bill Brooks wasn't so comfortable in his new role. It's a big change for a coach, to move from college back to high school. The other way around, from high school to college, it's more of a natural progression, but when you're used to working with young men, it's difficult to pull back and bring the same kind of approach to sixteen-, seventeen-, eighteen-year-old boys. There's a different level of expectation, a different level of commitment.

Coach Brooks never actually came out and said any of these things, but I could see how he ran practice, and I could see when he left the gym feeling frustrated. It occurred to me this might not be a good fit going forward, so I went to work on my own game. I'd already been attending a lot of coaching clinics under Coach Ryan, to learn what I could, but now I looked to step that up even more. Now I looked for opportunities to gain some experience and to develop my own approach. To seek out other coaches who maybe had something to teach me. To sketch out plays on the backs of napkins. Up until this point, my style as a coach tended to reflect Coach Ryan's—or now, Coach Brooks's—but I thought I should put a little more of my own stamp on things, so I looked first to the areas of fitness and preparation.

The way you practice is the way you play. It's an old coaching cliché, but you'd be surprised how many coaches don't embrace it in a full-on way; their practice sessions are loose, disorganized, where they should be planned into the ground. Each session should have a set of goals attached to it, a bunch of things you're trying to accomplish. Each drill should have a purpose, each touch should have a lesson your guys can carry with them to the next game.

With these things in mind, I started "writing" our practices. I'd break down each session ahead of time, allowing so much time for shooting, so much time for drills, so much time for scrimmaging. It got to where I had each practice worked out to the minute, because I didn't want to waste a second of our precious gym time. In our case, this was especially important because we didn't have our own gym. We rented space, so court time was like gold. That's one of the big reasons I placed an emphasis on fitness, because that was something we could work on away from the gym. That was an area where we weren't coming at it from any kind of disadvantage.

St. Anthony teams had always been known for defense— again, because that's one of the few aspects of the game a coach can influence. You can't teach height, or pure athleticism, and if you're a small school, the odds of filling out your roster each time out with talented big men and exceptional ball-handlers and shooters run pretty long, so you work with what you have. You fix what you can. You find ways to instill a tenacious defensive mind-set, to get your guys to play to their strengths, to lift their basketball IQ so they can better understand the game and how to work it to advantage. Basically, you teach them to focus, to prepare, to approach each game like it matters—but even more, like it's within reach. This last is key, because if you allow your players to go into a game thinking they're overmatched or outgunned, then that's probably how it will go. They'll be overmatched and outgunned. They'll be scared, tentative. That's not what you want as a coach. You want your guys to play with confidence—even when they've got no good reason to be confident, other than what you've drilled into them in practice.

Almost as soon as I got the junior varsity job, I started scouting teams on our schedule, which was not something you saw a whole lot of on the JV level—you still don't, by the way. But I wanted to put my teams in a position to win each game. And it worked. We kept winning, and winning, and folks in and around New Jersey schoolboy basketball took notice. I started getting calls from other schools, offering me jobs. I hadn't counted on this, although

I must say I was flattered at the attention—and careful not to jump at just any offer, because I wanted to make sure it was the right move. I wanted to think through how my schedule would fit alongside my full-time job in probation. Plus, Chris and I were starting a family—our son Bobby was born in 1971, just before the start of my third year as junior varsity coach—so my time wasn't entirely my own. I knew my way around at St. Anthony, I knew my schedule and what was expected of me, so there was a certain comfort in that. I remember telling Chris I wouldn't move just to move.

We'd gone undefeated my second year, so we had some nice momentum going, a good group of players, and I didn't want to leave the program just for the chance to be a head coach. It had to be the right situation, and for a while I thought I'd found it at Hudson Catholic, which had always had a strong basketball program. I was inclined to take the job there, but there was one wrinkle: my brother Timmy played for Hudson Catholic, and my mother didn't think it was such a good idea for me to come in as his coach. I didn't exactly see it the same way, but I couldn't argue. The timing just wasn't right, she said. There'd be other head coaching jobs, she assured me. And she was right, there was—at St. Anthony the following year, after Coach Brooks stepped down and Father Walewski and the St. Anthony administration decided that after yet another undefeated junior varsity season, and no more locker room outbursts (at least none that had come to their attention), I was finally ready to take over the program.

The promotion came with a big bump in pay—all the way to $1,000. It wasn't going to make us rich, Chris and I were realizing, but it was something.

———

It's not like I was jumping onto a moving train when I started coaching the St. Anthony varsity. I'd coached the junior varsity for the past three years, which had put me on the bench for the varsity games as well. And a lot of my junior varsity players were moving up to the varsity with me, so there was a level of familiarity you don't always get as a new coach. This was a good thing and a not-so-good thing. It was good because I knew my players, their strengths, their tendencies, but it was not so good because they had that same level of familiarity with me. They knew me as a big kid from the neighborhood. They knew me as someone who used to run with a lot of their older brothers and who'd coached them on local teams at the youth level. They'd seen me play at the playground or maybe followed my career in college. And so, because of all this familiarity and proximity, I spent a lot of time worrying how to exert my authority over these kids. Today it's not really an issue. I've been at it a while by this point. I'm a lot older. I've got a whole bunch of gray hair and a whole bunch of state championships, and I've learned how to raise my voice to make my point (and scare the crap out of some of my players!), so the authority kind of comes with the whole package. But when I was just starting out, I thought my age and my circumstance might get in the way of what I was trying to do.

First thing I did, and I made a big point of it, was to get them to call me Mr. Hurley. John Ryan had put the idea in my head back when I first joined the program as coach of the freshman team. Left to my own, I might have gone the other way on this, but Coach Ryan stressed how important it was to get some kind of separation with my players. He said the easiest way to do this was to have them address me in a formal way. I felt kind of funny about it, but at the same time I knew I had to find a way to empha- size my position. Nowadays a lot of my players will call me Coach, or Coach Hurley. Very rarely will someone call me Mr. Hurley. But during those first couple seasons, when I was still in my early twenties, still close enough in age to my players that I could have been their older brother, I thought it was the best way to put it out there that I expected to be treated with respect—even though I hadn't earned it just yet.

I still remember my first game as head coach of the varsity. We went up against St. Joseph's of West New York, at Dickinson High School, where I used to be a substitute teacher. St. Joe's always had a decent team. They were coached by a guy named Frank Grasso, who became a great friend of mine over the years, and they were known as a tough, aggressive group, but I felt good about our chances. We'd played well in a few scrimmages to start the season, and our guys looked strong. It helped, I think, that I knew my players as well as I did, because I was able to slot them into roles early on. I knew what to expect, all through the lineup. A lot of times, with a new coach, it takes awhile before all the parts are moving together, before everybody's contributing like they're supposed to contribute, but when you have a good feeling for your personnel, you can make a smooth transition.

We ended up winning that first game, but a couple things have stayed with me about my varsity coaching debut, other than the victory. One was Frank Grasso getting tossed. Frank was a very emotional guy, coached with a lot of intensity, liked to work the officials, and all during that first game I kept thinking of the kind of coach I wanted to be. I was too young, too green, to have any type of style or approach to call my own. All I could do was mimic what I'd seen from other coaches—from Jerry Halligan, my high school coach; from Joe Palermo, my freshman coach at St. Peter's College, who also coached Bill Raftery at St. Cecilia High School in Kearny, New Jersey; from John Ryan and Bill

Brooks on the bench at St. Anthony. I didn't know if I wanted to be one of those coaches who rides the officials all game long, the way a guy like Jim Calhoun did so effectively at the University of Connecticut, hoping to get a couple close calls to go my way as a result. I didn't think so. I was more interested in getting good possessions by working our bench and keeping a dialogue going with my players during the run of play. And all these years since, that's been my approach. I might even miss a possession or two every game because I'll be huddled with one of my players, trying to work on something or to reinforce a point, but I'm okay with that. In a typical game, we'll have the ball sixty to sixty-five times, and I've become pretty good at eyeballing all five of my guys, all at once; if there's just a time or two down the floor when I don't see everything we're doing, every twitch and feint and stutter step, because I'm going over some important something with one of my players, I consider that a good trade. I'll take that.

But I didn't know these things about myself just yet. I'd started to get a good feel for the Xs and Os, the fundamentals, but that was about it. I'd only coached at the youth level and in a hundred or so games for the freshman and junior varsity squads, and now it was a whole different ball game. Now it was all about maximizing your opportunities and playing all out for the win much more than it was about trying new things or developing players. Also, I had to think about motivating my team—and by that I don't mean to suggest my guys didn't want to win. You always play to win, even as a kid on the playground; as long as you're keeping score, you want to come out on top. No, this was a different kind of motivation I needed to find, a way to get them up for each and every game, for each and every practice, and to keep them up throughout the long season. At the youth level, as guys are coming up and coming into their own, it's mostly about talent. But here at the high school level, against good competition, it was mostly about drive and determination, about being prepared, about being mature and even-tempered and playing the right way.

A good coach leads by example—I knew that even then—but it would take awhile to figure out exactly what example I wanted to set for my players. As I watched Frank Grasso work the officials and get tossed I told myself I'd try a different way. And do you know what? Over the years I've stuck close to this ideal. If you've watched me work a game, you'll get that I'm vocal. You'll hear me yell at the refs if we're not getting any calls. You'll hear me chew out one of my players if he fails to execute or messes up an assignment. I'm loud, but I'm in control—most of the time. If we play thirty to thirty-five games a season, I'll maybe draw one or two technical fouls the whole year. And I can probably count the number of times I've been run from a game on the fingers of one hand, so it's interesting to me now, looking back, that the opposing coach was ejected in my very first game. Nothing against Frank Grasso, a good coach with his own style, but that set it up in my head as a real contrast in style to the ways I saw myself as a coach.

The other thing that's stayed with me from that very first game was a fluke play you hardly ever see at the high school level—and you'll never see it twice on the same possession, but that's just what happened. We had a guy on our team that year named Walter Majkowski. He hadn't played a lot of organized ball, but he came out for the team and busted his butt and earned his way on. Walter kept improving all during preseason, and I liked having him around. This was important, because one of the other things I was figuring out was how to cut a kid. When I was coaching the freshman team and the junior varsity, I basically took all comers. That was the St. Anthony way—and John

Ryan's philosophy. It wasn't my program, and the varsity coaches let it be known that it was my job to keep as many kids playing basketball as possible. Why? Because you never know how players will develop physically, how they'll grow their games. You cut a kid in ninth grade and he steps away from the game, he might have turned out to be a Division I–type player, so you try to be as accommodating, as welcoming, as possible. That gets tougher to do when you coach the varsity, because the demands on these kids are so much greater and you want to make sure your upperclassmen get their minutes, but I was finding my way on this. In fact, I don't think I cut anyone that first year, and Walter was like the poster boy for this attitude. To this day I don't like to cut a kid. If he's willing to put in the time and the effort, and if he's shown that level of commitment on our freshman or junior varsity team, I'll find a way to keep him.

And the thing of it is, Walter Majkowski ended up playing in college—so, like I said, you never know. Early on, though, Walter was mostly a good, hustling practice player, and that was about it. The other kids all got along with him and seemed to admire his work ethic. He didn't see a lot of time on the floor as the season wore on, but I found a way to get him into this first game, late in the fourth quarter. We were up by a comfortable number, so I tried to empty my bench and get everyone in the game—thought it was a good way to begin the season, spreading around some minutes.

Almost as soon as Walter went in he had a chance to make a play—only it wasn't the sort of play any of us had in mind. Rick Jablonski grabbed the rebound off a St. Joe's miss and fired the ball out to Walter, who must have been so excited to be in the game that he panicked. He was still down at the St. Joe's end of the floor, but he stepped and shot anyway—at the wrong basket!

Now, this kind of thing happens from time to time. Not a lot, but it happens, only rarely at the high school level. Still, a lot of our guys thought this was the funniest thing in the world, even though poor Walter must have been mortified. Luckily, he missed, and I think Jablonski got the rebound a second time, although it might have been another one of our guys. Whoever it was pitched it out to Walter again, and sure enough, Walter went right back up with it. Two shots on his own basket, in just a couple seconds. This follow-up shot didn't go in either, but now Walter's teammates were giving it to him pretty good, along with the crowd, and as we finally moved the ball toward our own basket I turned down to the other end and saw Walter, face down on the hardwood floor. It looked like he'd been shot. Then he started pounding on the floor in frustration. I felt for this kid, I really did, but there was nothing I could do for him. He'd made his own mess, and he'd just have to learn from it.

To Walter's great credit, he did. He lifted himself off that floor and found a way to become an important role player for us. He even came off the bench to score in the state finals that year. A lot of guys never get to play in the state finals, let alone score. And he went on to play Division III ball at New Jersey Institute of Technology, so he clearly got past that one fluke moment.

One of my first innovations as a coach turned out to be one of my only innovations as a coach. I wasn't exactly what you'd call a great innovator. Mostly I was a sponge. I borrowed certain approaches from coaches I admired; I pinched certain drills, even certain inspirational quotes, and reimagined them in my own way. If it's true that imitation is the sincerest form of flattery, then I was flattering the hell out of every coach I came across at a clinic, every coach I ever coached against, every coach I ever played for. Chances are, if I saw you in the gym with a whistle or a clipboard, I grabbed a little something from your playbook and found a way to make it my own. Occasionally, though, I'd find myself with nothing to go on, so I had to scramble—or I'd go completely against how things had been done for years and years if I thought I could go at it in a new way. That's how it shook out here, with this one innovation. Actually, to even call it an "innovation" is to give it more weight than it deserves, but I saw something I wanted to change—a small thing, really, but I believe it's paid big dividends for us over the years, so I'll share it here.

Up until I started coaching the St. Anthony varsity, I'd been a kind of lone wolf on the sidelines. As a youth coach, and later as a freshman and JV coach, it was just me on the bench with my kids. I'd sit with Coach Ryan and Coach Brooks during varsity games, but I didn't really have much of a role, except to observe how the head coach handled the run of play, how he managed the clock, how he talked to his players when they came out of the game. All that good stuff.

Traditionally, the St. Anthony bench was like every other bench in basketball. The coach would sit on one end, closest to the scorer's table, and his assistants would sit next to him, filling the next two or three or however many seats they needed until we got to the players. You saw the same setup on most college benches, most pro benches—only now that I was a head coach, with freshman and JV coaches on hand as assistants, it didn't make a whole lot of sense. I mean, I'd logged my time in one of the "suggestion" seats—the assistant spots on the bench—but once I stepped up to the varsity I wanted to be close to my players. I like to pull a kid out of the game as soon as I can if he messes up. I'll even call a time-out to get one of my guys off the floor double-quick if he makes a particularly boneheaded play—not because I want to chew him out, but because I want to reinforce what was wrong about what he did, get it done and out of the way while it's still fresh. (It might *seem* like I want to chew him out, especially once you hear me yelling, but there's usually a method to my loudness.) I didn't need to have this false buffer of assistant coaches between me and my players, and I certainly didn't need to be at midcourt, right on top of the scorer's table. These days, with six or seven assistants, I'd be half a gym away from my players and I wouldn't be able to talk to them at all during the game if I stuck to this tradition, so I flipped it around. I had my assistant coaches fan out away from the scorer's table, and I took the last seat before the players, closer to the middle of our bench. This way, I'm in the heart of the action, right where I need to be to get the attention of my guys and to give them my attention in return.

Like I said, it's a small thing, really. But it's made a big difference in how I interact with my players. Anyway, it's not like I sit all that still during the game. Like a lot of coaches, I'm up and down the sidelines, pacing, stepping onto the floor to bark at a ref, calling out plays over the crazy din of noise that can sometimes fill a high school gymnasium. Over the course of a game, I towel off as much as any player. I drink as much fluid. I sweat. It's a real workout—but mostly, it's emotionally draining, and I didn't see the need to make it any tougher on myself by sitting as far away from the action as possible.

Very quickly my kids knew if they were coming out of the game to take the open seat next to me. It was drilled into them. Half the time I'd chew them out and send them right back onto the floor because the guy who went in for them would invariably make a screwup of his own. I was a regular "Captain Hook" the way I was yanking kids in and out of games, but I believed this was the best way to get inside a player's head. Talk to him on the floor, middle of the game, and he'll nod like he's listening, but he won't hear you at all. Talk to him on the bench, when the whole gym knows he's made a stupid play, when *I* know that *he* knows he's made a stupid play, and there's no avoiding me. He's got no choice but to listen . . . and, hopefully, learn.

Another innovation was to step up my efforts on the scouting front—in a way that seemed to fit with this in-the-mix approach I'd adopted on the bench. You have to realize, there wasn't a whole lot of advance work in New Jersey high school basketball back in the early 1970s. You played your game and hoped like hell you could keep your opponents from playing theirs. But I always believed there was a lot to learn about an opponent that went beyond their style of play. It was easy enough to figure out another team's strengths, to spot their best shooter, their best ball-handler. And it was easy enough to figure out an opposing coach's tendencies too. Go up against the same coach a time or two and you'll know his set plays, the tempo he likes to play, the fitness and fortitude of his team. You're scouting without even realizing you're scouting. In recent years, I've had some big help in this area from my assistant coach Ben Gamble and from alumni and friends of St. Anthony who have scattered about the state. They'll be my eyes and ears at an upcoming opponent's game if I can't make it, and I've come to trust their take, their insights. Also, they've come to know what I'm looking for with their assessments.

But back then it was mostly on me, and I found that I was most interested in the action on the sidelines. I'd want to put myself in the middle of *their* bench as well as ours. I'd fix on the way a kid came off the floor on a substitution. I'd take note of everything. Does he take the seat next to the coach, the way my players do? Or does he go to the end of the bench and sit by himself with the towel over his head? Does he listen—*really* listen—to what the coach has to say to him when he comes out of the game? What I wanted to know was how a kid responded when things were not going well, because that was a piece of information we could exploit. That was a kid we could pressure, maybe find a way to frustrate him and get him off his game.

Again, wouldn't really call it an innovation, this type of scouting, but it was something new—on the St. Anthony bench, at least.

Oh, and one last improvement I tried to make on the Coach Ryan/Coach Brooks way of doing things at St. Anthony. This one came off the court, in the form of a contract I started asking my players to sign. There was a code of conduct in place when I took the job, but it wasn't really enforced; you saw the same type of thing at a lot of schools in those days, at Catholic schools especially, but I got to thinking it was something the kids were taking for granted, so I presented it in the form of a contract. I thought if it was something they had to discuss with their parents, if it was a document they had to study and consider and endorse with their signature, in an adult-type way, they'd have to really take it seriously—and they'd get that I took it seriously.

It's evolved over the years to bend to societal changes, to technology, to the ways my players live away from the gym, but at its core it's basically the same. Here's the current version:

STUDENT-ATHLETE ST. ANTHONY
BASKETBALL CONTRACT

1. I will represent myself, my family, my school, and my team properly at all times, including on social networks such as MySpace and Facebook.
2. I will take my education seriously, knowing that my education is for a lifetime. I will treat my tutors, teachers, etc., with the proper respect.
3. I will refrain from the use of tobacco, alcohol, or drugs of any kind.
4. I will not take out or use a cell phone during school hours other than the cafeteria at lunchtime. Failure to comply with this rule will result in an immediate and indefinite suspension from the program.
5. I will always wear both my school and team uniform properly.
6. I will adhere to my curfew hours of 10:00 PM for school nights and 12:00 midnight on weekends.
7. I will maintain a clean-cut appearance with a short haircut (absolutely no Mohawks) and no facial hair.
8. I will not get a tattoo during my time in high school.
9. I will actively attend my church of choice.
10. I will stay away from people and places that will not have a positive effect on me.
11. I understand that any legal difficulties will result in automatic suspension until such time as this has been reviewed and resolved.

(continued)

STUDENT-ATHLETE ST. ANTHONY
BASKETBALL CONTRACT *(continued)*

12. I will attend any counseling or tutoring sessions recommended by the school coaches or staff.
13. I will adhere to the rules regarding the appropriate use of jewelry.
14. I will refrain from the use of profane language or derogatory comments about others.
15. I will never involve myself in any hazing of another student.
16. I will be on time for classes, school or team activities and practices, and games, and understand that I must communicate in advance when I will not be able to attend via a parent or guardian.
17. I will involve myself willingly in all community service activities as a member of the team and in school.
18. Finally, I understand that it is a privilege to play at St. Anthony High School, and my participation will be determined by my adherence to the rules and my further development as a player.

Clearly, we weren't worrying about tattoos, Facebook, and Mohawk haircuts back in the early 1970s, but every generation came with its own set of challenges. (Don't get me started on my players and their cell phones!) By asking my players to sign a contract, indicating their willingness to follow the guidelines appropriate to the times, I thought I'd be able to deal with any issues that might come up during the season. This way, if a kid stepped out of line in any way, I could hold up this document with his signature on it and remind him of the pledge he'd made to me, to his teammates, and to the program.

My first year as coach we lost only two games the entire season—on our way to a state championship—so it wasn't just Walter Majkowski who figured things out. We figured it out together, as a team, from the coach on down to either end of our bench. And it set us up with a story line for my second season—the 1973–74 season—because it gave me an unexpected way to motivate my players. We'd finished that first season at 27–2. Our only losses were against Hudson Catholic, away, and Bergen Catholic, also away—not a bad start to my high school career, but only because it came with a state championship. If it had turned out we lost in the state finals and finished at 26–3, it would have been a disappointment. Just that swing of one game would have made all the difference, even though those two losses were tough to shake.

Remember, we hadn't lost a game my last two years as junior varsity coach—we went 20–0 each season, as I recall—so I didn't have a lot of experience on the short end of a final score. Not as a coach anyway. I'd never been a good loser in all my years as a player, but I'd usually managed to leave my frustrations on the floor. As a coach, though, I tended to carry the sting of a loss a little longer than I would have liked. This was another thing I was figuring out, about what kind of coach I was going to be. Wasn't quite sure how to accept a loss and set it aside. I kept going over the game in my mind, wondering if there was something else I could have done in the Hudson Catholic game, the Bergen Catholic game, a substitution I could have made to get a better matchup, a time-out I could have called to put an end to a momentum run . . . something. I just hated the thought that I might have done something—or *not* done something—that cost my kids a game. As a coach, the tough losses, the close losses . . . they're on you. As a player, I was finding, you can shake off a defeat and turn your attention to the next game, but when you're the one in charge of moving all the pieces around the floor, of setting out a game plan and getting your guys to respond to any surprises the other team might throw at you, it always feels like you didn't do enough to help your team get the win. And that's how I felt about these two losses, all during that first off-season. I wanted those games back, so I could go at them another way. Really, I couldn't shake them for trying, even though on a purely rational level I knew my players had probably moved on. Even though we ended up winning the state championship.

That's supposed to be what you play for, right? That's the ultimate prize. No coach in his right mind sets out to record a perfect, undefeated season. It doesn't happen that way. Even a guy like Bill Belichick, the head coach of the New England Patriots, one of the greatest football coaches of all time, has said it can be a huge distraction. Remember when his Patriots went to the Super Bowl after going 16–0 during the 2007 regular season? All the talk that year was about how the Patriots had a shot to make NFL history, instead of just winning the Super Bowl, and Coach Belichick said all along he wished the focus could have been on just this one game.

It's tough enough to play for the championship without also playing for history. It got in the way, in the end, because in football it's all about winning the Super Bowl. In New Jersey high school basketball, it's all about winning the state championship.

And here we'd done just that, so why was I beating myself up over a 27–2 record?

I'm almost embarrassed to admit it, but I still think about those two first-year losses. Two tough games, against two tough opponents. The loss to Bergen Catholic is especially hard to take, still, because it's become an annoying stain on St. Anthony basketball history. I know I just said history shouldn't really enter into it, but in my forty years as head coach, guess how many times one of my teams has lost to a team from Bergen County, New Jersey. Just this once. That's all. So it's not hard to see why the loss has stayed with me over the years.

One of the silver linings, heading into my first off-season, was the thought that we'd get to wipe out those losses, sooner or later. In fact, we were supposed to play Hudson Catholic the following year in the back end of a home-and-home, so right away that became a focal point. As a coach, you're always looking for ways to motivate your players, for a little extra something they can put into their tanks and call on at a crucial point in the game, so I decided going into my second season that this grudge match against Hudson Catholic would be our litmus test as a team. The only problem with this strategy, it turned out, was that Hudson Catholic had a scheduling problem heading into the season, and they had to cancel our game. Hudson Catholic had a good team that year—Jim Spanarkel, who'd go on to be a first-round draft choice of the Philadelphia 76ers after an excellent college career at Duke, was their go-to player—so it was especially disappointing that we didn't get another crack at them, but that little extra something I'd tried to put into my guys' tanks seemed to pay off, because once the regular season had come and gone it still looked like we might meet up with Hudson Catholic in the postseason.

We were on opposite sides of the bracket in the county tournament that year, and it worked out that after we won our semifinal game we sat together as a team to watch the second semifinal—Hudson Catholic against St. Mary's. Our guys were rooting hard for Hudson Catholic, so they could take another shot at them, and when Hudson Catholic took the lead with a couple seconds to go in the game, it looked like we'd have our chance. But then St. Mary's hit a half-court shot at the buzzer to win the game and head into the county finals with all kinds of momentum.

Of course, back then, I couldn't know any of that. All I knew heading into the season was that I wanted to avenge those two losses. I wanted my guys to want the same thing. I wanted those two losses to matter, so we could build on them, learn from them. In reality, they didn't matter at all, but I wanted the sting of losing to get into our system in such a way that my guys would do everything in their power to avoid the sting a second time. Most of my team was coming back that year, so this became one of our themes, going into my second season. Each year, I was realizing, there'd be some sort of theme to our efforts—some way to unite our group and make sure we were working together toward a shared goal. During my first year it was all about starting a new chapter in St. Anthony basketball history and extending the winning tradition that had begun under Coach Ryan.

This year it was all about payback.

Turned out we didn't play Bergen Catholic *or* Hudson Catholic that year—but the idea that we might was the spark that lit our season.

The first few Friars teams I coached were built on quickness and speed. Part of the reason for that was that we had some talented ball-handlers, but it was mostly because running was pretty much the only thing we could do with these kids before the season started. In some ways, we're still facing down the same deal. Remember, without a gym, our court time has always been limited. So I decided early on that we would be the best-conditioned team in the state. That became the foundation. I got it in my head that my guys should run every day in Bayonne Park for thirty-two minutes, since that was the running time in a high school basketball game. If we couldn't run at the park, for whatever reason, we'd run around a vacant lot next to the school. For thirty-two minutes. After that, we'd run some more.

The great thing about running is that it creates some very tangible goals for your players. At the start of a season, when everybody's a little out of shape, you run for about five minutes, hard, and you're sucking air. But then you find a way to get your second wind, and when it kicks in you're good to go for another five minutes, and at that point you have to reach for another gear. Basically, you have to keep pushing yourself and pushing yourself until eventually you've pushed yourself right past whatever it was that was holding you back. You push the pain and fatigue from your mind and power through.

Most times, I would run right along with my players. I wasn't sure how it would work, me wanting to separate myself from them in terms of my age and my position of authority, but like I wrote earlier, I wanted to send the message that I was willing and able to do whatever it was I was asking them to do. When we finally got into the gym and started scrimmaging, I'd run the floor with them as well, and these kids just weren't used to that. A lot of them had played for coaches who were much, much older than them, who couldn't keep up, but I could still play. I could still show these kids a thing or two, and I think they appreciated that; I think it added a layer of respect, to put myself down on the floor with them.

We were individually talented, that 1973–74 team. We had a kid named Daryl Charles who was probably our best all-around player; he ended up having a nice college career at LaSalle. Pat Rochford, at power forward, was also a big asset for us; he went on to play at Manhattan, along with Howie Wilson, who went on to play at Temple. Tony Gentile, the catcher on the baseball team, was probably the toughest player on the team; he had a real rough-and-tumble demeanor to his game. And we also had Bob Kilduff, a hardworking, playmaking guard who went on to play at Bloomfield College.

That team had a lot of character, I'll say that. Probably one of the scrappiest teams I've ever coached, but at the time I didn't think in just this way. I had nothing to compare them to, really. I'd coached a lot of these same kids the year before, and a lot of them the year or two before that, on the junior varsity. Somehow they'd always found a way to win, even when their shots weren't falling or the calls weren't going their way or their heads were someplace else—to the point where I almost took it for granted that they'd come through.

And they did. They always did.

The thing of it is, all season long, I don't think we paid any attention to the fact that we had yet to lose a game. I certainly didn't give it a thought, and I never heard any chatter about it from our players. And even when it did occur to me that we were undefeated, I pushed the thought right out of my head. Our focus was always on our next game, our next opponent—not on the string of victories we were putting together. That was almost beside the point. Our goal, all along, was to make it to the post-season—and, once there, to make it to the state finals. Obviously, once you reach the knockout phase of your season, winning each and every game takes on a whole new significance—but up until that point, we weren't playing with the kind of urgency or single-minded focus that can attach to a winning streak as it grows and grows.

We were just playing . . . and winning.

And playing . . . and winning.

All the way to the state finals and a rematch against St. Joe's of Camden. We'd beaten these guys the year before, and here we were defending our title on the back of an undefeated record. We were the number-one team in the state, and I think it finally went to our heads a little bit. And the kids from St. Joe's, it went to their heads too. I'm sure their coach had set it up like a revenge-type game, same way I had our sights set on Hudson Catholic. We'd beaten St. Joe's the year before, so they wanted payback.

We were their motivation.

They were our obstacle.

Now, I'd made a point all along not to talk about our season in any kind of historic terms with my players; I tried not to attach any great weight or significance to any one game. Winning was the endgame, but it wasn't the be-all and end-all, if that makes any sense. But inevitably, the streak came up in the couple days leading up to this St. Joe's game. Reporters started writing about it, asking questions about it. Folks in and around the game started bringing it up, and I don't think I did such a good job preparing my guys and helping them to keep their focus. I let a lot of distractions get in the way. I was no longer a rookie coach, but I made a bunch of rookie mistakes. For one thing, the game was being played at Brookdale Community College, in Lincroft, so I decided to make a real road trip out of it. We got in the night before and stayed over, and that was the first time this group had made an overnight trip. Probably not a good idea to set it up for right be-fore our biggest game of the season, but I was still learning. And like everyone else, I was caught up in the excitement, and since there was money in the budget that year for a low-end motel-type stay, it seemed like a good idea to take my guys away from their home environments so we could live and eat like a team the day before the big game. Just like the pros.

Not a good idea, it turned out.

Our guys just weren't ready for that kind of responsibility. They weren't mature enough. And I wasn't mature enough as a young coach to recognize that I was putting them in a tough spot. I thought that if I gave them a curfew, I could expect them to honor it—but that's not how it went. They were kids, after all, so they ended up staying up a little later than I would have liked, making a little more trouble than I would have liked. Nothing major, just goofball antics and horsing around, but I had this fan-tasy in my head that we'd talk basketball over dinner, and then our guys would break off into groups of two or three or four and talk a little more basketball before lights out. But the adventure was a little too big for them to get their heads around, I think, and the trip was a little too much about being on the road, away from home, and not nearly enough about St. Joe's and what we needed to bring to the floor the next day in order to beat them.

We came out flat. Pat Rochford was sick. He'd made the trip, but he was unable to contribute, said his legs felt like rubber, so that left a big hole down low. He suited up, but I wasn't planning to play him unless we absolutely needed him—and even then, it wasn't clear that he'd be in any kind of shape to play—so right away we were at a disadvantage. It was like starting out a game of chess without your bishops.

Daryl Charles was a couple points shy of a thousand for his

high school career, so that was a whole other distraction. A thousand points is a big milestone for a high school player, so guys were looking to get the ball to him early and often in ways that took us out of our game.

Plus, the facility was disorienting: the court was lined in a multipurpose way, with markings for volleyball and badminton and, from the looks of it, every conceivable gymnasium game you could think to play on a hardwood floor. It was tough to tell from all the lines if you were coming or going, or if you were inbounds or out of bounds. And then, to make matters worse, the gym was lined with big picture windows, in such a way that the light came in during the day and made it difficult to shoot. Of course, these facility-related distractions cut both ways—St. Joe's had to make the same adjustments—but I could have been smarter about it and brought my guys in the day before for a shootaround to get them familiar with the court and the lighting.

All these years later, our point guard Bob Kilduff, who now works as the chief of detectives for the Jersey City Police Department, remembers that we laid an egg. It still bugs him—probably always will. Last game of his school career—last game for most of that team, in fact, because we were a veteran team of mostly seniors—and we laid a big fat goose egg.

St. Joe's went out to an early lead—they were up 17–9 at the end of the first quarter. Then they stretched their lead to thirteen points by halftime, so we were clearly in trouble. It was shaping up to be one of those blah days. Every team runs into a game like this every once in a while, but you hate it when it happens in such a big spot. There's not a whole lot you can do as a coach to turn things around at halftime. It's a chemistry thing usually. You can create chemistry over the course of a long season, but you can't flip a switch at halftime and make things happen the way you want them to happen. Not all at once, just like that. You can't take a kid like Pat Rochford out of the mix and expect the pieces to all fit back together, same as always. He was a big part of our offense that year, so it was a blow, and St. Joe's was playing a wacky zone, some defensive scheme we'd never seen before, and I had no answer for it.

Didn't help that we weren't hitting our shots. Didn't help that when I finally put Pat Rochford into the game, he could hardly move. If anything, that upset our chemistry even more, because we'd made some tiny adjustments and put the ball in the hands of some other guys who could score for us—and now that we had Pat back out there, we had to switch things up all over again.

And yet, somehow, we battled back. We pulled close and then pulled out ahead and held on for the win. But it was an ugly, ugly win. It left a bad taste in our mouths because we'd played so poorly—it was like ending the season on a down note. And you could see it in the way our guys came off the court. They weren't whooping it up and high-fiving and jumping all over each other, the way you'd expect after winning a state title. There was a little of that, but not as much as you'd think—certainly not as much as I'd been expecting going in. Really, it was the most halfhearted celebration, the most ho-hum ending to what should have been a storybook-type season, because none of us were happy with the way we played. Okay, Daryl got his one-thousandth point. Okay, we were state champions. But to a man, our players wanted that game back, same way we wanted those Hudson Catholic and Bergen Catholic games back from the season before.

And it cost us, that game. We'd gone into the final as the top-ranked team in the state, but we were so listless, so off, we ended up dropping to third or fourth in the polls. Of course, you can't control the rankings; all you can control is the outcome of the game you're playing, and here we'd barely managed to do just that. Even though we'd found a way to win, the great lesson to our guys, and to me as a young coach, was that St. Anthony basketball was not just about winning and losing. Sometimes it's how you win—and even how you lose—that matters most of all. There's winning, and there's playing to your potential, and here we'd succeeded in one and not the other.

Yeah, we won the game. Yeah, we won the championship. But somehow this wasn't enough—not for me and not for my players. I don't mean to suggest that it was a full-on disappointment, to eke out this last win, only that it wasn't the rousing victory I would have wanted for this group. These kids had been with me long enough by this point to get that the manner in which we win is just as important as whether or not we win at all. If you mean to be great, your performance is more significant than winning or losing, and that day my team just didn't have it. We were flat. It wasn't at all typical of how they'd played their whole two seasons together.

And so, on the one hand, we had something to celebrate— heck, we had *everything* to celebrate, we'd just won the state title! But on the other hand, we had this great takeaway, a lesson to carry with us into the off-season. We had something to work on, some way to grow our games.

For the kids who'd be coming back to play for me the following year and the kids who were going off to play in college, the takeaway was the same: we could do better.

And underneath that takeaway was a promise we all made to each other: we would.

HARD WORK

We'll play anyone.

We'll take on all comers.

That's been my philosophy ever since I took over the program. We play as independents, so we're not bound by any league schedule. Nothing's set except the games we set for ourselves. The invitations we accept to showcase events. The long-standing agreements we've made with our traditional rivals, with home-and-home games in alternating years that stretch back over many seasons.

In the beginning, I inherited a lot of commitments made by my predecessors, John Ryan and Bill Brooks, but after a while I was free to make my own schedule. There's an art to it, I realized. You develop a feel for how many games you look to play early on, when your team is still finding its way; how many games you need to play in the middle of the season as your guys are hopefully hitting their stride; how many games you want to play heading into the postseason as you start to worry about injuries, fatigue, burnout, and all the other sideline variables that can mess with a postseason run. That's always the goal—to play for the state championship. It has a lot to do with pacing. Variety too. The idea is to throw a bunch of different looks at your team, a bunch of different styles of play. To vary the space between games. To keep your team fresh, focused. Basically, you want to give your guys a shot, that's all—and you certainly don't want to cost them that shot by loading them up with three or four brutal games in a single week, with no time between contests to install any new plays or to rest or to try someone out in a new role if one of your regulars is hurt or struggling.

What you're looking for, really, is a balance. You want to vary the level of competition, first couple weeks of the season, so you can look at your guys in different roles, maybe shake up your rotation a little bit, get into a decent rhythm, but at the same time you want to push them to play at the highest level, as a unit, so you want to be sure you're going up against some talented teams.

This season's schedule looked good on paper. The plan was to get in four or five games ahead of our holiday tournament in Boston, which would hopefully leave us well positioned for a clash with St. Benedict's on New Year's Day. And that's just how it has worked out, only we weren't quite ready for St. Benedict's, a strong team out of Newark where my son Danny used to coach. We've shown ourselves to be a solid defensive team, holding our opponents to an average of just twenty-eight points over our first six games, but we're having trouble scoring—one of the emerging concerns of our season. We've managed to run up some big numbers against a couple weak teams, but overall we're inconsistent. Overall, we're underwhelming. We keep winning, each time out, but I don't like the way we're winning. I don't like the way we're moving the ball, the choices our guys are making on the offensive end, and I worry how we'll measure up against St. Benedict's, which this year features a talented junior guard named Tyler Ennis, one of the top players in the state.

In fact, St. Benedict's is ranked as one of the top ten teams in the country heading into this game—a showcase at Hackensack High School. They've played a bunch more games than we have at this point, because as a prep school they're not bound by the same rules as we are as a public school. They're free to start practicing at the beginning of the school year, which is a huge edge, and they're just crushing everybody in the early going, so I know we're in for a battle. Turns out we're not quite up to it. We manage to win, by a single point, but we play lousy. Make a ton of stupid turnovers. Almost cost ourselves the game a half-dozen times down the stretch. But somehow we hang in there. Somehow we come back from a six-point deficit to start the fourth quarter and manage to build a small lead.

It's one of those games that can go either way at the end. UCLA-bound Kyle Anderson goes to the line with a chance to put us up by four points with less than a minute to go, but he only hits one of his free throws, so it's still a one-possession game. St. Benedict's ends up calling a time-out with just a few seconds left on the clock and sets an inbounds play for Ennis, who's already hit three three-pointers, but our two junior guards, Hallice Cooke and Josh Brown, are able to swarm around Ennis and disrupt what he's trying to do, and he can only get off a desperation shot at the buzzer.

It feels to me like we've dodged a bullet. If we could play that team a month later, we could give them a better game, but we're happy to come away with the win, deserved or not.

Later this month we face another test—at the Hoophall Classic Hall of Fame game at Springfield College in Massachusetts, against Miller Grove, a powerhouse out of Georgia. They have a senior on that team named Tony Parker who's one of the most highly touted big men in high school—the kid is such a big deal that both Duke coach Mike Krzyzewski and Kentucky coach John Calipari are in the stands to watch him play. But here again, our defense comes through. Our guys do a great job containing Parker, holding him to just six points—on one field goal! Take him completely out of his game.

This isn't any kind of rout, though. It isn't what you'd call a convincing victory or a "statement" game. We win by twelve points, a nice margin, but it's a four-point game at the half. It's close all the way. One momentum run could have turned the game either way.

Still, it's a good win for us, and it starts to feel like we're finding our way as a team—but then the bottom falls out of our schedule. That Miller Grove game was on a Monday—Martin Luther King Jr. Day—so our kids were off from school. But then our opponents have to postpone a game that Thursday, and then on Saturday, January 21, there's a dusting of snow in our area, and the other coach calls two hours before game time to bail. He says there's a problem with transportation, that traffic is snarled—but, really, to call it a "dusting" is probably an overstatement. Our guys are already at the gym, so we run a split-squad scrimmage instead, but I would much prefer to stick to our schedule, because it now means we're going over a week between games. That's a long time for our guys to be out of action.

(The snow has pretty much melted by the time we leave the gym, by the way.)

And then the layoff stretches longer still. We have a game on Tuesday, January 24, against East Orange, which is meant as a final tune-up for the SNY Invitational that weekend, on Long Island University's Brooklyn campus. The folks at SNY have been running that tournament for years—first at NYU, and now at LIU—and it always features some of the best teams in the region. It has become one of the centerpieces of our schedule, and our players look forward to it because the games are shown live on the SNY cable network. It's a chance for them to play on a big, big stage, against big, big competition. This year we're in a field along with St. Raymond, Cardozo, and Thomas Jefferson—all dominant teams in our area—so the games are huge for us.

But we never get to play them.

NCAA officials pull the plug on the tournament the day before it's meant to start. Apparently, the tournament is in violation of a new rule, enacted last season, prohibiting nonscholastic events from being held on Division I campuses—one way to keep schools from using these types of showcases as a recruiting tool. I understand the rule, but I don't get why it's being applied at the eleventh hour. I mean, we played this same tournament last year, under these same circumstances; the tournament itself has been running for a bunch of years; this year's schedule has been set for months; and now it's too late to get those games moved to another venue.

It means a lost weekend for us—and a missed opportunity. It also means that whatever rhythm we've managed to achieve over the first month of the season is now completely out of whack, with just one game in a two-week period, so I go from thinking we're moving in the right direction to thinking we aren't going anywhere.

We aren't just snakebit on the calendar. There are a mess of personnel issues that threaten our season. Jimmy Hall has been in and out of trouble, in and out of my doghouse, to where I never know if I can count on him, one game to the next. At six-eight, he's our starting center, and he's got good skills, good athleticism, good presence down low—but the problem with Jimmy's game is Jimmy himself. Even when he's on the floor, you never know what you'll get out of him in terms of effort.

Jerome Frink is nursing an early-season ankle injury, and he's off and on, hot and cold. He was a mainstay of last year's national championship team, so I've been counting on him to return to form, but he hasn't been right in the early part of this season—and I catch myself hoping that when he's back to 100 percent physically, the rest of his game will follow.

You have to expect a certain number of injuries, but we also had a couple midseason and preseason defections that left some big holes on our roster. Rashad Andrews got himself suspended again and ended up transferring to Boys and Girls High School in the city, so he's out of the mix. Jordan Forehand, a sophomore guard who looked like he might make a real contribution over the next couple years, wasn't happy with his minutes, so he transferred to St. Benedict's. Chris Regus, a junior guard who'd played big for us in the tournament last year, and Paul Collado, a transfer from Memorial High School, were also gone from the team, along with a guard from last year's JV team named Tyrinn Shannon, who ended up as the starting guard at Ferris, a public school around the corner from St. Anthony.

That's a lot of talent to shed from your depth chart. A lot of holes to fill.

A few too many question marks.

Despite our unblemished record, our season has been a crapshoot. We're 19–0, going into tonight's game, but it's like we're treading water. I've taken to telling reporters we're a "perfectly imperfect" team, because that's how it feels. Like at any time we'll start sinking.

All of which takes us to today's game, the new centerpiece on our schedule, against one of the top teams in the country—Huntington Prep Basketball Academy from West Virginia. We're coming off a hard-fought contest against another state power, Plainfield, in a rematch of last year's Tournament of Champions final. That game was a struggle. Our outside shooting was dreadful—by my count, we were 1–16 from fifteen feet out. You can't win with outside shooting like that, especially against an efficient team like Plainfield. And yet we once again played a pressure cooker–type defense; we chased down every rebound; we kept the game close and pulled out a double-digit win—despite ourselves.

At the end of the game, the Plainfield coach, Jeff Lubreski, told a reporter that our team played more the way we wanted to play, while his guys played less the way they wanted to play, and I read the comment in the paper and thought, *Yeah, that about sums it up.*

This Huntington Prep team, though . . . I'm not so sure we can dictate the terms of this one. When I accepted the game, I knew next to nothing about the program. We were supposed to face them at the Prime Time Classic, over in Mercer County. We'd always gotten some pretty good games at that tournament, so I figured they'd push us, but then the tournament organizer called and told me the sponsors had pulled out. This Huntington Prep team still wanted to play us, however, so I took the game, so long as we could keep it local. We didn't have the budget for a bus ride to West Virginia, but money didn't seem to be a problem for these guys. They were happy to come to us, and since they're a big draw, with a national profile, we needed a neutral site to accommodate a good turnout.

So now here we are at Roselle Catholic High School in Union County, in front of a couple thousand fans, taking our warm-ups. We're on the floor first, which is not the way I like to play it. I like it when the other guys take the floor ahead of us. It gets in their heads a little bit, worrying what we're up to, what's taking us so long—only here we're the ones doing the worrying. Here they're in my head. Ben Gamble has done his usual thorough scouting job, but I still don't know what to expect. Their starting lineup stands six-ten, six-seven, six-eight, six-six, and six-three. They've also got

a seven-two kid on the bench and a six-eight junior who
might not even get into the game and who's still being
recruited by some top schools. Not to mention their
sixth man, a six-six forward who'll be playing in the Big
East next year, for South Florida.

I watch the other team step onto the floor, finally,
and I wonder what the hell we're doing here. I turn to
my buddy Tom Lalicito, the longtime head coach of
St. Mary's, another Jersey City basketball power. Tom
and I have known each other for forty years, and when
St. Mary's was forced to close its doors last spring, I
jumped at the chance to bring him on as an assistant.
Didn't matter that we'd been rival coaches all that time.
Tom knows the game as well as anyone, and here I
catch him looking at these giants and wonder if he's
thinking what I'm thinking.

I say, "Pretty big, huh?"

He says, "Pretty big."

One of Huntington Prep's big guys, the six-seven
Andrew Wiggins, is probably the best sophomore in the
country. People talk about him like he's the next Kobe
Bryant, and just watching him move in these warm-ups,
it's not hard to see why. Just a tremendous, tremendous
player.

It's not that there's something in the water down in
West Virginia that accounts for all this height, all this
talent. Not at all. Huntington Prep is like a finishing
school for college-bound athletes. The players come

from all over and live together as a group and attend a nearby high school, but they don't play for that school. They play their own schedule, do their own thing—and here they mean to do their own thing against us.

They go out to an early lead—ten points—before I can even think about making an adjustment, but we bring it down to five by the end of the first quarter. Our guys are a little intimidated, I think. They've never gone up against such height, such talent, such strength.

Right away it's clear Huntington Prep doesn't have a single weakness. Everyone can play. The only way they're weak, I realize, is the game itself. I mean, a high school game is short, only thirty-two minutes. That's not a lot of time, and there's only one ball, so it's tough to keep everybody happy on a team like that. Our guys are used to filling different roles; they're used to sharing the ball; they've been playing together for years. These other kids, they've been thrown together like a kind of Dream Team, so I start to think, if we keep playing to our strengths, we'll be all right. If we keep the game close, we'll be all right.

We go into halftime down by just four points, and I have to laugh. My players, they don't know what to make of me, laughing. They don't get what's so funny. So I tell them. I say, "This team is unbelievable, but they're only up by four. We've missed a bunch of shots, a bunch of free throws, but we're only down four."

Something clicks, because our guys come out in the third quarter and start hitting their shots. They play a little smarter, a little crisper. Tariq Carey, a senior transfer from East Side High School in Newark, really comes up big for us. He's one of our best shooters, but he's yet to put it together in a game—until tonight. Here's a kid who was motivated enough to switch schools and join our program, where he'd have to fight for minutes and carve out a new role, and I've yet to figure him out. He's got tremendous skills, but sometimes it seems like his head's not in the games. In practice, he'll never seem to know what drill we're running, what's expected of him, and then when he's left to kind of freestyle, his instincts kick in and he'll just light it up. That kind of player can be frustrating to coach, but I've learned to hang with them and kind of shoehorn their approach into what we're trying to do as a team, on the thinking that they'll eventually come around and make a meaningful contribution. That's just what happens here. Tariq comes off the bench and hits a three, a layup, plays tremendous defense, gives us a real shot of energy. We end up outscoring them by five points in the third quarter to go up by one, on the back of a couple fast breaks, a couple smart possessions, and a couple big stops.

All of a sudden, it starts to feel like we can win this thing. Our guys start to feel it too. You can see it in the way they come off the floor at the end of the third quarter. And now the crowd is with us. We're not used to being the underdog, the Cinderella team, but against these Huntington Prep kids, we're clearly the fan favorite, so it helps to have the fans on our side. Helps a lot actually.

All game long, and into the fourth quarter, we've taken the paint away from Huntington Prep. We're keeping them from their game. They're firing up threes when what they want is to get the ball down low.

We go up one with about a minute to go, when Kyle finds Jerome on a tremendous feed for an easy basket, and after a quick stop Huntington Prep has to foul Jimmy Hall. Jimmy's a decent free-throw shooter, so I'm thinking he can give us a small cushion, but he misses the front end of the one-and-one.

Huntington Prep grabs the rebound and calls time.

We've got two fouls to give.

In high school you don't advance the ball to half-court on the back of a time-out, so they have to run their inbounds play from the baseline.

The crowd is going completely crazy. By now, they're all the way with us, so our guys are drawing on all that emotion, all that energy. They'll do whatever it takes to protect our one-point lead. We do a good job keeping the other team in the backcourt off the inbounds, and with twelve seconds to go in the game, Josh Brown gives a foul to stop the clock.

This time the ball is at half-court, so Josh gives another foul. Stops the clock with four seconds left.

What happens next is kind of amazing. Huntington Prep gets the ball to Elijah Macon, a six-eight kid who'll be playing for West Virginia next year. Macon gets the ball off the foul line and looks to drive past Jerome Frink toward the basket, hard. Remember, it's a one-point game, so all they need is a bucket, so this is the right move, but for some reason Macon kicks it back out to the six-six kid on his way to South Florida, who fires up a three at the buzzer.

The ball rims out, and we win the game, and as the ball drops harmlessly to the floor and our guys start to celebrate I can't shake thinking why Macon didn't just take it to the hole. It made no sense. I mean, they'd just come off of a time-out. And another time-out just before that. This kid had to know the score. This was a well-coached group. A top player like that, he had to know a layup would give his team the game. But we'd denied them the paint all game long, so maybe we were in his head. They'd been living by the three-pointer all game long—thirty of their forty-nine points came from downtown—so I guess if you live by the sword you die by the sword, right?

4.

The St. Anthony Way

CHAMPIONS AREN'T MADE IN GYMS. CHAMPIONS ARE
MADE FROM SOMETHING THEY HAVE DEEP INSIDE THEM:
A DESIRE, A DREAM, A VISION. THEY HAVE TO HAVE
LAST-MINUTE STAMINA, THEY HAVE TO BE A LITTLE
FASTER, THEY HAVE TO HAVE THE SKILL AND THE WILL.
BUT THE WILL MUST BE STRONGER THAN THE SKILL.
—*Muhammad Ali*

IF I WAS GIVEN EIGHT HOURS TO CHOP DOWN A TREE,
I WOULD SPEND SEVEN HOURS SHARPENING MY AX.
—*Abraham Lincoln*

I should probably double back and fill in some of the blanks at home, at work, and at St. Anthony, because it adds up to how I found my identity as a coach.

When Chris and I got married in August 1970, I was still finishing college at night, working a bunch of different jobs during the day, coaching in the afternoons and on weekends. I was also tending bar a couple nights a week at Dahoney's. Summers, I ran leagues—first for the parish and later on for the Jersey City Department of Recreation.

Money was tight, but I wouldn't want to suggest we were living from paycheck to paycheck. We had so many different paychecks coming in, they couldn't help but add up—and besides, Chris and I had simple tastes, so we were doing okay. Each week we'd sock away a little money for a down payment on a house, and it got to where our only real worry was that we never saw each other. Chris was working as a teller at Chemical Bank in Greenwich Village, which meant one of us was always coming or going.

Chris worked banker's hours, so at least her schedule was consistent. My shifts changed with the seasons, and when basketball season came around I was busy on top of busy. Those first few years when I was coaching the freshman and junior varsity teams at St. Anthony, I was also working at the post office for a stretch—and then, for another stretch, in roadway trucking. Whatever I could find, if I could fit it into my days, I jumped at it. I even delivered pizzas for a while—which meant we ate a lot of end-of-the-night leftover pizza.

(Poor Chris hated all that stale pizza, said it tasted like cardboard, but it was what we told ourselves we could afford—and frankly, it wasn't half-bad.)

The one constant in that early part of my career was the work in recreation. The other part-time jobs would come and go, but I always ran those summer leagues. Started out running the same league I used to play in as a kid, which for years and years had been run by our parish athletic director, Jack McCoy. It was a good gig. The hours were flexible, and I was already coaching a lot of these young players, so it was no big thing to hire some kids to keep score or keep time, to order a couple boxes of different-colored T-shirts for uniforms, and to coordinate the referees. Didn't take much to get everybody registered and set up the schedules; once you did it a time or two, it kind of ran itself, so I wasn't about to give it up. I ran that parish league up until 1978, when I was asked to run a much bigger league in the northern part of the city. By that point, our parish leagues had started to attract some really good teams. The competition was becoming more and more intense, so it made sense to kick it up a notch, and before long these city leagues were drawing some of the best players in the metropolitan area. We had pro players trying to stay in game shape over the summer, college players hoping to lift their games, top-level high school players looking to keep sharp . . . all playing in this one league. Games were played outside, inside the boards of an ice skating rink. We brought in fiberglass backboards, a twenty-four-second clock, bleachers, a big outdoor scoreboard. It was tremendous. People came out in big numbers to watch all these great players. From all over. We had Kelly Tripucka play with us, when he was home from Notre Dame. We had Butch Lee the summer after he'd been named Player of the Year in the NCAA tournament, for Marquette. We had Chris Mullin, a future NBA Hall of Famer, home from St. John's. Each team had two or three guys on its roster who were playing big-time college ball, wanting to stay in game shape over the summer.

Kelly Tripucka was a good example. He'd played at Bloomfield High School, graduated in 1977, and of course he went on to star at Notre Dame before becoming a first-round draft choice of the Detroit Pistons. He ended up becoming an instrumental figure on the Jersey basketball scene. Not because he had a tremendous high school career, which he did, and not because he went on to a great career in college and in the NBA, which he also did, but because his family decided to challenge a long-standing state rule that restricted how or where you could play basketball outside of high school. The case ended up changing the landscape of the sport. It used to be that you could only have two or three kids from the same school on the same summer league team; the idea, for high school athletes, was that you could play, but you couldn't play together. Kelly's parents took the position that the state athletic association had no authority over what these kids did outside of the school season. I looked on and thought, *Good for them.* And, *Good for the St. Anthony Friars,* because it would mean more time for us to work on things as a team, to integrate our younger guys into the group.

Eventually, the ruling came down in the Tripuckas' favor. After that, teams were allowed to play together during the summer, and a lot of schools took advantage of that. We certainly did at St. Anthony, although I was never really available to coach my guys; there was always a game I needed to ref or some other league business that needed my attention, but I was usually able to recruit one of my former players to help out. These days I have a long list of terrific assistant coaches to fill in for me over the summer, but there were no Ben Gambles back then. My players got the benefit of playing with each other over the summer, but they didn't get the full benefit the way they would have with a hands-on coach. If I could break free, I'd find a way to coach during their games; sometimes, if I had to ref, I'd be whispering to my guys while I had the whistle. Wasn't exactly legit, but I made up for it by calling the game the other way; I went out of my way to make sure no one ever thought I was playing favorites. Whenever there was a close call, I went against our group from St. Anthony, so my guys knew they had to play doubly hard to win; if they were fouled, they had to be really whacked to get the call.

If I had to characterize our program for the first ten years I was head coach, I'd say we were always able to run out a competitive team. We were good, but not great. We won a whole lot more than we lost, and some years we hardly lost at all, but in many ways we were indistinguishable from a lot of the better parochial schools in the area. Put us up against a team from St. Peter's Prep or Hudson Catholic, Marist or St. Joe's West New York, and it would have been a toss-up. They were also good, but not great. Like a lot of these more competitive schools, we still tended to draw mostly from the parish district, mostly local kids—in our case, mostly from blue-collar Polish-American families. You never really knew what you'd have to work with from one year to the next; you never really knew which team would be a power from one year to the next; all you knew was that we'd be in the mix.

I was still learning, still figuring out what kind of coach I wanted to be. Whenever I could swing it, I'd go to coaching clinics, and if I saw something I liked—a drill, a set play, a defensive scheme—I wasn't shy about borrowing it. In fact, I made sure to tell the coach that I was planning on stealing from him, and whoever it was, to a man, they never seemed to mind. Mostly, they were flattered—long as I didn't come back and use whatever I'd stolen against them in a game. I accepted every invitation I could to work various summer camps in the area, and here too there was a lot I could soak up, just from being around. It was like hanging out with John Ryan all over again, doing Xs and Os over beers, so each season I'd come to our first practice with a list of new things I wanted to try.

My personality on the bench and during practice . . . that was on me. My style with my players was a lot like it is now. I tended to yell a lot in practice, which I found was the only way to get some of these kids to listen to you. I yelled during games too, but a little less loudly; I didn't need to chew someone out in front of his friends or his parents, although from time to time I couldn't help myself. I expected my guys to focus, to prepare, to play hard. I took an in-your-face sort of approach. In the beginning, I think I had to overcompensate in this way because I was so close to my players in age, but as I got older and had a little more time and success (and probably confidence) under my belt I kept yelling. More and more, my players started coming to me with a level of built-in respect. It wasn't something I had to keep earning each time out—but that didn't mean I dialed down on the yelling. No, sir. If anything, I might have started yelling even more, even louder, because I finally had their attention, and once I did I pushed them. Hard. It was no longer about me earning their respect—it was about them earning mine.

And then, the next day in practice, they had to earn it all over again.

I was tough, but I tried to be fair. I gave my players the benefit of the doubt, but only once. If they messed up a second time or missed an assignment, I was all over them. And their teammates too. If one player couldn't follow a play or a drill, I let it be known that it was on everyone else, not just him. It was up to each player to lift the others.

Looking back, I think a lot of my demeanor as a coach came from the work I was doing as a probation officer. Wasn't just the hours that fit together well; there was a lot of the same mind-set, the same persona. I needed to be a kind of drill sergeant on the job, so it made sense that I became a kind of drill sergeant in the gym. Folks who know me, guys who've played for me, might tell you I'm a drill sergeant with heart, but I tried not to let them see the heart part. Same thing for my guys on probation. When I started out in December 1971, as a provisional (or temporary) hire, I was given a caseload of about 150 men on probation. It was an eye-opening experience. I was assigned to the Greenville section of Jersey City, where I'd grown up, but this was a whole new world to me. I'd lived a certain way as a kid, ran with a certain crowd. Yeah, I hung out on a lot of street corners, but only with guys just like me—guys who played ball all the time. We didn't know all this other stuff was going on, and now I had to walk these same streets, looking out for heroin addicts and gang-bangers, people involved in all kinds of things. Like I said, it was a whole new world even though it was right in my own backyard, so I had to develop a tough exterior to get these guys to take me seriously. Some of my cases, I knew the family, so it was a big adjustment—for them, for me, for the folks we knew in common. You grow up looking at the world a certain way, and then you cross to the other side of the same street and look at the world a whole other way . . . it shakes things up, I'll say that.

The biggest adjustment from working as a provisional to being hired off the list on a full-time basis was in our training. It was the same job essentially, only now someone took the time to tell me what the hell I was supposed to be doing. Before that, filling in, they just expected us to wing it. All along, my guidelines had been common sense and whatever seemed reasonable, but I had a lot to learn. My caseload stayed about the same in terms of size, only now I had to track the same cases over a longer period of time. Now I had to do a little more than just hope for the best. I wasn't just subbing or covering someone else's book.

The other change, obviously, was in the job security. I finally had a steady paycheck and a pension. It meant I didn't have to go chasing all these odd jobs. It meant Chris and I could maybe settle down and focus on starting a family. For the first time, I had a set schedule, which fit in great with my coaching schedule, and I could finally feel like I was building something for our future. When I was just starting out full-time working for the state of New Jersey, just finding my legs as a coach, I thought of myself as a probation officer first and foremost. It was who I was, most of all. The basketball stuff—the coaching, the leagues, the clinics—it was all a sideline, something I was passionate about, something to do to keep me sane and whole. But there's no way I could have relied on basketball to make a living, so I never thought of myself in those terms.

Even with my full-time job, we were on a tight budget. We lived for a time with my family on Linden Avenue. My folks owned a small building with four apartments, so we rented one and lived right upstairs from the apartment I'd grown up in. My siblings were still living at home, so we were like a Jersey City sit-com—one *really* big family living underneath one not so big roof. Chris and I kept our own kitchen, did our own thing, but there was pretty much an open-door policy between our apartments. What happened in one house tended to spill over into the next.

It was a great setup, but only for a while. Things got pretty crowded, pretty quick. Bobby was born in 1971. Danny came around a year and a half later, and somewhere in there Chris's dad passed away, so her mom came to live with us as well. We only had a four-room apartment, and we were running out of room, so when Bobby was starting first grade, we scraped to-gether what we could and bought a small home in Country Vil-lage, just a couple short city blocks away. Same neighborhood basically, but to me it felt like we were on the other side of the city. I can still remember what we paid for that first house—$32,000, a big number at the time, although I've since bought cars for more money than that, so it's hard to remember what that money meant when we were just starting out except that it was just barely within reach.

The few thousand dollars I earned from basketball—a stipend from St. Anthony and a small fee from the city for running the leagues—really helped fill in some of the gaps for us, especially once Chris stopped working and it fell to me to cover the shortfall.

But our needs were not so great, so we considered ourselves extremely fortunate; we had just enough.

Once Danny was born, Chris and I had to stop double-teaming Bobby and pay attention to his little brother. The old joke, which you hear a lot in basketball families, is that when the third kid comes along, you switch from man-to-man to a zone. But even with just two kids, we were spread pretty thin, so I started taking Bobby with me to the gym on Saturday and Sunday mornings, just to give Chris some alone time with Danny. Bobby was too young for basketball, of course. He'd only been walking a couple months, so the only kind of dribbling he was doing was down his chin. Still, I packed up some of his toys and made a kind of playpen area for him in the corner of a gym, throwing a couple chairs together to protect him from any loose balls and keep him from running out onto the floor during our scrimmages. From time to time, I had the team manager check in on him to make sure he didn't get into any trouble, and it seemed to work out fine. It got to where Bobby started looking forward to these trips to the gym. He was like our team mascot, and as soon as Danny was old enough to join him, I brought him along as well so Chris could use those mornings to recharge her batteries.

From that point on, Bobby and Danny were fixtures of our program—two Hurley mascots for the price of one. They were always around, always with a ball, always playing. And always together. They were close enough in age that they could have been twins, and on the basketball court they were inseparable. Unfortunately, there was no room for a hoop in our yard at the Country Village house, just a small patch of indoor/outdoor carpet we laid down in the back, so I'd take the boys to the park and we'd shoot around, maybe get a pickup game going. When I started running summer basketball camps in 1975, they'd come along and soak up what they could. They became real students of the game, took to it naturally—which I guess made sense, because they were basically born to it.

We suffered a great sadness during this period: Chris and I lost a child, our son Sean, who was born prematurely. There was a problem with the pregnancy, and he only weighed about two pounds, and we were all devastated. He lived a little less than a week. We were already preparing ourselves for the worst, but as a parent you can never get your head around the loss of a child. It knocks you down and sends you reeling—and even now, all these years later, I choke up when I think about Sean.

There will always be a hole in our lives that he was meant to fill.

Obviously, this was a difficult, anguishing time for our family, and Chris and I have always been private about it, but I mention it here to give a sense of how things were for us back then. How we grew as a family. On the one hand, I felt incredibly blessed for the riches we had—two healthy sons, a comfortable home in a great neighborhood, a solid career, and a fulfilling sideline in high school and rec league basketball. But on the other hand, we were racked with grief and shaken over the loss of little Sean. The boys were too young to really grasp the heartbreak of losing a baby brother like that, but I do recall that they'd been tremendously excited to become big brothers. And Chris and I both remember some painfully difficult conversations with Bobby in particular (Danny was a little young), trying to help him sort through his emotions and understand what was happening.

And so we pressed on—what choice did we have, after all?

———

Soon as it made sense, we started thinking about having another child, and Bobby and Danny finally got the chance to be "big" brothers. (I know, Bobby was already a big brother to Danny, but the two of them were so close in age, I don't think he saw himself that way until much, much later.) Our daughter, Melissa, was born in October 1980, and almost from the moment her little hands could hold a basketball she started going through the same motions as her older brothers. She played all through grammar school, same as them. But basketball was never her "thing," the way it was with Bobby and Danny. She played softball too, and by the time she started high school at Holy Family Academy in Bayonne, basketball was just another after-school activity. It was a take-it-or-leave-it sort of deal. No big thing. Melissa played for a couple years, but then gave it up—and at first I was disappointed she didn't stick with it. Chris too. Melissa knew the game better than most of the other girls who played; she had good size, good skills. But she preferred to watch our games at St. Anthony, where basketball mattered most of all.

The culture of our program really started to change around the time Melissa was born. As I've written, during my first decade as head coach of the St. Anthony varsity, we were a strong, solid team—again, good but not great. Up until 1977, 1978, the team consisted almost entirely of kids in our neighborhood. We found our strengths wherever we could and learned to play to them—where we were weak one year we were strong the next—and even though the goal at the start of each season was to win the state championship, the realistic expectation was to make it to the post-season and put up a good fight. That's all. But then, slowly, we started to see a shift in Jersey City basketball. Hudson Catholic was probably the first school in the area to draw kids from all over the city instead of just one community. We followed soon after, beginning in the early 1980s. We had a really good team in 1980, and again in 1981—led by Ben Gamble, who's been my top assistant for a bunch of years, Mandy Johnson, Phil Robinson, Felix Rivera, and Jared King, mostly local guys who just happened to come along at the same time.

It's no coincidence that Sister Alan Barczewski came along at St. Anthony at around this same time. Back then, most of our teachers were Felician Franciscan nuns, and most of them lived in a convent around the corner from the St. Anthony grammar school, on Sixth Street. Sister Alan joined the nuns at a young age, and this was one of her first assignments, but she took to the school immediately. She was a great sports fan, from Philadelphia, which meant she was fiercely devoted to her Phillies, her Eagles, her 76ers. She was also a big Villanova fan—she went to masses there. We hit it off immediately. We talked a lot of sports at first, but she taught English and history, so we were also trading books and ideas, and it worked out that her arrival as a young teacher came about a year or so before our guys really started to gel on the court. She really warmed to this group—and they responded to her as well—and in a whole bunch of ways she started doing more and more to help us out.

Sister Alan was a terrific supporter, showed up at every home game; she even took the bus to some of our away games. But she also took on a lot of the responsibilities of our athletic director, Tony Nocera, the guy who'd hired me. Tony was only a part-time AD; his real job was in the sheriff's office, so there was nobody around during the school day to arrange gym time, to schedule games, to deal with all the different things that come up during the course of a basketball season. Gradually, Sister Alan took on some of this role. She also let me know if she didn't like a substitution I'd made, late in a game, or if she thought one of the guys on my bench wasn't getting enough playing time. She really knew her stuff, and she wasn't shy about letting me know it.

More than anyone else on the St. Anthony faculty, in the parish, in the archdiocese, Sister Alan was the one who helped to integrate what we were doing on the court into what we were trying to do in the classroom. Over the years, first as a classroom teacher and later on as the school's athletic director and vice principal, she lifted our basketball program to a place of real significance at the school—and she became our biggest fan.

That 1980 team, with Ben Gamble and them, seemed ready to take us to a whole other level. We had a deep, talented bench, which allowed me to push my team in practice and all during the season—because, let's face it, when you're only five or six deep in talent, it's tough to motivate your guys to play at any kind of optimum level. As a coach, you want your players to compete for their roles on the team, the same way you want them to compete to win.

The real change came in 1981, with the arrival of an incredibly gifted freshman named David Rivers. David actually started that season on the junior varsity, but I let him run with the varsity at the end of the year and dress for our games, and that team went on to win the state championship, so the idea that we'd be returning a core group from that team and adding a talented sophomore for the 1981–82 season was terrifically exciting. And David exceeded all of our expectations. As a sophomore, he was named Player of the Year in Hudson County, and he led our team to the county championship. By the time he graduated two years later, he'd become the most heavily recruited basketball player to ever play at St. Anthony. It felt to us like every major college coach in the country came by to check him out, including Jim Boeheim from Syracuse, Jimmy Valvano from North Carolina State, and

Digger Phelps from Notre Dame, where David ultimately went to play.

What this meant for St. Anthony was that a whole new set of eyes was watching us. It meant the basketball world was taking notice, and all of a sudden we started seeing a different caliber of ballplayer, from other parts of Jersey City and beyond. All of a sudden, kids wanted to be a part of whatever it was we'd started to build with David Rivers—as we set off on a record run of nine consecutive state championships. Nine! I can still hardly believe it, but one good team led to another. In 1985 we were led by Kenny Wilson, who went on to Villanova, and things really began to accelerate from there, and by the time Bobby got to high school, there was a tremendous culture of winning and excellence that had taken shape. It was a wonderful thing to see, but we didn't go looking for it.

Meanwhile, David Rivers had an outstanding career at Notre Dame, where he set all kinds of school records. He played in the NBA for a few years—first with the Lakers, later with the Clippers—but his professional career never really took off in the States, so he went to Europe. He played in France, he played in Italy, he played in Greece and Turkey. He was the first American to earn European League MVP honors, which was a great big deal. David ended up having an outstanding career overseas, played for well over a decade, and I couldn't have been prouder of the ways he carried himself after leaving St. Anthony. He's now gone on to become a successful entrepreneur down in Florida, and he's one of those guys, with the opportunities he had at Notre Dame, who really built a life on the back of basketball. And along the way, he helped us build a championship mentality. We still talk every couple weeks, and I often point out to him what he meant, what his place is in the history of the St. Anthony Friars.

Really, he was the catalyst for the next phase of our program. He was the spark. He was like a Pied Piper–type character—all the kids in Jersey City, from Bobby's age on down, wanted to be like David Rivers. They followed him around. They'd seen him play on television, and whenever he played, the play-by-play guys would almost always mention St. Anthony, so we started seeing these talented kids from all over the city, wanting in. David's last couple years playing for me, there was such tremendous excitement, the whole school was connected to it. And not just the school—the entire community was lifted by what our teams were able to do on the basketball court.

Year after year.

It's like the game became a kind of maypole and the fates and fortunes of the school itself began to swirl around it.

Slowly, the culture of the St. Anthony student population began to change. Up until this time, our students tended to reflect the makeup of our basketball team, but by the late 1970s, early 1980s, our classrooms were starting to look a little different—basically because our neighborhoods were starting to look a little different. A lot of our middle-class families were moving out of the area. It used to be that if you lived in Jersey City and were looking to give your kids a coed Catholic school education, you had four options: St. Mary's, St. Michael's, St. Aloysius, and St. Anthony. But St. Michael's closed in 1983, and all those kids had to go somewhere else to school—and in later years St. Al's and St. Mary's would close as well.

All along, there had been three parishes in the city with deep Polish roots: St. Anne's, up on Tonnele Avenue, Mt. Carmel in Bayonne, and St. Anthony. Traditionally, those three parishes would feed our school, which had been up and running since 1952. Before that, the building was a public grammar school, but it had been abandoned by the Board of Education in the early 1950s, when the archdiocese purchased the property; it was never meant to house more than 250 to 300 students, but we've never really gotten close to those high-end numbers.

(St. Anthony historians take note: nothing's really been done to the physical plant of the school in over sixty years, other than a new coat of paint every here and there, so the place looks pretty much the same.)

Soon after the archdiocese took over the building, it was decided that we couldn't support the grammar school, and soon after that, we decided that we couldn't house all those Felician nuns in the convent either. Middle-class Polish families were moving away from downtown Jersey City and the parish kept getting smaller and smaller. By the time David Rivers came to school, we only had one Polish kid on the team—Joe Mikewicz—and only ten or fifteen more in our general student population. Ten years earlier, most of my kids had at least one parent who'd gone to college. Now most of them didn't, and more and more, our students were coming from single-parent households where college was hardly a given.

The dynamic of the school was tough to figure. It was a giant cultural shift, but on the court it was much the same. Didn't much matter what was going on at home—basketball was basketball. It was in the classroom, in the hallways, that you really noticed the difference. On paper, it was an archdiocesan school, but it started to feel like we were connected to St. Anthony Parish in name only. Only a small number of our students now came from St. Anthony families, and there were fewer and fewer of them each year. As a result, the parish was less and less likely to fund whatever budget deficits we carried, because it was less and less involved in the school. Without anyone really realizing it, or planning for it, or even adjusting to it, the identity of the school had changed—and for a while it's like we didn't even have an identity. If it weren't for the extra efforts and enthusiasm of good-hearted leaders like Sister Alan, I don't think the school would have had any personality at all. There was no sense of community to tie all these kids together. But then our teams really started to take off on that huge championship run, and folks started to take notice. Players started coming from all over the city to be a part of our program. They saw that our guys were playing at a high level and realized that if they were able to play at that same high level, they might be able to play their way into college.

Gradually, a new picture of St. Anthony High School started to emerge—and a new identity along with it.

Basketball—that would be our identity.

5.

1988–1989: FAMILY TIES

GREAT TEAMWORK IS THE ONLY WAY WE CAN CREATE THE BREAKTHROUGHS THAT DEFINE OUR CAREERS.
—Pat Riley

NO ONE PLAYS THIS OR ANY GAME PERFECTLY. IT'S THE GUY WHO RECOVERS FROM HIS MISTAKES WHO WINS.
—Phil Jackson

Growing up, the only time my sons Bobby and Danny ever played together on the same team was in the Our Lady of Mercy Pee Wee Basketball League, run by Father Miller. Their team was the Bucks, and I remember sitting on the sidelines and thinking ahead to their high school careers. Even then you could see they played with a little extra something. They worked off each other on the floor, looked for each other off the dribble. I don't mean to come across as a proud father, but they had a feel for the game. I could close my eyes and fast-forward to a time when the two of them might play together for the St. Anthony Friars.

I wasn't like a lot of the dads in our neighborhood. I couldn't coach my own kids, or even help out in practice, because my time was never my own. Between work, coaching at St. Anthony, and running summer leagues and clinics, it was all I could do to get to my sons' games from time to time. It was a priority, just as it was a priority to get to Melissa's activities, but there were a whole lot of priorities back then.

Of course, when your kids are eight or ten years old, you can't know how they'll develop or where their interests might take them, but I had a pretty good idea Bobby and Danny would be playing ball. They grew up as gym rats and lived and breathed basketball the same way their old man lived and breathed basketball, so I knew that's where they were headed. It was in their blood. They played baseball too. They ran track. But it was clear early on that basketball was their thing. Almost as soon as they could walk they were out on the floor at halftime during St. Anthony games, dribbling up a storm, bending their little knees to get enough *ooomph* on their shots to reach the basket. Soon, they were raining/draining threes, dazzling the crowd with their ball-handling skills, running the floor like they belonged no place else.

At St. Anthony home games, their antics were always appreciated; everyone knew them, rooted for them, wished them well. But when we were the visiting team or away at a tournament, folks didn't always want Bobby and Danny on the floor. No one ever stopped them of course. They'd sneak onto the court, and after just a couple minutes they'd have the crowd with them, and they'd run and shoot and dribble their little hearts out—sometimes while a school or arena representative tried to chase them to the sidelines.

All season long, year after year, that was the routine.

Like me, Bobby and Danny were late bloomers in the height department. The Hurley men are pipsqueaks starting out, but we grow into our frames soon enough. And the silver lining to our short stature is that we're forced to develop our dribbling skills right away; we've got no choice but to work on our handle, our passing, our outside shooting . . . it's all we've got, so we grab on to whatever edge that's within reach.

The boys had been coming to the gym with me for so long, it was almost inevitable they'd wind up playing for me—but it almost didn't work out that way. In 1985, when Bobby was finishing middle school, I got an offer from a friend of mine that Chris and I felt we had to consider. The offer came from Pete Gillen, who for years had coached high school ball in Brooklyn. We'd worked together at the Five Star Basketball Camp and remained friends. In fact, Pete went on to work with Digger Phelps as an assistant at Notre Dame, and he'd been instrumental in recruiting David Rivers from St. Anthony. When Pete left Notre Dame to take the head coaching job at Xavier, he started recruiting me to join him as an assistant.

He made a pretty strong case.

Now, I'd gotten a number of college offers over the years, but I'd never been all that interested. I liked working with high school kids. I liked that we were laying in a kind of template they could maybe follow the rest of their lives, to help them recognize and achieve their goals. I liked the hours. I liked that I didn't have to deal with alumni or recruiting or young men with puffed-up egos who thought they knew more about the game than their coaches.

This last issue was key. High school kids coming into their own are like a blank canvas; you can work on their game and their character and their approach; you can even help them reach their full potential as players and grow into the young men they're meant to be. Usually, they respond—and a lot of times, if they don't respond, it's on you as their coach. It means you haven't found a way to reach them. College kids, you sometimes have to sort through a bunch of bad habits and negative influences to get the most out of a player. A lot of times, if they don't respond, it's on them; they're who they are, for the most part—not quite fully formed or fully developed as players, but close enough to get them thinking they have it all figured out. There's just no way to reach some of these kids after a certain point, and I didn't think I had the head for that. I needed to see the upside in my players; I needed to know that they wanted to grow their game and that the extra efforts we were putting in on and off the court might amount to something.

Plus, I was a homebody. I'd never even been on a plane until Chris and I went to Miami on our honeymoon. I liked living in Jersey City; I'd been there my whole life, so I knew where everything was. But then Pete went to work on me, and I started to see the benefits of a college gig. The money was pretty great—way more than I was making on my civil servant salary, even with the modest stipend I was getting for coaching at St. Anthony, which back then was up to about three or four thousand dollars. Things went far enough on this Xavier job that Chris and I flew out to Cincinnati to meet with Pete, and he took us around to look at houses and schools for the kids. We came away thinking this was the right move for us as a family—but Bobby and Danny turned us back around. When we got back home and told the kids our plans, they kicked up a real fuss.

They made a pretty strong case too. They'd had their hearts set on playing basketball at St. Anthony, it turned out. We'd never really talked about it, except I guess it was always assumed that this was how things would go. Bobby and Danny didn't want to leave their friends. Melissa was still young at this point, so she didn't really have an opinion one way or the other, but the boys felt strongly about this. Bobby most of all. He was about to start high school. He had his basketball career all figured out. In his head, he was going to play for me at St. Anthony and then move on to North Carolina to play for Dean Smith. That was his plan, his dream. He didn't want to have to start from scratch with a whole new group of kids in Cincinnati.

What Bobby didn't say, what Danny didn't say, what *I* didn't say, was that we'd all been looking forward to this time in our lives for as long as any of us could remember—but there it was, and it took my kids to point it out and remind me it was something we'd been waiting on all along.

Sister Alan was another big reason I stayed on at St. Anthony. Already, by the time Bobby started high school, she'd become a fixture at the school. She gave the place a winning personality and helped our program enormously. Without Sister Alan, I would have never been able to build our schedule or deal with all the paperwork and organizing and nonsense that came with coaching. She ran interference for us with the administration, with the parish, with the archdiocese. She also had me convinced that our success on the court would in some way contribute to our never-ending fund-raising efforts, though I must say, I didn't see how the one had anything to do with the other.

Over time Sister Alan turned out to be right about this, as

she was about most things, but for the time being the school was doing okay financially. In fact, Bobby started high school at a time of peak enrollment for St. Anthony, so we were in good shape—at least for the next while.

It was a mixed blessing to be able to coach a kid like Bobby. For years I wasn't sure how I'd respond, whether I'd play favorites and cut my own kid a little more slack in terms of playing time, opportunities, expectations. If anything, I worried for poor Bobby, because I knew I'd go out of my way to make things a little tougher on him, to make him work a little harder than everyone else, to hold him to a higher standard. Not because I was out to bust his hump, but because I wanted to make double-sure no one ever accused me of playing favorites. That no one ever said Bobby was there on anything but his own merits as a player. For my sake as well as Bobby's.

Whenever I think back to that time in our lives, with Bobby about to start high school, I remember a comment Al McGuire made when he was coaching his son at Marquette and the kid was competing for minutes with another player. Al said, "If you're just as good as my son, you're in trouble, because he's my son."

I had a different view. I took the position that if you're my son, you need to outplay the other guy so nobody second-guesses your role. You have to earn your way onto the floor like everyone else, but then you have to do a little more besides. That wasn't exactly fair to Bobby (or, later, to Danny), but he knew what to expect.

And in some ways, I knew what to expect from my kids. I knew they'd work hard. I knew they wouldn't back down from a challenge. I knew they'd dive for every loose ball. I knew they'd drive opponents crazy with their ability to dribble and see the floor and find the open man. They played the game by instinct, like it had been drilled into them—and in many ways, I guess it had.

What I couldn't know was how they'd develop physically. When Bobby showed up in high school, he was five-four, maybe 110 pounds. Just to look at him, he seemed way too small to play varsity, so he started out on the JV. He wasn't too happy about it, but I think he half-expected it—and to his great credit, he made the best of it. First few weeks of the season, he was lights out, and when a couple of our varsity guards went down to injury, I had to look to the JV to replace them. Bobby was the obvious choice, even though he'd now give away a couple years, a couple inches, and a couple dozen pounds to his opponents.

He was up to it, though. First game he played, against my alma mater, St. Peter's Prep, he fired in the first three shots he took—*swish-swish-swish*—all from long range. That set the tone for the rest of his career, just in those first few minutes, and by the end of the season he had tallied ten points and ten assists in the state finals, so it was clear to everyone he belonged. He'd made his mark, together with his great buddy Jerry Walker, who started the season as a power forward in our rotation, a key part of our offense and a tenacious defender. So that first year with Bobby was unusual because we had two impact freshmen on the varsity—Bobby and Jerry. Doesn't usually work out that way, but this too set the tone. I don't think any of us realized it just then, but we were laying the foundation for a dominant run.

Bobby filled out, of course. He got taller, bigger, stronger. He went on to do some big-time things on the basketball court, including leading the Duke Blue Devils to back-to-back national championships in 1991 and 1992, as well as setting the all-time NCAA assists record with 1,076. (No, he never quite made it to Dean Smith and North Carolina, but it all worked out to the good at Duke, with Coach Mike Krzyzewski.) Bobby was selected with the seventh pick in the first round of the NBA draft by the

Sacramento Kings—and along the way he wound up playing with some great players. And yet, of all these great, great players, he still maintains that Jerry Walker was the single greatest teammate he ever played alongside—and I can't argue with him. Jerry was an absolutely tremendous player. Fearless. Smart. Talented. And even at fourteen, fifteen years old, he was a powerful presence on the court. He was the first freshman to ever start for the St. Anthony Friars, and he and Bobby had known each other for years and years, so once Bobby came up from the JV and joined him, they made a terrific tandem. Led us all the way to the state championship that first year. And the year after that. And the year after that.

Those three state championships with this core group, back-to-back-to-back, continued that great momentum run we'd started in 1982–83 with a team, led by David Rivers, that earned us six consecutive state titles.

(We'd go on to win another three straight, but I don't want to get ahead of the story.)

By this point, we'd added Terry Dehere to the mix, which made us the preseason favorites to repeat as state champs in 1988–89. Terry would go on to become the all-time leading scorer at Seton Hall, which helped to make him a first-round NBA draft choice, but he didn't start for us on a regular basis until his senior year. We also had a talented freshman on the team that year, Rodrick Rhodes, another future first-round NBA draft choice, and he figured to play a big role for us. So, on paper at least, we were looking like a dominant group. We were coming off a big season, winning our sixth straight state title, beating a bunch of tough, high-profile teams at big-time tournaments across the country—including a first-ever trip to a high-profile tournament in Hawaii, where we beat top national teams like Dunbar from

Baltimore (with Sam Cassell) and Tolentine from the Bronx (with Malik Sealy, Brian Reese, and Adrian Autry), only to come back home and lose to a local team, Ferris High School.

For some reason, we always had trouble with Ferris at their gym, but we came back to beat them in the county final that year. Ferris had also given us our only loss the year before, 1986–87, also at their gym. Both games were at four o'clock on school days—always a tough assignment for a visiting team, but especially tough against Ferris. Not to make excuses or anything, but we couldn't get our guys out of school and on the road until 2:45 or so, and then we really had to hustle to make it to the gym on time and get our full warm-up in, so we were up against it. We never really had a chance to get focused, but they beat us fair and square. Boy oh boy, those Ferris teams were good at home. They just didn't crack, and yet I think those lone losses really helped to set us up for our postseason runs in each of those years, because our guys had been pushed. They knew what it was like to lose— and what it would take to keep from losing again.

Here's how tough it was on Bobby to play for me. In those days, I was still able to run with these kids in practice, and every time Bobby messed up, I'd chew him out in front of the whole gym, same way I'd chew out any other player. But then, if Bobby messed up a second or third time, I'd pull him off the floor and take his spot in the drill or the scrimmage. I'd yell something like, "Why is this so hard for you?" Of course, some of this stuff was hard for him, because he was being guarded by three guys who'd go on to play in the NBA. It made sense that he couldn't complete a pass from time to time. Or run a play the way it was designed. So then I'd step in for him to show him it should be done. I was fortysomething years old—way, way past my prime as an athlete—but because I was the coach, these kids would hang back a little on defense. Out of respect, I guess. Or maybe they were afraid to guard me too tight because they thought I'd go off on them. So I was able to do whatever I wanted out there pretty much—whatever I wanted Bobby to do—so it couldn't have been easy for Bobby.

It was tough enough to step in as a freshman and sophomore and try to make your mark on such a talented team, and I only made it tougher, but to Bobby's great credit, he hung in there.

Jerry Walker made his own mark his freshman year when we went to a tournament in Johnstown, Pennsylvania. A lot of great players had played in this tournament over the years, and before the games began, we took our guys on a little tour, showed them where they kept the plaques for all the past MVPs, the past champions. Guys like Wilt Chamberlain, Hal Greer, and Maurice Stokes—legendary basketball players—had all played in this tournament. And there was Jerry Walker, all wide-eyed and bursting with confidence. He took a look around and said, "I'm gonna be up there with those guys."

The kid was fourteen, fifteen years old and thinking he belonged with some of the greatest athletes to ever play the game . . . but that was Jerry. Sure enough, we went out and beat the host team, Johnstown, in the opening game, in their packed gym, and then in the finals we managed to beat Ben Franklin—a big, impressive team from Philadelphia with six kids at six-seven, six-eight, or taller.

After the tournament, Jerry was named MVP, and as the tournament official called his name Jerry turned to me and said, "Told you."

We only graduated two players from that 1987–88 team with just that one loss to Ferris, and we were returning most of our core group and adding some real talent and depth, so expectations ran high heading into the 1988–89 season. There was even a new wrinkle to the schedule that year. For the first time, the winners of the state championships in every school classification would meet in a season-ending tournament to determine a true state champion. It had always been a topic of discussion in New Jersey high school basketball (and across the country, I imagine), whether a small private school like St. Anthony would be able to beat one of the big public high schools in the state. A lot of folks thought it'd be like comparing apples and oranges, or maybe like pitting a Division I NCAA champ against, say, a Division III NCAA champ. It used to be that there were three designations for parochial or private schools—Non-Public A, Non-Public B, and Non-Public C—and up until 1980, St. Anthony, one of the smallest schools in the state with an overall enrollment of around 240 students, was classified as a Non-Public C school. After that, the B and C groups were combined.

On the public side, dating back to the 1940s, there have been four groups: Public 1 (the smallest public schools in the state), Public 2, Public 3, and Public 4 (the largest). It gets a little confusing, I know, because the public groups go from small to big by number, while the non-public groups go from big to small by letter, but we've learned to figure it out.

The conversation regarding a *post*-postseason tournament to crown an overall state champion had intensified over the past six years as St. Anthony kept winning. We'd play some big public schools like Elizabeth and Camden and Plainfield during the regular season, but people in and around the game wondered how we'd do in a big-time, end-of-season tournament with statewide bragging rights on the line. Frankly, our guys were wondering the same thing, so this was a chance to settle the matter on the court. To really make a statement.

Over the years I've come to think of the Tournament of Champions as a drag on the New Jersey State Interscholastic Athletic Association's postseason schedule. It stretches out the season for another week or so and pushes the limits of what we expect of our kids, who've been playing hard for nearly four months by the time the state tournament is through. It's a lot to ask of them, to get up for a run at the state title and then to keep that level of play, that level of adrenaline, going for another two or three games—but the Tournament of Champions is now a fixture on the New Jersey high school sports scene, so we've got no choice but to give it our best shot. And for the first couple years at least, we were as excited as any other team in the state to compete on such a meaningful stage.

Really, it was a great big deal—and a great big honor.

In those days, as an independent, we tried not to play the Non-Public B teams in the northern part of the state during the regular season, because we knew we might see them again in the state tournament. There were enough strong teams in the state that we didn't have to give anyone a free look, so that was an internal, informal rule we tried to follow. Naturally, we'd break our own rule from time to time if we had an open date on the schedule or a long-standing rivalry that was good for the program, and sometimes we'd face a Non-Public B rival in a tournament, depending on the draw, but it was a general strategy we tried to keep in mind. And if it worked out that we were playing a team we thought we might see again in the postseason, we tried to hold back some pieces of our game plan, just so we could throw another look at them when it counted.

The other rule, in terms of scheduling, was that 70 percent of our games had to be against in-state opponents, up until the first Saturday in February. That was a state rule we had to follow in order to be eligible for the state tournament, so we did what we could to balance the formal requirements with our informal strategizing.

And so, heading into this 1988–89 season, there was this whole extra layer of anticipation, because our goal was not only to position ourselves to repeat as Non-Public B champions, but also to continue our postseason run into the Tournament of Champions and have a chance to prove that St. Anthony was a true basketball power.

On a personal note, I was especially looking forward to starting the season with my younger son Danny on the team, playing alongside his brother for the first time since Pee Wee ball, only it didn't exactly work out the way I'd imagined it. I didn't figure on Danny starting for us that year, but I expected to him to play some big minutes for us off the bench. He was a good outside shooter, so I was counting on him to spell Bobby and Terry from time to time, but he ended up getting hurt in our very first practice—just a fluke, freak injury.

We'd arranged a three-day preseason training camp in Port Jervis, New York, together with a team from Mahwah High School. We had to do some heavy-duty fund-raising to help pay for the trip, but I thought it was important to take these kids away from their home environment for a couple days, so we could really get our heads around the season. It helped to throw in with another team—to keep a lid on the cost, but also to provide some steady competition, a tough opponent to run up against once we were ready to start scrimmaging.

First day of training camp, I had my guys doing a monkey-in-the-middle type drill to work on mirroring the basketball. It's a simple drill, but it's the kind of thing you need to do to reinforce the fundamentals. A lot of coaches, they'll look to accomplish the same thing with a loose ball drill; where you roll the ball onto the floor and have two players chase it down and try to cover it, but I'd seen too many kids get hurt like that, so I used this drill instead. It was basic—two kids, passing the ball back and forth, with a third kid in the middle trying to intercept, deflect, or upset the pass any way he could.

We were at it maybe two, three minutes, when Danny reached for a ball and jammed his finger in just the wrong way. He was in a whole lot of pain, which is what happens anytime you jam your finger, but we could tell from the way his finger hung from his hand that it was bad. It wasn't something Danny could just ice and rest. He wound up fracturing his bone at the joint and sitting out the first two or three months of the season, which was a big disappointment and a big frustration for us as a team—and as a family. We'd all been looking forward to this season for years and years, and now Danny could only look on from the sideline.

My heart broke for him, as a dad. Bobby's did too, as an older brother. And my wife, Chris, was probably more upset than any of us, Danny included, because she'd had her heart set on watching her boys in their one-and-only high school season as teammates. But the focus for us as a team was on the opportunity that Danny's injury now presented for some of the other players on our bench—and we were a really deep team that year, especially in the post. We had Sean Rooney, our starting center, who went to Duquesne. His backup, Jose Ortiz, went to Radford University in Virginia. We also had a guard on that team, Lamont Street, who barely played a minute a game for us and still went on to score a thousand points in his career at Wagner College.

We went to Florida to start the season, to play at the Great

Florida Shootout in Kissimmee. First game of the tournament we
drew a team from Edison High School in Miami, and we got ourselves into trouble straightaway. In those days, pre-Internet, we
couldn't do the kind of advance scouting we do today. You'd go to
one of these destination tournaments, and you'd check out the rest
of the field when your guys weren't playing. That was the routine.
You'd study the brackets and look ahead to your likely opponents
in the next rounds. But that first game was always a cold call—
you never knew what you might get, other than what you could
piece together from word of mouth and anecdotal information.

We got off to a slow start. Jerry Walker committed two fouls
in the first minute and a half, so I had to sit him down before
he could even break a sweat. This messed up our game plan,
of course. By his senior year, Jerry had grown to six-seven, 220
pounds, so he was a real presence for us in the post. Everything
we did on the defensive end flowed through him, so as soon as
Jerry left the floor Edison started killing us on the boards and in
the low post. Luckily, Bobby played pretty well that game, and
we managed to hold on for the win, but Jerry never really got a
chance to get going, so I worried he'd still need some time to find
his game legs as the tournament progressed.

Happily, we got it going over the next couple games and made
it to the finals against Miami Senior—the second-ranked team in
the country—and here our perfect season nearly got away from
us, only four games in. These kids from Miami Senior were tough.
A lot of big bruiser types—and a deep, deep bench, with talent all
through their rotation. They had the crowd with them, to start.
Our shots weren't falling. We were a little out of sync, but we
managed to hang with them well enough, until halfway through
the fourth quarter, when we went down by three points. The
game seemed to turn on a technical foul. First it turned against

us, but our guys found a little extra something and turned it right back around. What happened was, Sean Rooney got clipped with an elbow and retaliated by throwing a punch. It was a stupid, bullheaded response, but in Sean's defense, his father was a boxer—and a great friend of Chuck Wepner, the heavyweight from Bayonne, New Jersey, who was thought to be the inspiration for Sylvester Stallone's "Rocky" character—so throwing a punch was second nature to him, even if it's not what you want to see on a basketball court. Miami Senior ended up converting the technical, and then on the ensuing possession one of their guards hit a three to give them that three-point lead, but after that the momentum seemed to swing back toward us. Miami Senior was all pumped up following the technical, but then the air just kind of leaked out of them. It was as if our guys needed to dig themselves one last hole before they could think about climbing back out— and somehow they did. Coming out of that three following the technical, we went on a 14–0 run, putting us back up by eleven points, and from there we won the game going away.

We were in a packed gym just outside Orlando, and the fans had been mostly leaning toward Miami Senior, but now they were all the way in our corner, and we rode that energy to really pour it on at the end. We couldn't miss for trying, and we kept stopping them on defense, and if the game had been just a couple minutes longer, we'd have won by twenty-five points, easy, so it was an important win for us. Sent us home thinking we could match up against the best in the country, even when things didn't quite go our way.

Our next big test came at the King Cotton Classic in Pine Bluff, Arkansas, just after Christmas. The story of the tournament reached all the way back to the previous season, to that one loss against Ferris. Those key wins against Dunbar and Tolentine had come in the semifinal and final of the Yolani Prep Classic in Honolulu—which also, by the way, came about on the back of a heavy-duty fund-raising effort. We beat Dunbar by a comfortable double-digit margin on our side of the bracket, while Tolentine just destroyed Flint Hill, a prep school team from Virginia, in their semifinal. In the final, we then knocked off Tolentine to take the tournament—another huge win for us, because Tolentine had been the consensus number-one team in the country going into the game. But that was last year. This year, heading into Pine Bluff, we were surprised to see that Flint Hill was seeded first in the tournament, even though we'd beaten the same Tolentine team that had routed Flint Hill the year before.

Nothing against Flint Hill, who'd won this same tournament the year before. That's how it works in most tournaments: if you're the returning champion, you're automatically given the number-one seed. And they were certainly a strong team; after Miami Senior lost to us in Kissimmee, Flint Hill took over as the second-ranked team in the country. They had a six-ten big man named Frasier Johnson, who went on to play at Temple; Arron Bain, who had a fine career at Villanova; George Lynch, who went to North Carolina and played in the NBA for a bunch of years; and Randolph Childress, who played a couple years for Wake Forest before setting off on his own NBA career. That's a lot of top-tier talent on just one team, so we couldn't discount them, but I put it in our players' heads that we were being disrespected by not being the number-one seed—by the tournament organizers, by the local crowds—and I let them think that the Flint Hill players were strutting around the complex like they were the team to beat, which they were, as far as we were concerned.

Jerry Walker picked up on this. He was always good at rallying the troops, getting under his teammates' skin. He was an intimidating defensive player—he would end up leading Seton Hall to two Big East titles and earning Defensive Player of the Year honors in the conference—but his real value came in the intangibles. Our guys respected him, followed his lead. He knew what buttons to push to get our team going. He hated that we were being treated like a contender in the tournament, and he said as much to anyone who'd listen. He hated that the kids from Flint Hill thought they were the team to beat. He especially hated that they kept showing up late to all the events the organizers had arranged—photo shoots, media interviews, and on and on. He even hated that the Flint Hill players traveled around in a team bus with a banner announcing that they were defending champions. He thought they were arrogant, and he got his teammates thinking they were arrogant. Yeah, they'd won the same tournament the year before, so they'd earned a little bit of swagger, but we hadn't played in that tournament—and Jerry set it up like we needed to take this team down a couple pegs. It wasn't just about winning; it was about making sure Flint Hill was denied.

There were other good teams in the tournament, but Flint Hill was the clear strength on the other side of the bracket, so they became our focus. Before we could face them, though, we had to get past a decent Catholic school team from New Orleans in the first game, and then an even better public school team from Memphis in the semifinal, but we were able to put them away without too much trouble. Flint Hill, too, was able to sail through the other side of the bracket, and by the time we met up in the finals, our guys were feeling like they had something to prove. The game was due to be televised on ESPN, on a tape delay, so that became a whole other something to prove—because it would be the first time we played in front of a national television audience. That kind of exposure meant the world to my players in terms of getting seen by college coaches all around the country. It was also an ego boost, a kick, so they had every incentive to want to play well.

One of the ways I like to get my kids up for a game is to really pump up our opponent, to get my kids thinking they need to be lion-killers. I'm pretty transparent about it, to the point where my players know exactly what I'm doing, but it's still an effective tactic. They see how concerned I am about an opponent, and they become concerned; they take care to put out their best possible effort, to make sure they remember what we worked on in practice that week. I've found that it's a lot easier to motivate your players when they think they're the underdog than when they think they're expected to win, and here I liked it that we were thinking like upstarts.

And we did have something to prove—but only to ourselves.

In many ways, that Flint Hill game signaled our arrival as a team. Our guys came out strong, ended up outplaying this team from Virginia in every way. There was one play in particular that seemed to set the tone for our entire season. Bobby made a steal at half-court and pushed the ball the other way. Randolph Childress scrambled back on defense, and he appeared to have a bead on Bobby, but just as Bobby made what looked to be his final move toward the basket, he dumped off a neat little throwback pass over his shoulder to Terry Dehere, who was trailing the play. Terry took the ball and soared to the rim and threw it down, and as he did, Childress kind of turned and stumbled and lost his footing. This alone was remarkable, because Childress was one of the top players in the country, but he was so turned around and discombobulated by our quickness and athleticism that he could barely keep his feet. It was something to see. And his teammates appeared to falter as well. The game went from a convincing, comfortable margin to a rout, just on the back of this one play—really, we sent that team reeling—and I remember looking on at this one exchange with Bobby and Terry and taking it as a sign of things to come.

I left thinking we could run circles around the competition.

The way the game shook out, we were up by more than twenty points for most of the second half, and I sat on the bench once the game was in hand knowing this Friars team had a chance to do something special. Remember, we'd gone down to Florida and beat Miami Senior, the number-two team in the country. Then, a couple weeks later, we went to Arkansas and beat Flint Hill, the new number-two team in the country. Doesn't matter that we were the number-one-ranked team each time out—it's still a difficult assignment to knock off *two* number-two teams, almost back to back. And yet I worried we might be peaking too early. There was no good reason to worry—no logical reason, anyway—but I worried just the same. That's how it goes when the breaks of the game are falling your way—you still find a reason to worry. What you want, as a coach, is to build a certain kind of momentum into your season. You want to make strides every game, every week, always with a goal in mind, but here we were looking ahead to a mostly local schedule for the next six or seven weeks, against teams that really didn't match up with these Miami Senior and Flint Hill squads, and the danger was that we'd coast for a while, maybe become a little too complacent, a little too full of ourselves.

Turned out we almost didn't get out of Arkansas. There was a problem with our plane, and we spent most of the night in the airport in Little Rock. We were sprawled out on the floor by the gate, propped up against our bags, trying to catch a couple hours' sleep, but a lot of our kids were restless and wired from the game. I tried to catch a couple winks, but it was useless—and besides, somebody had to keep an eye on all these restless and wired kids. All these years later, I still remember Danny and a couple of the other guys just yukking it up, middle of the night, giving the business to one of our players, Darren Savino, for the patented up-and-under move he'd tried to pull against one of the Flint Hill big men.

Darren Savino was a kid from the neighborhood who'd grown up with Danny and Bobby. He's now an assistant coach at the University of Cincinnati, and it's possible he would have never gotten into coaching if he and Bobby hadn't been such great pals when they were all little. Same way Bobby and Danny were bitten by the basketball bug, Darren was bitten too, by association. He was a role player for us, didn't get a whole lot of minutes, but when he played he went at the game with a big man's mentality. That's been his strength as a coach, working with players in the post. He was only about six feet tall, but he was like an undersized post player, and toward the end of the game he was being guarded by the backup Flint Hill center, who must have been about six-eleven. They made an odd picture, the two of them, battling for position, because the big kid had almost a foot on Darren. So what does Darren do? He gets the ball beneath our basket at one point and pump-fakes like he's taking it hard to the rim, tries to get the big man to commit, and as soon as the kid leaves his feet, Darren kind of ducks beneath the defender's outstretched arms and scoops the ball underneath for an old-school layup. For some reason, this struck our guys on the bench—Danny especially—as just about the funniest thing in the world, and as our long night dragged on, stranded in the airport, they started razzing poor Darren pretty good.

Oh, one thing I forgot to mention: the six-eleven Flint Hill kid who was guarding Darren just kind of swatted the ball away. Like it was an annoying mosquito. It was a pretty emphatic rejection. If Darren had sunk the layup, our guys would have had no reason to ride him about the shot, but because he'd made such a soft, dainty move and still managed to get rejected like that, it was open season. And there was no end to it. At one point, I opened my eyes and saw Danny, his hand still in the cast he wore the first month or two of the season, doing his version of Darren's up-and-under move to howls and howls of laughter from his teammates. At four o'clock in the morning, it was even funnier than it had been during the run of play—but Darren shouldered the ribbing with great good cheer.

It was a tight-knit group, that team. They'd been playing together for a long, long time. They'd gotten used to winning—and winning big—but they could always find a way to laugh at themselves.

You know, in many ways this 1988–89 team was blessed. We were blessed with enormous talent, excellent team chemistry, and a couple tough matchups that happened to go our way. But we were also cursed. For all of our triumphs and hard-won glory, there's a pall that hangs over that season for me and my guys. It's been less than twenty-five years since the seniors from this team graduated high school, and already we've lost three members from that core group—four if we include a young man who'd played with us the season before, when our key guys were still juniors.

That's a heartbreakingly big number from a team of just fourteen or fifteen players. And it's not like these kids had to wait all that long to start facing their own mortality, because one of our players didn't even make it out of high school. Jermaine Rivers, David's brother, would have been a big part of this special season, but he succumbed to a brain tumor during his junior year. He was another one of Bobby's pals, another kid from the neighborhood. We used to pick him up every morning on the way to school, along with Jerry Walker. Jermaine stopped playing ball in his sophomore year, when the treatments became too much for him, but he hung in there at school for as long as he could. He never really made it all the way into a varsity uniform, although we had him pegged to make a contribution as an upperclassman. Guess you could say he was more like an honorary member of this group, and here the emphasis would have been on the word *honor*, because the way he shouldered his illness was such an inspiration. His death was such a devastating sadness for Jermaine's family. For the entire St. Anthony community. It hit my boys especially hard, because they'd all been close. In fact, it hit the entire team pretty hard, because Jermaine died just before the start of this charmed season, and these kids were all friends, so his spirit kind of filled the gym as we went about our business.

He was with us even when he was no longer with us—and for every good turn that found us, for every big win, there was an aching reminder that one of our own wasn't there to share in it. Even now, all these years later, when I sit with my boys and think back to this one season, I think of Jermaine and what he missed. Not just on the court, of course, but how the rest of his life might have gone. We talk about how he would have fit himself into the mix. He was a part of what we accomplished that year, even though he couldn't be a part of it.

And lately, my thoughts drift to three other players as well— Mark Harris, Sean Rooney, and Sydney Raeford. Mark, first guard off the bench for us while Danny was out, was hit by a rare form of cancer—the same cancer that claimed Walter Payton. Mark's death was tough to accept for his St. Anthony basketball family, because we all knew Mark as an incredible physical specimen. No one wanted to face this kid in practice, because he would pound the crap out of you. He fouled you every which way, just about every time he touched you. There was nothing dirty about the way Mark played, but he was relentless. He was all muscle and bone; if you ran into him, you got hurt, and it was a kind of art form with him, getting opposing players to run into him. Really, he was the prototypical practice player, the kind of guy you want on your side, because he went at it hard. Like he had something to prove. And he did. Every time he took the floor, he played like his role on the team depended on it, and the starters used to bellyache every time they scrimmaged against him, because they knew they'd be black and blue the next day.

At the time, I used to think Mark's hard-charging work ethic in practice made us better as a team. It pushed Bobby and Terry to a whole other level. With Mark, it didn't matter if you were his teammate or his best friend—he played like it meant something, like whatever was going on in his life, in school, in Jersey City, in the whole wide world, basketball mattered most of all. And then, when I learned he'd been diagnosed, after he'd been out of school a couple years, I remembered how he'd carried himself as a young man. I heard about his illness one Thanksgiving, just as our season was getting under way. I figured Mark would put up a good fight. I figured he'd beat the crap out of his cancer, same way he used to beat the crap out of his teammates, but by the end of March he was gone—and to this day it strikes me as a cruel irony for such a beast of an athlete to be cut down at such a young age.

Sad to say, we've lost a bunch of former players over the years. That's what happens when you've been coaching high school basketball as long as I have, but we've never lost so many, so young . . . from the same group. It's a sadness on top of another sadness. And it would get sadder still. We lost our starting center, Sean Rooney. He died of a massive heart attack just a couple years ago, and his loss struck me like a punch in the gut. As hard as Mark Harris used to play in practice, that's how hard Sean Rooney used to play in games. He just wouldn't back down from a fight—and as we saw in that game against Miami Senior, he'd sometimes start one, just for the hell of it.

When I heard the news about Sean, that a kid who'd played with so much heart and absolutely no quit somehow had his heart quit on him during what should have been the prime of his life, it shook me up pretty good. Sean always played with such joy, such abandon. He didn't have the pure athletic talent of a Jerry Walker or a Terry Dehere, but he was just as determined to win, just as passionate about the game—and he played just as big a part in our success. He didn't always fill up the stat sheet like Bobby or some of his other teammates, but he made his presence known every time he took the floor.

Sydney Raeford graduated a year before this group, but they all played together on the 1988 team. He'd come to us from the Number 14 school in Jersey City—another kid from the neighborhood. Sydney went to Xavier on a basketball scholarship, finished his career at St. Peter's College, then fell to cancer too. That's three kids out of this one group who'd all grown up within a couple blocks of each other, all struck down by some form of cancer, way before their time. Syd grew up on Atlantic Street, Mark was on Virginia, and Jermaine's family lived on Ege, so of course everyone assumed there was some environmental trigger. I guess it made sense folks were thinking that way, because there was a lot of industry in that part of the city; there'd obviously been a lot of dumping over the years, but no one was ever able to make any kind of definitive connection, so all we could do in the end was chalk it up to a run of devastating bad luck—one sadness after another.

Don't think I'll ever get used to the idea that these good kids are no longer with us. It's not supposed to happen that a high school basketball coach outlives his players, but sometimes life gets in the way of what's not supposed to happen. Life . . . and death. And now I can't look back on the great success we enjoyed that year as a team without thinking of the pieces that are now missing. It doesn't take anything away from what we were able to accomplish during this one perfect season, from the great run we had with this core group. But it colors the time we all shared and leaves me thinking about why we play, why basketball matters.

It does matter, I've come to believe. Because, while we're playing the game, it's who we are. And when we're through, when we leave this world, it's how we'll be remembered.

Back to basketball.

There weren't a whole lot of teams in a position to test us that year, especially the teams close to home. Elizabeth High School was probably the second-best team in the state, and we'd beaten them handily in a game at St. Peter's College, winning by about twenty points. They had a left-handed seven-footer, Luther Wright, who'd started his career at St. Anthony, so it was a bit of a reunion for some of our guys. Not exactly a grudge match, but there was a little extra incentive for us to play well—and a little extra pressure on Luther to give his old teammates a push, maybe hand us our first loss of the season.

Luther would go on to play with Danny, Terry, and Jerry at

Seton Hall, and he was a first-round draft pick of the Utah Jazz, but he just didn't have it that day at St. Peter's. Elizabeth was a good, deep team, with all five starters going on to key roles at Division I college programs, but we were on an unbelievable momentum run, playing out of our heads. Whatever those public school kids threw at us, we were able to throw it right back, and the game was never even close.

Probably the toughest game on our local schedule that year was against Solebury Prep, last game of the regular season. We were convinced the entire starting lineup was in their twenties. A lot of programs, they reclassified players of postgraduate age who still had some high school eligibility. At St. Anthony, our guys were all "by the book," of regular high school age; most of the teams we faced during the season also followed the traditional classification rules, but this Solebury Prep team was one of the schools we faced where it looked like the entire roster had been reclassified. I can't say for sure, but it certainly appeared that way. The contrast in their physical characteristics was apparent. Even just a couple years, at that age, can make a tremendous difference in the size and strength of a young athlete. Physically, the Solebury Prep players were much bigger, much stronger, but we found a way to outplay them and come out on top—by a comfortable margin that didn't really reflect how uncomfortable we looked going up against these guys.

Danny returned from his injury in the state tournament against Don Bosco Tech in a game that turned out to be a real romp—one of the few times in my career a St. Anthony team scored over a hundred points in a game. It happens maybe once every three or four years, and it's not always a welcome thing. In a thirty-two-minute game, if you get eighty points, it's a big deal. To score another twenty points . . . well, the other team is probably cooperating. And it usually means things will get ugly. If you're in someone else's gym, you'll hear taunts and nonsense about running up the score, even though you've got your second and third units in. These kids, they're on the bench most of the season, you can't exactly put them out there and expect them to sit on the ball. They'll be looking for their shots—and on this Friars team in particular, that whole second group ended up playing in college, so there was some talent all through our lineup. They were like thoroughbreds, itching to be let out of the gate. Everybody wound up scoring for us in that game. Danny came off the bench in the fourth quarter and poured in ten quick points, and it was good to see him back in the mix. It was a big deal for him to finally be able to contribute, even in a one-sided game. And it was a big deal for me to finally see him on the floor for us. Wasn't running alongside his brother just yet, because Bobby was out of the game by the time Danny checked in, but it was a glimpse of what this season could have been . . . and what it might be still.

Danny's return coincided with an injury to Bobby's hamstring. Bobby had suffered a tear in his upper hamstring with about two weeks to go in the season, but he was trying to play through it. The injury had me worried—but not too, too worried. Bobby wasn't about to miss the last postseason of his high school career, especially with so much on the line, so we kept running him out there. We were careful with his minutes, though, careful with how we used him, and now that we had Danny back, our bench was a little deeper.

We weren't really tested in the state tournament that year and ended up beating a decent team from St. Rose in the Non-Public Group B final by a big number. But then we had to look ahead to this new Tournament of Champions format. Any other year, we would have finished the season as state champs, undefeated, the consensus number-one team in the country—but now we had to play another couple games to keep all of that in place. No one could take away our state title, of course, but if we faltered now, we'd lose our perfect season and the number-one ranking right along with it.

As a coach, you never like to press your luck or keep going back to the same well, over and over. In all my years at St. Anthony, we've never shied from a game. We'll play anyone, so long as we can fit it into our schedule and our budget. But here it felt a little bit like we were pushing the limits on our good fortune. By every measure, we'd had an amazing season—a *perfectly* amazing season. Only here we had to keep it going for another couple games. Bobby was battling this injury, and I would have liked to shut him down and let him get going on his healing and rehab so he'd be fresh and fit and ready to start his college career in the fall. And Luther Wright and his Elizabeth teammates were waiting for us as the number-two seed in the Tournament of Champions— a nationally ranked team looking to avenge their regular-season loss and spoil our undefeated season.

I tend to be fairly confident as a coach. I always like our chances. But at the same time, I worry. Always, I worry. Ask my wife, Chris, how many sleepless nights I've passed, obsessing about our matchup the next day, only to see us win the game by twenty or thirty points. So this was my worry, going into this season-capping tournament. The last time we'd played Elizabeth, it was in Jersey City, so it was essentially a home game for us. Now, meeting up in the Tournament of Champions final, we'd be playing in the Brendan Byrne Arena at the Meadowlands—a big-time facility in front of what would probably be a big-time Elizabeth crowd. They were one of the biggest high schools in the state; we were one of the smallest. Put together all of their current students, alumni, and boosters, and the Elizabeth community could fill the place. Put together all of our students, alumni, and boosters, and we could maybe fill a couple sections.

My biggest concern was that we were beat up. Bobby was hurt. A couple of our other key guys were dragging. Terry and Rodrick had been playing well down the stretch, but as a team we were hobbled, hurting. And Elizabeth head coach Ben Candelino was an excellent game strategist, so I knew he'd done a careful study of our regular-season matchup and made some adjustments. We could count on him to throw us a different look and to find a way to counter whatever strengths he'd seen in our game plan and turn them into weaknesses.

Whenever you play a team a second time, the team that loses the first game is at an advantage. At least, that's how it almost always seems to go—especially at the high school level. The losing coach has a lot of information he can now use, a lot of ways to motivate his team, whereas the winning coach has to find a way to manage his team's expectations and keep them from taking their opponents for granted.

Basically, we had everything to play for, everything to lose—never a good scenario heading into a big game. We hadn't really been pressured all season, other than that one game against Solebury, but even that game went our way by a big score. Our margin of victory had been in the double digits every single game that season, and most times we won by twenty, thirty, or more. So we weren't used to playing under pressure. Of course, I had no reason to think my kids wouldn't respond—but that still left me with every reason to worry.

In the end, we played well enough to win—but *just* well enough to win, almost the same way we'd ended that first perfect season back in 1974. We came out on top by a score of 62–55, but we could never separate ourselves from Elizabeth and put the game away. Whatever we threw at them, they seemed to have an answer for it. Also, Bobby's hamstring was bothering him. He usually set the tempo for us, and he was only at 60 percent or so, which left the rest of our guys running the floor at 60 percent or so. We were sluggish, out of rhythm. It never felt to me like we were in danger of losing the game, but at the same time I never got the feeling that it was in the bag either. We didn't play all that well. We looked tired. It had been a long season. A lot of travel, a lot of hard work. And so, for most of those thirty-two minutes, it felt like the game could have gone either way. A couple bad possessions for us, and we could have handed the game to Elizabeth. We were just trying to hold on, to get to the finish line, and at some point in the fourth quarter I liked our chances enough to finally pull Bobby from the game. He wasn't doing the things he was usually able to do; he was really hurting. Still, he was an important presence, extremely confident with the ball, so I'd kept him out there as long as I could, as long as I felt we needed him, and when I finally sent Danny to the scorer's table to sub in for his older brother, the boys had a nice exchange at midcourt. I hadn't planned it just this way, but it worked out, like something out of a movie. Bobby crossed to Danny and said, "It's on you now."

And that was that—but in that one brief moment, my two sons on their ways in and out of the game, Bobby passing the St. Anthony torch to Danny, I caught a glimpse of what this season might have been. Not that I'm complaining, mind you. Not that the season turned out anything less than spectacular. But deep down I caught myself realizing it could have been all that and more. It was one for the record books, that's for sure, but it could have been one for the family scrapbook as well.

Here again, the way we ended this championship season left

me thinking of the importance we've attached to winning. It's never about the outcome of just one game. It's an attitude, an approach. Remember, we'd been the number-one team in the country the previous year and then stumbled with a regular-season loss at home to Ferris High School. At the end of the season, that one loss cost us the top spot in the national rankings—which went to a team we'd already beaten head to head. So of course our guys felt like they'd left something on the table, like there was unfinished business, like their accomplishments had not been fully recognized, and it worked out that this year's team was largely the same as last year's team.

My returning players all felt like they had a little something extra to prove, and that had become the theme of this season—to reclaim that top spot. And for a while it looked like they were about to do just that. We'd played in two national tournaments during the season and beat the second-ranked team in the country each time out. Then we ran the table the rest of the way. That was our stated goal, going into the season. With this group, it wasn't just about winning the state championship. It wasn't just about winning this first ever Tournament of Champions. It was about winning it all . . . and then some. Doesn't always happen that you set the bar so high for a team, for a season, but you have to consider that this was a group that included three NBA first-round draft choices and a fourth player who'd go on to become the Big East Defensive Player of the Year. The talent was abundant on this team, so I don't think we set any unrealistic goals for ourselves. I don't think we set the bar too high. This was just our mind-set, heading into the season. It wasn't just about winning. It was about winning big, and sending a message that we would not be denied, and this final against Elizabeth was the only game that was even close. Every other game had been decided early.

And here, in the end, we could only squeak out this championship game—against a very good team, mind you, but a team we
should have dominated. A team we'd beaten pretty handily earlier
in the season.

I think we all would have liked to have won this game going
away, but sometimes the ball doesn't bounce the way you think it
might—the way you plan for it to bounce, all season long. Sometimes you run out of gas, just a little shy of the finish line, and it's
all you can do to hang on and hope like crazy you make it the rest
of the way.

HARD WORK

Saturday, February 18, 2012

What a week.

First, we've had to get through three tough games—on Monday, at home, against a very mature team of postgrads from the Each One Teach One Academy in East Orange; on Wednesday, at Lincoln High School in Brooklyn, against Thomas Jefferson, one of the top teams in the metropolitan area, who'll go on to play for the city championship at Madison Square Garden; and finally, on Thursday, at Bishop Eustace, all the way down near Camden.

We've gone from hardly playing at all over a stretch of a couple weeks to playing three games in just four days, leading up to one of the biggest games of the season for us—on Saturday, against Long Island Lutheran.

Feels to me like leaving a sports car in the garage all winter, then rolling it out to the driveway, expecting it to start.

We win the first two games, but it ends up costing us, because Tim Coleman goes down with a season-ending knee injury against Jefferson. Tim, a six-four junior, was slotted in at small forward. He's been playing well—especially in practice, where he's the only one of our second-team guys who can challenge

Jerome Frink and give him a run. We don't know the extent of Tim's injury just yet, but we know he's out for at least the next while, which means we have to play Bishop Eustace shorthanded. They've already won twenty games, a magic number for a high school team. You get to twenty wins, you're doing something right, and here Bishop Eustace has the luxury of hosting us at the tail end of a grueling midweek schedule, with one of our bigs on the shelf, so they have a bit of an edge. Our guys are tired, dragging, but Jerome has a big game for us, filling up some of the spaces Tim Coleman might have been, scoring sixteen points to lead us to another double-digit victory.

The real drama, though, comes the next day, a Friday, when it's brought to my attention that a group from our team has been involved in an incident that will result in the expulsion of one player from the team and the suspension of three others. I want to be careful in describing the incident, because there were no criminal charges filed, but I think it's fair to say that all four players showed monumentally poor judgment. Basically, all four of them were idiots.

Yeah, they're just kids, and sometimes kids do stupid things, but when you play for St. Anthony, the idea is that you're not like other kids; you're supposed to stay out of stupid situations. I couldn't be more clear about this, with the contract I ask each player to sign. We hold our players to the highest standards—and we

expect them to pay the price for their transgressions.
If they mess up, they let their team down, they let their
school down, they let their family down.

They let themselves down.

Here's what happened. We had a team meal
scheduled at a nice restaurant in Jersey City—the Light
Horse Tavern, on Washington, where the owner, Bill
Gray, takes good care of us—which had become our
routine on home game days. At St. Anthony, we depend
mightily on the kindness of the community to help
knit us together as a team, and here it had been a kind
of godsend to have a place where we could gather as
a group and get our heads around whatever we were
working on as a team. Our players know these team
meals are important, a big part of what we do. More
than that, they know they'll get a good meal, which is
more than a lot of them get at home.

And yet four of my guys had something better to
do. Jimmy Hall, Tariq Carey, Josh Brown, and Kyle
Anderson skipped out on the team meal and went off to
make trouble. The kind of trouble you're not supposed
to make when you wear the maroon and gold of the
St. Anthony Friars. The kind of trouble you're not
supposed to make if you expect to be treated like a
responsible, respectful member of the community. The
kind of trouble you're especially not supposed to get
involved in or be anywhere near when you're expected
at a team event.

Kyle Anderson should have known better. This is a kid who has the basketball world in the palm of his hand. He's headed off to UCLA in the fall. He's widely considered to be one of the top five high school players in the country. He's got the physical gifts and the raw talent to play the game at the highest level. And yet he still allowed himself to go against his better judgment, to put himself where he wasn't supposed to be—until the very last moment, when he finally realized his teammates were up to no good, so he stepped away. Not all the way back to the Light Horse, which was where he should have been, but at least he knew to put some distance between himself and his buddies who were up to no good.

Tariq Carey should have known better. He came to us as a transfer, hoping to get a couple longer looks from college coaches. The kid can play. He doesn't always make the best decisions on the court, but he can certainly play—and if he doesn't screw things up, he'll land a full scholarship at one of the better local colleges. He'll get a shot at a good education. At some point, he too realized it was probably a good idea to step away from his buddies.

Josh Brown should have known better. He's already committed to Temple, as a junior. He's lifted his game dramatically since last season, when he was mostly a bench player for us. Made himself into one of the best perimeter defenders in the area, with the kind of

quickness and instincts you can't teach. He's got the
next five years of his life all mapped out—one more
with me, and four more down in Philadelphia with
Temple coach Fran Dunphy—but he was willing to risk
all of that for a little mischief with his pals.

And finally, Jimmy Hall should have known better.
He's headed to Hofstra, where head coach Mo Cassara
thinks he'll be worth the hassle—and with this kid,
there's been a whole lot of hassle. I'm still hoping Mo is
right on this, because when Jimmy wants it, when he's
focused, he can be a factor on the floor. He's got good
size, good presence. But off the court, he can't get out
of his own way. He's been suspended from school for
academic reasons. He's been suspended from my team
for disciplinary reasons. He's a senior, a ringleader, so
the other kids seem to want to listen to him and follow
his lead—and here he was apparently able to convince
three of my guys to go off with him to kick up some
dust, until one by one they all realized they were better
off being someplace else.

Before Jimmy could do anything too, too stupid, a
security guard came by. He recognized Jimmy as one
of my players and called one of my assistant coaches.
That's how it sometimes goes in Jersey City, which for
a good-size city is a lot like a small town. Our players
are well known, and here the guard must have thought
he was helping us out. Well, he was and he wasn't.
The guard could have called the cops, which is how

I would have handled it. But instead, he called one of my coaches, so it fell to us to deal with these kids internally.

There was nothing to think about as far as I was concerned. I huddled briefly with Ben Gamble to look at our options—but, really, there was only one option. Jimmy Hall would be kicked off the team. The other three would be suspended for our next game.

End of story.

But of course, there's a little more to the story. We still have a basketball team to consider, right? We're still undefeated on the season, still one of the top-ranked teams in the country, still looking to defend our state and Tournament of Champion titles—only now we're looking to do so without most of our starting lineup.

And we've still got this next game, against a top Long Island Lutheran team. We've already run our practice and prepared for this opponent, so we're up against it. Not a whole lot we can do, on the fly, so I get to the gym early to watch the JV game, and it's like I'm on a shopping spree. I see kids I like, kids who can maybe help us, I give them a uniform. I tell the JV coach to sit these kids in the second half so they'll be eligible to play for us.

When our guys start arriving, I lay it out for them. I don't waste my energy on Kyle, Tariq, or Josh. I tell them not to bother getting dressed. Tell them to leave us alone, that today is for the team, for everyone who buys into what we're doing. My focus is on the game we now have to play, not on the nonsense that happens away from the gym, so I look right through these kids. They're three of our best players—heck, Kyle is one of the top high school players in the country—but they're of no use to me just now, so I turn my attention to the rest of the group.

I huddle with my assistant coaches, come up with a new game plan. I decide to start Tarin Smith, a sophomore guard; Kody Jenkins, a six-five junior swingman; and Kentrell Brooks, a six-eight junior who'll start to see more time for us now that Tim is out. They'll join starters Jerome Frink and Hallice Cooke. Edon Molic, a senior guard from Brooklyn, becomes our first guy off the bench. Shaquille McFarland and Cheddi Mosely, two of the JV players I've tapped, will get some time off the bench.

Everybody's role is changing, so what I want to do with the kids who are usually substitutes and who are now going to start, and with the kids who are deeper on the bench but are now going to be key reserves, is sit them down and go over in very defined terms exactly what we think we can do with this change in personnel. We take some things out of our game plan that no longer fit and put in some other things that now make sense.

A good example for this game is Kody Jenkins—a

junior guard who's been stuck playing behind a very, very good player. We've been on this kid all year, reminding him that he's playing against Kyle Anderson every day in practice, telling him what a tough assignment that is, and how it's preparing him for the role he'll have for us as a senior. So before this game, I pull him aside and tell him this is his shot. I say, "Listen, you're not Kyle. We don't expect you to be Kyle. We just want you to be the best Kody Jenkins you can be. We want you to be our poor man's Kyle Anderson."

He's heard that phrase before, of course. We've drummed it into him, which is what happens when you play behind one of the top high school basketball players in the country. You're always being compared to the star player, even though there's no comparison. Even though you can still be a great player by any other measure. To his great credit, Kody doesn't hear this as a negative, and it's not meant that way. Not at all. Kody sees Kyle dominate players every game, and he's been going up against him every day in practice, so he knows what Kyle means to our team. He knows all the hype and publicity that seem to follow Kyle around. At the same time, Kody also knows what he himself is capable of, so this is an opportunity for him to strut his stuff a little bit. To emerge from Kyle's shadow.

Another good example for this game is Hallice

Cooke, who's been pigeonholed by me and the other coaches as mostly an open shooter and a perimeter defender; now we have to ask Hallice to take more of an all-around role. To handle the ball a little bit more. To distribute. To drive to the basket. Basically, to do some things he hasn't been asked to do for us—some of the things we always look to Kyle to do.

Jerome Frink, too, has to take on some of the scoring we've come to expect out of Kyle—so basically we'll have three players stepping up and filling the role usually taken on by just this one player.

You might think that these younger players would be a little tentative, a little nervous about being put in this situation against a good team like Long Island Lutheran, a team that won their state championship the year before, but actually it's just the opposite. They're pumped, confident. It's the St. Anthony way, and they've been preparing for this moment their entire high school careers. They're good and ready. All along, they've been taught to believe their time is coming— and here it is.

The Long Island Lutheran players can see something is up. They all know Kyle—by reputation, at least. They've prepared for Kyle. They know Josh and Tariq. They see these kids dressed in street clothes, sitting in the stands, their entire game plan goes out the door—but at the same time they start to think they don't need a game plan. With Tim Coleman out and

Jimmy Hall gone from the program, we're down five key players—so if they scouted us earlier in the week, they've probably got no idea what to make of us now.

One of the great ironies of this game, I'll learn later, is that a group of high school coaches from Long Island have come to the gym just for the chance to see Kyle play. They've heard about him for years, and this is their chance to see what all the fuss is about, so you can just imagine how disappointed these guys are to see Kyle sitting in the stands in his street clothes. A couple of them stand to leave, once they figure out Kyle and our other starters aren't playing. They can't imagine we'll even give Long Island Lutheran a good game. But one of these coaches, Frank Alagia, who was a terrific ballplayer himself—had a nice career at St. John's playing for Lou Carnesecca—turns to his fellow coaches and says, "You guys don't get it. This is St. Anthony basketball. These kids Hurley's putting in, they expect to win. You should hang around. They'll give them a good game."

Sure enough, most of the coaches leave anyway, but Frank calls it just right. Our young guys are psyched. Our bench players are determined to show they deserve more time on the floor. We come out sharp and manage to hold a slim lead the whole game. It's a battle—not quite back and forth, but there's not a whole lot of forth. We're playing well, but we can't seem to push the lead. At one point in the first half, Long Island Lutheran goes on a bit of a run, but Edon Molic comes off the bench and hits a big three to turn the game back our way. The kid's one of our best pure shooters, but he doesn't get a lot of meaningful minutes, so it's good to see him make a contribution. Tarin Smith, too, starts to light it up. This kid's been making great strides all season long—a sophomore guard from Monmouth County who figures to play a bigger and bigger role for us. Really, there's a lot to like about Tarin's game—and what sticks out is his motivation. He lives in Monmouth County, takes the train up every day, which right off the bat tells me he's into it. He's motivated. Plus, he's an outstanding student—a candidate to play Ivy League ball when the time comes.

I sit back and watch Tarin and the rest of his teammates take the floor with all kinds of swagger—like each one of them, to a man, belongs on this floor and no place else. Like going into battle without five key players is no big thing.

We wind up winning 48–39, our biggest margin of the game, and it's all because the guys who are with us put the team on their shoulders. Because they find a way to pick up the guys who let us down.

6.

A Dark, Dark Night

EVERY SEASON IS A JOURNEY. EVERY JOURNEY IS A LIFETIME.
—Mike Krzyzewski

NEVER UNDERESTIMATE THE HEART OF A CHAMPION.
—Rudy Tomjanovich

L ife never goes the way you think.

Doesn't even come close.

As a kid, I thought I'd play in the NBA. Never occurred to me I wouldn't even make it off the freshman team at St. Peter's College, but that's just what happened. Never thought my sons would go on to play big-time college ball, for two of the top coaches in the country—Bobby for Mike Krzyzewski at Duke and Danny for P. J. Carlesimo at Seton Hall—or that they'd face each other in the Sweet Sixteen round of the NCAA tournament, but that's just what happened. Never once imagined I'd have an opportunity to coach at a school like St. Anthony, or to grow its basketball program into one of the best in the country, but that's just what happened too.

And Chris and I certainly never thought that for every happiness and success we enjoyed as a family there might be a real heartbreak waiting just around the corner—but of course, there's no avoiding heartbreak. We lost our parents eventually. We lost our son Sean. And one night in December 1993, we nearly lost Bobby.

I'll share this last story here, because it has to do with the "undefeated" theme that runs through this book, and because it's an important marker in our family and in the St. Anthony community. It's with us always. And it's emblematic. Like the seven perfect teams profiled in these pages, Bobby had to have an iron will and a bottomless supply of grit and perseverance to fight his way back after a terrible car accident that almost cost him . . . everything.

First, a little setup. After a great career at St. Anthony, Bobby kept it going at Duke, where he ended up winning back-to-back NCAA titles. Set all kinds of school records, conference records, NCAA records. I couldn't have been prouder of him, as his former coach, or more excited for him, as his father. It felt like everything was going his way. After his senior season, the Sacramento Kings selected Bobby in the first round of the NBA draft and signed him to a big contract. My brother Brian went out to California to help Bobby transition from the life of a student-athlete on the East Coast to the life of a professional athlete on the West Coast. Bobby was smart enough to see that my brother would help him to keep his focus, or maybe he just liked having his Uncle Brian around; either way, it worked out.

The transition into the Kings' lineup was a little less smooth. The Sacramento coach, Garry St. Jean, had a set rotation he used to deploy, with two different units. Typically, it meant Bobby would play either the first and third quarters of the game or the second and fourth quarters. Spud Webb was the other point guard on the team, and he usually played the other quarters. As a fellow coach, I could understand Garry's thinking, if you had a deep bench and certain guys who worked well together on the floor, but as a dad, I found it frustrating. I kept my mouth shut—not usually one of my strengths—but I couldn't shake thinking that if you're playing well, you should keep playing; if you're struggling, you should sit. It's tough for a guy to get into the flow of a game if he knows he's coming right back out; he'll never find his rhythm. Bobby, to his credit, was a little less frustrated than me; he was just worried about making the most of his minutes, making an impression. He'd always call after his games to let us know how things went; we'd talk about what he could have done better, what he could have done different, what he could work on going forward. Remember, this was back before you could get the NBA league package on satellite, before all these wall-to-wall cable stations, so we couldn't always follow the Kings, but seventeen games into his rookie season, we'd still managed to get a good handle on how things were going. When Bobby played well, his postgame calls were filled with all kinds of details and analysis; when he struggled, the calls were a whole lot shorter. Either way, he always called as soon as he got home or back to his hotel room.

The Kings had just been in Philadelphia on Friday, December 10, for a game against the 76ers. I'd already seen Bobby play in a game against the Nets at the Meadowlands, where he handed out nine assists, and in a game against the Knicks at the Garden, where he struggled. That's how it was for him the first month of the season: he was on and off, hot and cold. He'd play with confidence one game, and then he'd be unsure of himself the next, so I was hoping to catch him on a good night against the 76ers. We'd arranged for a whole busload of people from Jersey City to go down to Philly, and it was tremendous. Bobby played pretty well: four points, six assists. He only played about half the game, as usual, but he ran the floor like a demon and showed everyone he could play at the NBA level. Absolutely, he could play. I left the Spectrum that night thinking it was only a matter of time before Bobby really established himself as an NBA player.

Two days later, Sunday, December 12, the Kings were back in Sacramento for a game against the Los Angeles Clippers. We were all looking forward to the game, Bobby especially. He was going up against his old friend and teammate Terry Dehere, who also went in the first round, after a fine career at Seton Hall. Their plan was to get together for dinner to compare notes and catch up. And we were excited back home because the game was the featured Sunday night game on television, so we could tune in. Still, it was late for us, Chris and I both had to get up for work the next day, but we watched the first half and went to bed, thinking Bobby would check in afterward with his report.

Right around one o'clock in the morning, about an hour or so after the game was due to end, we got a call. My first thought was that it was Bobby, checking in. But it wasn't Bobby. He'd been in a car accident, we were told. We didn't really know anything else at that point, only that he'd just left the Arco Arena, so we just figured it was a fender bender, some kind of minor accident in the parking lot, because there hadn't been a whole lot of time after the game.

Ten minutes later, we got another call—this time from the Sacramento team doctor, Richard Marder. Chris answered the phone, and the first thing Dr. Marder said was, "We think he's gonna make it."

Oh, man. To have to hear something like that, from out of nowhere like that . . . our whole world went dark. From that first call, we weren't thinking life and death. We just thought maybe the car was a little banged up, maybe Bobby was a little banged up, that's all. In fact, we both thought this next call would be from Bobby, to tell us what was what.

Chris dropped the phone and fell to her knees; she was in shock. I slipped into some kind of autopilot mode—not really thinking, just doing what needed to get done. I picked up the phone and tried to get some more information, but all this doctor could tell me was to make arrangements to get out to Sacramento as soon as possible.

We were frantic, trying to find a flight.

We were frantic with worry.

Just, frantic.

By this point, one-thirty or so, we started getting a ton of calls. The accident had been on the news, on ESPN, all over. Still, we couldn't get any real information, only that Bobby had been taken to the University of California–Davis Medical Center, that he'd gone into surgery, and that there had been blood coming from his ear when they found him, probably from a head injury. The details that managed to come our way had us sick with worry, and it didn't help that the details kept changing—like the fact that the blood coming from his ear was really coming from a cut under his eye, something it would have been good to know sooner rather than later.

Somehow we were able to get on a 5:00 A.M. Northwest Airlines flight to Denver, so we had to hustle a few things together and head to the airport. Before we left, we turned on the television and saw a picture of Bobby's car, and we knew it was bad. The car was almost unrecognizable.

Danny was home from school on break, and Melissa was home as well. Chris's mom was still with us too, so we had a full house. Even so, some friends came over to stay with my mother-in-law and the kids while we raced to the airport, still pretty much in the dark about what was going on. The whole flight to Denver, we were in agony because we had no real information, other than that grim prognosis from the doctor on the phone, the horrifying pictures of Bobby's car on the news, the unreliable details we kept hearing on the news. One of us had been on the phone to the hospital the whole time before we left for the airport, but there was nothing anyone could tell us. Nothing reassuring anyway.

Chris was able to use the phone on the plane to reach Dr. Marder, who told us that there was no brain damage. A part of me heard that and thought, *What a relief!* But another part thought, *Brain damage?* It killed me to have to think of my son in such life-and-death, touch-and-go terms.

We managed to get through to the hospital when we switched planes in Denver—but still there was no real news. Bobby was still in surgery, that's all we knew. By now the story had been all over the news for hours, so people were coming up to us at the airport to show their support, but we were desperate to know what was going on in Sacramento. Either we couldn't get through to the right person at the hospital, or the right person didn't want to give us too much information. All we knew was that Bobby was in bad shape.

We were literally flying blind.

To this day I've got no idea how we made it through those long, terrible hours of not knowing. Chris doesn't have any idea either. It's like our lives had been put on pause, and all we could do was get out to California and race to Bobby's side. There was nothing to talk about. We just held on to each other and tried not to lose it in front of all those good people.

———

We were met at the airport in Sacramento by Travis Stanley, the Kings' director of media relations. He was in a very somber mood. Already, I'd been imagining the worst, and then putting it out of my mind, and then imagining it all over again. Before we got to see Bobby in the hospital at Cal-Davis, the doctors and nurses took us into a private room and tried to fill us in, telling us what to expect. Bobby was unconscious, but they didn't want us to break down in front of him, because he could still be plugged into what was going on in the room. They wanted us to be up and positive and hoped maybe Bobby would pick up on that.

Well, they could have prepared us all morning for this and it still would have been a real shock. Less than three days earlier, we'd seen Bobby play in Philadelphia, and he was 165 pounds, in the best shape of his life, running like a marvel, and here he looked like he'd ballooned to 300 pounds. His entire body was inflated from the trauma, the same way your knee might swell after an injury, because the body attempts to heal itself by sending fluids to the site of a trauma. Bobby was completely swollen, from head to toe. He looked like a stranger.

I knew it was my son, but only because that's what they told me.

Chris and I sat with Bobby for as long as they let us, one of us on each side of the bed while they continued to work on him, to monitor him. We rested our hands on him and sat and prayed and tried not to cry.

As we sat, we learned that if there hadn't been a perfect storm of life-saving miracles, Bobby might never have made it this far. What happened was, the guy who ended up hitting Bobby's car was driving without his lights on. Another driver happened to be on the same dark country road right by the arena just as this reckless driver sped by, and this second guy knew instinctively that a car approaching from the opposite direction would be in serious trouble, so he tried to follow the vehicle without the headlights and maybe get out in front and signal the driver and prevent an accident.

Meanwhile, Bobby was a little dejected after the game, frustrated that he hadn't played well, and he was heading back to his condo; turned out Terry didn't have a great game either, and neither one of them felt like going out. Bobby didn't even have his seat belt on yet, because he was just pulling out of the arena parking lot—turning left onto the county road that ran by the arena— and as he did, this guy came crashing into the driver side. Bobby never saw him coming, never had a chance to react.

The guy was a painter, driving a station wagon filled with paint cans, and the impact sent Bobby through the passenger side door and about fifty feet in the air, into an irrigation ditch on the side of the road.

If Mike, our Good Samaritan, hadn't set off in the direction of the speeding car, who knows when they would have found Bobby.

And if Mike didn't happen to have a cell phone—which in 1993 a lot of people still didn't have—he would have never been able to call 911 and get help on the way. This probably saved Bobby's life, because the road surrounding the Arco Arena was in the middle of farm country. The arena parking lot had already emptied. It could have been hours before another car spotted the accident scene.

Another Mike, Bobby's teammate Mike Peplowski, pulled out of the arena a couple moments later, and he of course noticed the damage to Bobby's car, so he pulled over. This, too, was a lifesaver. Both Mikes started looking for Bobby, and Mike Peplowski got to him first, found Bobby lying with his head in a puddle. It's a wonder Bobby didn't drown, which takes us to another miracle:

there'd been a drought that year, that part of California, so there was hardly any water in that irrigation ditch.

It worked out that the emergency room resident on duty that night at Cal-Davis was Dr. Russell Sawyer, an expert on trachea surgery. In fact, Dr. Sawyer had just written a chapter for a book on the subject, compiled by the National Thoracic Society, so he was able to take one look at Bobby and make an immediate diagnosis. It also worked out that the hospital's head of thoracic surgery, Dr. John Benfield, heard a report about Bobby's accident on the radio, so he immediately called the hospital and got on the phone with Dr. Sawyer. Amazingly, Dr. Benfield was the head of the National Thoracic Society; he was the one who'd actually compiled the book on the subject featuring the chapter by Dr. Sawyer; Dr. Benfield had been traveling, but had cut his trip short, and it was pure luck that he was in town to perform Bobby's surgery. Another doctor, F. William Blaisdell, head of the hospital's automobile trauma unit, was also on hand to assist with the surgery, so Bobby had a kind of dream team working on him.

Bobby's injuries were so severe, most people wouldn't have survived them. The trauma of being thrown that distance from the car and hitting the ground with that kind of impact tore his windpipe. He broke his ribs, and both lungs were collapsed. Amazingly, the injuries seemed to match up almost exactly with the new surgical procedures that had just been outlined by Dr. Sawyer and Dr. Benfield in this new book, and Dr. Blaisdell was one of the top automobile trauma guys in the country, so the entire team knew exactly what to look for.

Bobby was taken to Cal-Davis by chopper. The medics didn't think there was time for an ambulance; it would have taken forever. As it was, Bobby was in surgery for over seven hours. They told us later he stopped breathing on two separate occasions while he was on the table. All of this happened while we were up in the air, flying blind, imagining the worst but hoping for the best.

What we also didn't know until many years later was that Bobby came to once Mike Peplowski found him in that ditch. Bobby was out, unresponsive, when Mike got to him, but then, as Mike cradled Bobby's head in his arms, Bobby kept saying, "Mike, am I gonna die?"

All these coincidences, coming together like that . . . one Mike spotting the speeding car with no headlights and calling it in; another Mike finding Bobby in the ditch; a record-setting drought that left the water levels low; an expert surgeon who'd just written a paper on the procedure Bobby required; another surgeon who'd compiled a book on precisely these injuries and who'd just returned to town and happened to hear about the accident on the radio; and there was still another surgeon on duty who'd devoted his career to working with car crash victims . . . there's no way Bobby could have survived if just one of those pieces had not fallen into place.

That's how it sometimes goes when you will not be defeated. You can be the fittest, most hard-charging competitor on the planet, but you'll still need to catch a couple breaks if you hope to prevail—and here Bobby caught a whole bunch of them. Of course, you can make the flip-side argument and say that all of this good luck and coincidence wouldn't have even come into play if everything hadn't already lined up against Bobby that night. If he'd had a better game and maybe left the arena with Terry Dehere by some other exit. If he'd taken just a split-second longer getting to his car. If the painter in that station wagon had turned on his headlights. Yeah, there were a whole lot of "what ifs" that put Bobby in just the wrong place, at just the wrong moment, same way they put the two Mikes and these fine surgeons at just the right place, at just the right moment, so I've chosen to celebrate the positive outcomes to this accident and set aside the rest—otherwise, I'd just go crazy.

And the positive pieces kept on coming. A couple days later, Bobby was a whole lot better; we sat with him for three days, until he finally appeared to turn a corner. We went from not knowing if he would make it through at all to not knowing what the quality of his life would be going forward—but we took it as a good trade at the time. Bobby's body was completely broken: there were cuts and bruises all over his face, all over his body; broken bones in his arms, his fingers, his wrists; five broken ribs; a shattered left shoulder blade; compression fractures in his back; torn ACLs. Just then, no one was thinking about basketball. No one was thinking anything. We just wanted to get our Bobby back, and whole.

The outpouring of love and support over those three days was tremendous. Mike Krzyzewski flew out immediately. Bob Delaney, the NBA referee, came by, and so did Orlando Magic rookie coach Brian Hill, along with Shaquille O'Neal. Dennis Rodman sent flowers. Bill Cosby called to say he felt a special connection to Bobby, since he'd just been in Philadelphia two days earlier. Ronald Reagan sent a letter telling Bobby how much he and his wife enjoyed watching him play.

Even more incredible than these individual visits and calls were the thousands and thousands of letters and "get well" wishes that poured into the hospital. Bobby had no idea how many lives he'd touched, just by playing basketball—how many people were rooting for him to get better. He was lifted by each note, each call, each visit . . . we all were, really.

———

It was tough to think about basketball during that time in the hospital, but at the same time it was tough to turn away from it. The game ran through our lives. Every night I was on the phone back home to my assistant coach, George Canda, who filled in for me at St. Anthony. We had our season opener coming up that Friday, December 17, and we needed to go over a few things. George took to calling every night when we got back to the hotel. It was late for us, even later for George because of the time difference, but it was a good distraction. For an hour or so each night, we'd go over practice, talk about our game plan. Our season opener was against a really good local team, Essex Catholic, but our guys were playing well. We'd had a good preseason, so when George called that night to report on the game, I wasn't surprised to hear we'd won.

It was our second game that would be a problem. St. Anthony was scheduled to play DeMatha, a Catholic high school in Maryland coached by the legendary Morgan Wootten, who would go on to post more wins as a head coach than anyone else in basketball history. Ever. At any level. At that point, Morgan had won more than a thousand games, and George had won only one.

It hardly seemed fair.

Truth was, I'd forgotten all about that DeMatha game, but it had been set up with great fanfare. DeMatha was coming up to Jersey City for a tournament, so folks who followed high school basketball started talking about it like this great big showdown— and I guess it was. Morgan was approaching the end of his career (he'd finish with 1,274 career victories), and St. Anthony had been good for a while, so this was a chance for our two teams to play, but when the game finally came around on the calendar, my head was elsewhere. Still, I wanted our guys to do well, so I spent some late-night time with George on the phone, going over strategy, although in truth I was no help to George at all. DeMatha ended up beating us in a close game, but these early-season games were way beyond my focus.

We stayed out in California through Christmas. At some point, Danny and Melissa came out. Bobby made great strides, but some days I'd walk into his room and he'd be arguing with the nurses or the physical therapists. He was in a lot of pain. His injuries were no longer life-threatening, but it was like the motivation had been sucked out of him. He didn't see why he had to move, to sit up, to start in on the long, hard road of rehabilitation. Instead of fighting through the pain, he seemed to want to fight with everyone who wanted to help him. So what did I do? I got in his face, that's what I did. I yelled at him, same way I used to do in practice when he was flagging. Same way I yelled at all my players. I told him he didn't have any choice in the matter. It wasn't about basketball, or fighting back into game shape. That would come later, or not. For now, it was about getting his life back, getting his blood circulating so he didn't come down with pneumonia, which was a big concern in those first weeks after the accident.

Poor Bobby, he was really down. We all were, but I tried to look past all of that. I told Bobby he needed to lift himself up and out of his hospital bed and back into the rest of his life. The doctors could patch him up and set him right, but now he was on his own. I was hard on him, and it killed me that I was hard on him, but I didn't see that I had a choice. He had a lot of work to do. We *all* had a lot of work to do, because it was a full-on family effort. Bobby needed a push, so we took turns pushing. He had to do his breathing exercises, his sitting-up exercises, his moving-around exercises. We couldn't let him sit still or feel sorry for himself, so every day we'd descend on his hospital room like personal trainers.

For a long time, Bobby wasn't himself. He was in so much pain, the doctors had him on morphine at first, and they kept him on morphine those first couple weeks, so that kind of sapped him of all his energy, his motivation. This was a kid who'd been like a pit bull his entire life, putting in all those hours in the gym to make himself better, faster, stronger . . . and here he was in such agony and shot through with all these poisons, he was out of character. It was like he was in a fog and we were all waiting for it to lift, Bobby included. Soon as they could, the doctors dialed down on the morphine and put Bobby on codeine, and soon after that he was on Tylenol with codeine, and eventually just straight Tylenol. But with each change to Bobby's prescription, it was like he was going through detox—getting off the morphine especially. He was miserable, depressed. He got these terrible headaches. He was like a junkie, really—going through some of the same things I'd see with my guys on probation.

But he got through it. He did. Somehow, we all got through it together.

Day after Christmas, we took Bobby home from the hospital to his condo in Sacramento. It had been just two weeks since the accident, two weeks since hearing from these doctors that they weren't even sure he would make it, so he was making remarkable progress. Unbelievable. On the night of the accident, flying cross-country with all those dark thoughts and worst-case scenarios, Chris and I would have signed on for a two-week hospital stay in a heartbeat. It would have been nothing compared to what we were facing, but now that we were in the middle of it—now that we'd reached the end of it—those two weeks felt like the longest two weeks in the history of mankind. And looking ahead, we worried there'd be no real end to it.

I flew back to New Jersey the next day. Chris stayed out in

Sacramento for another couple days, along with Melissa and my brother Brian. The idea was to get Bobby well enough to travel, so he could do his rehabilitation back home in Jersey City, but it would be another month or so before his lungs were healed and the doctors cleared him to get on a plane. Brian stayed with him the whole time, and in that month we started to think about Bobby's basketball career. I suppose we'd been thinking about it all along, in a back-of-our-minds sort of way, but now we pushed it front and center. Now Bobby started to talk about it. At first we were just worried about his life, and then it was the quality of his life, and then it was clear that basketball was a huge part of the quality of Bobby's life, so we all started thinking about what it would take to get him back to playing.

Dr. Marder and the Kings were concerned about the ACL tears, because that was potentially the most career-threatening of Bobby's injuries. They were also worried about his shattered shoulder, and it was decided that they would have their team doctor operate and put a plate in Bobby's shoulder, because that was something they believed they could fix. The ACL tears, by a whole other miracle, somehow knitted back together and healed themselves.

Bobby flew back to New Jersey with his uncle, and we set him up in our old house on Linden Avenue, in the front apartment upstairs. He started going to physical therapy with Carl Gargiulo and Dan Strulewicz, who used to work with all of our St. Anthony players back then, so Bobby was familiar with them. They set him up with a routine. It was slow going at first. Bobby couldn't even do five minutes on the treadmill. He could last a little longer on the stationary bike, so that's how he started working on his cardio, but walking was difficult. His body was completely out of alignment.

I'd spend some time with him each day—and each day it broke my heart to see him struggle, to see him in so much pain.

By mid-March, he was able to move about under his own steam, and he came down to see us play in the state tournament. There was a lot of excitement in the gym when people started realizing Bobby was in attendance. The entire St. Anthony community—heck, the entire Jersey City basketball community!—couldn't have been more supportive of our family during this time. They loved Bobby. They treated him like a favorite son, so when he turned up to cheer on his old man and his old school, people were pretty emotional.

We ended up losing in the second round of the state tournament that year, to St. Pat's Elizabeth, but what's stayed with me most of all from that postseason was a moment away from the crowds, away from the cameras. We were in the gym for our final practice before the St. Pat's game, and when practice broke Bobby walked to the basket. Someone handed him a ball, and he rolled it around in his hands for a bit, getting the feel of it. I don't know if he'd handled a ball since the accident, but it was the first I remember seeing him with a ball in his hands. Anyway, it was the first time he'd had a ball in his hands while standing beneath a basket—so naturally, he tried to shoot it.

Weren't a whole lot of people in the gym, wasn't a whole lot of activity, but everything kind of stopped as Bobby turned and squared to shoot. It was like something out of a movie—but it was a tearjerker movie, because Bobby couldn't even reach the basket. It was a brutal, heartbreaking thing to see. This great, great player who'd lit up this same gym on so many occasions, unable to get the ball over the rim from right underneath the basket because his body was so completely broken.

At that point, a lot of people would have just packed it up and

A shot from my "Mr. Hurley" days. Here I am huddled with my assistant coach Jerry Dailey and members of our 1973–74 team at a home game at Dickinson High School. Get a load of my sideburns and jet black hair.

RIGHT:
David Rivers—probably the most exciting, most charismatic player to ever play for St. Anthony.
Taro Yamasaki, Getty Images

BELOW:
Rodrick Rhodes—such a talented athlete, and one of the only players to ever start for me as a freshman.

Tyshawn Taylor going up for a shot in his senior year, showing the potential that would take him all the way to the NBA.

Myles Mack, who joined us for his senior year and helped to lead St. Anthony to a #1 national ranking.

Kyle Anderson, the most complete player I've ever coached, hitting the court for the big game against #1 St. Pat's.

On the bench with assistant coaches Ben Gamble and Jason Hassan.

Sister Alan—for decades, the heart and soul of St. Anthony, she helped to steer the school and our athletic program to great success.

LEFT:
Danny and family.

BELOW:
Bobby and family.

BOTTOM:
Melissa and family, with a proud Pa and Mimi.

With the entire Hurley clan, to celebrate my induction into the Basketball Hall of Fame, Springfield, Massachusetts, 2010.

Posing for pictures in our new Hall of Fame jackets with other 2010 inductees. It was a crowded ceremony that year, because in addition to the individuals being honored, the Hall made room for members of the 1960 and 1992 Olympic teams.

With my beautiful wife, Chris, at the Hall of Fame dinner.

quit, but not Bobby. He was miserable, but he wasn't done. And
we knew he wasn't done, so we all took turns riding him pretty
hard. His brother, Danny. His uncles. His physical therapists. Me.
By April he was able to hit a golf ball. In May he ran a twelve-
minute mile—a pace that was probably twice as slow as he ran
back in grade school, but to us it was like Roger Bannister breaking the four-minute-mile barrier.

Really, he was making phenomenal progress. He was relentless.

First week of July, he played in a Jersey Shore league game.
His timing was off, and he was moving slow, but he was playing.
To me, that was all that mattered—but to Bobby, he could see
how far he still had to go, and he came to me after that first game
and said he was thinking about quitting. He said maybe he felt
like he was beating his head against the wall, like he'd never be
able to play at the professional level. He was pretty down about it,
but at the same time he seemed resigned to it. Like he'd given it all
he could and had to face reality.

I didn't want to hear it. I refused to hear it. So I got in Bobby's
face all over again, told him to meet me at the gym after work the
next day and we'd see about quitting. I put him through a bunch of
drills. Cutting. Shooting. Passing. Running the floor. Worked him
hard—harder than he'd been working himself. But he needed this
kind of push, he said. He needed to see if his frustration was from
the fact that he'd been away from the game for so long or from the
fact that he'd never be able to get his body to do the things it used
to do. If it was cobwebs or a new set of physical limitations.

We went at it again the next day. And the day after that. Soon,
I started to realize that the only thing keeping Bobby from playing at a high level was Bobby. He was rusty, that's all. He hadn't
played in over six months. So I took him aside and told him there

was no reason he couldn't fight his way back into NBA shape. No reason he couldn't lift his game close to where it was. Would he ever be able to run the floor like a demon and light up the gym the way he did for the Duke Blue Devils or the St. Anthony Friars? Only Bobby could answer that—but I saw no good reason why he shouldn't give it a shot.

And so he did.

Now, it would be nice to be able to write here that Bobby returned to the NBA and tore up the league, but that's not how it went. He did make it back, though. He did return to the Kings in time for their training camp the following season. He did read in one of the California papers that there were some people in basketball—in fact, some people in the Sacramento organization—who thought he'd never make it back, but that just drove him harder to prove them wrong. He did pour in twenty-one points in just twenty-two minutes in his first preseason game, against the Lakers—to go along with three rebounds, five assists, and one steal. And he did manage to honor the balance of the big contract he'd signed with Sacramento when they made him their number-one draft choice; he didn't miss a game the rest of the way.

But he was diminished by the accident, no question. His body wasn't right. He could fight his way back into the league and play at a professional level—hey, he even put up a double-double his first year back, also against the Lakers, with fourteen points and seventeen assists—but he would never lead his team to a championship. He would never dictate the outcome of a game the way he had in high school and college.

And yet it was a thrilling, uplifting thing to see, the way Bobby battled back.

No, he would never be the same, but he would not be denied. He would not be defeated.

A final few words on my kids before I turn the focus back to these winning seasons. I'm happy to report that all three of our children have drifted in one way or another into what I guess you could call the family business—coaching, teaching, working with young kids and sending them down some sort of purposeful path. In some cases, that meant drifting away and coming back to it; in others, it meant this had been the goal all along.

My younger son, Danny, was the first to think in this way. Soon as he finished playing basketball at Seton Hall, he went to work teaching at St. Anthony and helping out on my bench. He understood the game as well as anyone, and he understood the culture of St. Anthony basketball, which was just as important. After just one season coaching with me, he moved to Rutgers and spent four years there as an assistant coach under Kevin Bannon, and after that he interviewed with Father Edwin Lahey, the headmaster of St. Benedict's in Newark, who hired him to be the head coach of the boys' basketball team, a job Danny held for nine seasons. He had a great run at St. Benedict's, turning a nothing-special .500-type program into a national powerhouse.

As a prep school, we never met St. Benedict's in our state tournament, so Danny and I never had to face each other head to head. His team played in the prep school tournament and went to a ton of national events. We didn't start playing them until Danny left to take the head coaching job at Wagner College, which was just as well with me. It was tough enough preparing to face all these top teams without having to go up against my own son on the other bench.

(And as tough as it would have been for me and Danny to

coach against each other, it would have been even tougher for my wife, Chris. Talk about being torn!)

Bobby, meanwhile, didn't take such a direct path to coaching. Like his younger brother, he also came to work with me for a year after he was done playing, but he wasn't so sure coaching was for him. Anyway, for a while his focus was elsewhere. He kept his hand in the game as an advance scout for the 76ers, but his main interest once his NBA career was over was in racing and breeding horses. He stayed around basketball, did some color commentary, coached a little bit at the youth level, but then, as time went on, he started to realize the horse business wasn't the way to go—and it was around this time that Danny was offered the head coaching job at Wagner, so the two of them got to talking.

It's funny, the way opportunity finds you when you're not really looking for it. Bobby wasn't ready to give up on the horse business just yet. He was building a horse farm in Ocala, Florida, where he was planning to breed and train thoroughbreds. Danny was teaching history and coaching at St. Benedict's and starting to think he'd be happy making a career there, and all of a sudden there was this college job at Wagner that Danny had to consider. It was a whole other level of coaching, an exciting challenge, and Danny knew he was up to it, and he knew Bobby would be a tremendous asset to him on the bench and in practice. I couldn't have agreed with him more. I mean, Bobby had played for Mike Krzyzewski, he'd played in the NBA, he'd scouted in the NBA, and he'd even had that year coaching with me at St. Anthony, so he clearly had the pedigree.

The only question, really, was whether Bobby was too far removed from basketball to make an impact—but that was never an issue as far as I was concerned. You have to realize, this was a kid who'd lived and breathed basketball his entire life. That doesn't change just because you step away from the game for a while—and happily, it worked out that the two of them went to Wagner and transformed that program. The team had been 5–26 the year before Danny took over as head coach, and after two years they'd improved to 25–5, one of the most dramatic turnarounds in NCAA history, and folks took notice. All of a sudden, Danny was getting a lot of well-deserved attention as one of the best young coaches in college basketball. His name was mentioned for just about every coaching vacancy that came up, particularly at schools in the Northeast, where it was thought he wanted to remain. Sure enough, at the end of the 2011–12 season, Danny accepted the head coaching job at the University of Rhode Island. It was a chance to compete in the Atlantic 10 Conference, on a much bigger stage, so of course he grabbed it. Bobby went with Danny as his assistant.

My daughter, Melissa, has also made her mark. She graduated from Monmouth University with the best grades of any of our kids and ended up taking advantage of a special education program being offered in Jersey City. The way it worked was, if you came in as an inclusion teacher, working with kids who'd been mainstreamed, you'd earn a master's in special education along the way, so she set off in this direction and found some of the same fascination and satisfaction in working with these students and their families that her brothers and I did as coaches. And lately she's been an enormous help to me, keeping me connected to my players in meaningful ways off the court, away from the gym. Why do I need her help in this way? Well, I don't text. I don't use Facebook or Twitter. But these days that's how high school kids communicate, so Melissa keeps me plugged in. She stays on top of all this social media stuff and makes sure I'm never out of touch.

(Or, at least, never *so* out of touch that I can't get a message to a kid on my team.)

As a bonus, she married a coach. Melissa's husband, Gabe, is a terrific high school soccer coach, so now it looks like all of my grandchildren will grow up in coaching households—and Chris and I look on and think this is a great good thing.

After all, we tell ourselves, our kids didn't turn out too bad. They know what it means to set and keep a goal. They know what it means to work hard. And mostly, they know what it means to win.

7.

1995–1996: GUARDING KOBE

NO ONE HAS EVER DROWNED IN SWEAT.

—Lou Holtz

**I'VE MISSED MORE THAN NINE THOUSAND
SHOTS IN MY CAREER. I'VE LOST ALMOST THREE
HUNDRED GAMES. TWENTY-SIX TIMES, I'VE BEEN
TRUSTED TO TAKE THE GAME-WINNING SHOT
AND MISSED. I'VE FAILED OVER AND OVER AGAIN
IN MY LIFE. AND THAT IS WHY I SUCCEED.**

—Michael Jordan

Sometimes the game gives back to you and your players way more than you put into it—and when you're fortunate enough to find yourself in the middle of a season for the record books, it makes it so much sweeter when you're able to send your players off the court with a couple lessons learned, to go along with your string of victories.

It doesn't always work out that you're able to set the right example, the right tone for your players and still find a way to play at the highest level, but it's something to shoot for. That's how things shook out for our 1995–96 edition of the St. Anthony Friars—a team that featured several players who'd won the state championship the year before and the Tournament of Champions that followed it, with just a couple bumps along the way. In fact, we only had two seniors on that team—Ned Felton and Eugene Atkinson, who both went on to play for Lefty Driesell at James Madison University—so we had every reason to think our returning squad would be strong. We ended the season as a nationally ranked team—after losing an important Christmas tournament in Florida, along with a couple other tough losses early on—so I was excited about our returning group.

I thought we had a shot to do something special.

When I think back on our 1996 team, I think of Rashon Burno. It wasn't all about him, of course, but he was key. As much as anybody else on that team, whatever happened that year, good or bad, he seemed to have a hand in it.

Here's a kid who had a real rough patch. Rashon had lost both of his parents by the time he was out of grammar school, ended up being raised by a grandmother who had to cash a Social Security check each month to put groceries on the table. He lived in the Duncan Projects, surrounded by all kinds of negative influences. Those buildings were a real blight on the community (they were recently knocked down), a magnet for trouble, but somehow Rashon managed to emerge as close to unscathed as any angel could have hoped.

Guess you could say that angel was Rashon's grandmother, and she did a good job with him early on, but then she was in and out of the hospital with Alzheimer's and Rashon was pretty much left on his own. He didn't have a whole lot of support in that kind of environment. At some point, he drifted down to the Boys' Club and started playing ball with my friend Gary Greenberg. Guess you could say Gary was another one of Rashon's angels, because he was looking out for him. This alone wasn't so unusual, because a lot of kids from the projects found their way to Gary's gym, but in Rashon's case, he didn't seem to have the build for basketball. To this day he's barely five-seven in his high-tops, which meant there was no NBA in Rashon's future, but he was able to turn his difficult surroundings into a fierce competitiveness and mental toughness that came out in the way he played. This kid, he would not be denied. He would not quit. Didn't matter what kind of lousy hand he'd been dealt—he'd find a way to persevere and play it to some kind of advantage.

Just to give you an idea what the game meant to Rashon—and what it continues to mean—he went on from St. Anthony to a first-rate career at DePaul, where he was a three-year captain. After graduation, he became a financial planner in Chicago, and he was doing well, but after a couple years he found himself missing basketball, so he started coaching high school. It was something to fill in the spaces where the game had been. And that's all it was at first, but then he found those spaces were bigger than he'd thought. He took a head coaching job at a prep school just outside the city, and from there he moved to an assistant's position at Towson, under Pat Kennedy, who had been his coach at DePaul. Now he's moved on to another assistant job at Florida, and it's a real wonder to talk to this kid and hear his philosophies on coaching.

Rashon first popped up on our radar when he was in grammar school. He showed up at one of our camps when he was ten or twelve years old, and after that he kept coming. And like I said, Gary Greenberg had his eye on him as well. The thing about Rashon was that he was smart enough to see basketball as his ticket. A lot of times kids get caught in the swirl of what goes on in public housing and can't see their way out of it. It becomes this self-fulfilling prophecy of doom. They only know what they see, and they mimic what they know, but Rashon got hooked on basketball just in time. He saw enough kids get their shot, either playing with me or playing for another one of the good competitive programs in the area. I'm not so full of myself as to think I'm the only coach who could have whipped this kid into shape and sent him on to college. St. Anthony isn't for everybody, and I'm certainly not for everybody. Basketball, that's what this kid needed. A lot of it. With a heavy hand to guide him.

Rashon came up with another freshman, Anthony Perry. Rashon had gone to Number 39 school, and Anthony went to Number 14—two of the worst grammar schools in the city. Gary Greenberg kept bringing them out to see our games, even our practices, to give them a goal. He'd say, "You want to play for Coach Hurley, you've got to stay off the street corners."

My big concern with Rashon when he first joined us was whether we could build enough of a family around him to help him. Like I said, he didn't have that at home. Anthony, he was being raised by his mom, but Rashon was on his own more and more, at a time in his life when he was having more and more freedom, facing more and more temptations, and that was a bad recipe. It's tough enough stepping up to our program as a freshman, but without some solid footing at home, it can be damn near impossible. I expect a lot from my players. They've got a lot of pulls on their time, and school of course comes first, but I can be pretty demanding, and if you don't have a responsible adult at home helping to keep everything straight . . . well, it can get away from you quick.

In forty years as head coach, I've only had about ten freshman players make the varsity, and here again I had two in the same season. It was easy to work Anthony into a lot of what we were trying to do as a team because he was tall—probably six-two that first year. He wound up leading our team in scoring, as a freshman, so he made the adjustment.

Rashon, his contributions were more subtle at first. A lot of the older kids, they could see Anthony putting up all those points, so it was maybe a little bit easier for him to feel accepted. His efforts were right there on the scoreboard. With Rashon running our offense, I'm sure some of my guys felt like this kid was taking away their minutes, but by the end of that first season even the seniors had to admit this kid was something special. I didn't start him, because I felt that Ned Felton, one of our seniors, deserved to start, but Rashon came off the bench and became an integral part of the way we played.

Still, he had a lot to learn. There was one game his sophomore year when I realized I had a lot to learn as well. This was one of the bumps I hinted at earlier, a rough patch that found us on the way to the 1995 state championship. We were playing Miami Senior late in that key Christmas tournament game. We were up by a point with seven seconds on the clock, and we had a foul to give as the other team prepared to inbound the ball. We'd just missed the front end of a one-and-one, and Miami Senior had called a time-out. In high school ball, you don't automatically move the ball to half-court on a change-of-possession time-out, so we had them pinned at their end. I liked our chances, but only if we played it smart. I told my guys during the time-out that we wanted to let them burn a couple dribbles and then give a foul. This way, they'd have to take the ball out again and there'd be even less time on the clock for them to run a play.

Well, Rashon's man got the ball on the inbound play, and it turned out Rashon didn't quite know what it meant to "give a foul." Instead, he went for the steal, but all he could do was wave at it, and his man drove to the basket for what should have been an easy layup to win the game. But it's never easy, is it? This kid from Miami Senior missed his "gimme" layup, but two of his six-eight teammates crashed the boards behind him, and one of them tipped it in at the buzzer.

As I watched that play unfold, my heart sank. Then, on the miss, it lifted. Then, on the tip-in, it sank all over again—this time all the way to where I couldn't shake this one loss. If there's one thing you need to know about me, it's this: I don't like to lose. My wife knows this. My kids know this. My players know this most of all. Really, it just about kills me to lose. Stays with me a good long while. And when we lose a close one . . . well, then it kills me in a dozen different ways.

And yet this loss was on me. Why? Because the longer you do something, the more you realize that people who are really good at something tend not to talk about it. They just get it done. That's how it was with Rashon Burno. The game came easy to him. What he didn't know, he made up for with his athleticism and his instincts. He just didn't know that the phrase "give a foul" meant I wanted him to intentionally foul an opposing player, and he didn't know to ask. He understood the concept—because, hey, you play enough ball, that kind of thing is innate—but he didn't get the language. He'd never heard the phrase before.

So now we have a drill called the command drill. In a

command drill, I call out what I want my players to do during the run of play. If I call out, "Give a foul," which I do regularly during the season when I want to get a substitute into the game late rather than use one of my time-outs or watch the clock run down, they know exactly what I expect. There's no room for doubt or confusion, not anymore. Also, coming out of that one loss to Miami Senior, we now have charge drills, loose ball drills, giving foul drills. We cover it all.

I learned from that one game against Miami Senior that you can't assume these kids know anything. They can have all the basketball knowledge in the world and play with all the confidence a coach could want in his players, but if you're not completely clear with them on every last thing, it can cost you.

Okay, so that's the first big lesson this team took in: accountability. In this case, it was up to me to "own" this one mistake against Miami Senior. Yeah, Rashon didn't do what I'd asked him to do on this one inbound play—but only because I didn't ask in a way he could understand. Only because something was lost in the translation, because I didn't take the time to communicate clearly, effectively.

But Rashon had a couple things to learn about accountability on his own—and here he had some company with his classmate Anthony Perry. Early in their junior year, December 1995, we had a game on the schedule against Lower Merion High School, a public high school on the Pennsylvania Main Line, just outside Philadelphia. A lot of folks who follow high school basketball will know that Lower Merion was where Kobe Bryant went to school—and this was his senior year. You have to remember, the buzz on Kobe Bryant was huge by this point in his high school

career. We'd played them at home the year before and managed
to beat them pretty soundly. By now, though, it was generally
known that Kobe planned to skip college and go straight to the
NBA, and it was generally agreed that he would make an immediate impact at the professional level, so last year's game didn't
much matter. Kobe was bigger and better; his teammates were
bigger and better; this would be their last season with one of the
greatest high school players to ever get his hands on a basketball,
so all season long I had to think they'd be putting it all out there.

When you look at your schedule at the start of the season,
there are certain games that loom larger than others, and this
was one of those games. I'd circled it on my calendar. With or
without Kobe, Lower Merion was a big-time program. Their fans
were real die-hards. They packed their home gym and cheered
like crazy, so they had a real home-court advantage. This game
was to be played in a sold-out gym at St. Joseph's University, but it
would still be a home game for Lower Merion, packed with their
own fans, their own energy. It was being shown live on a local
cable station, and there were sure to be all kinds of NBA scouts
and executives in the arena, so we were expecting a pretty electric
environment—and privately I worried that none of that electric-
ity, none of that energy, would be for us.

It was still early in a long season, but in many ways this game
would stamp our year. We had another tough matchup a bit later
on, against St. John's Prospect Hall, another nationally ranked
opponent, but other than that, it didn't appear we'd be pushed until
the postseason tournament. And remember, we'd won the state
championship the year before—the first of three straight state titles
for our Friars. We'd only lost those two seniors to graduation, and
now I had guys like Rashon Burno and Anthony Perry, who'd be
coming into their own as upperclassmen and full-fledged leaders.

Okay, so that's the setup to this showdown with Kobe, and it was lining up to be a real battle, but then nature got in the way—and by "nature" I mean the natural elements as well as human nature. You see, the Lower Merion game was set for a Friday night, but earlier that week there was a killer snowstorm all up and down the northeast coast. The storm started late Monday, and by the time Jersey City woke up on Tuesday the streets had been swallowed up by almost two feet of snow. You couldn't move, so obviously school was canceled. And then it kept on snowing. Next day, a Wednesday, school was canceled again, but I managed to track down the custodian at the gym we were renting for practice, and he opened the place up for us so we could get in a run and keep sharp before our big game.

In those days, back before my players all had cell phones, we had a phone chain set up, so we were able to get the word to everyone. By this point, the kids had been trapped in their houses or apartments since Monday night, so they were itching to get out and let off some steam, and I remember leaving the gym that night thinking practice had gone well and that we were in good shape for the game on Friday.

On Thursday, St. Anthony was finally able to open its doors—but for whatever reason, Rashon and Anthony didn't make it in that day. Anthony told me later that he just assumed we'd be closed, since he had two siblings in Jersey City public schools and they were closed that day. And Rashon insisted that he had followed protocol and called the school office that morning—but before the office had changed its outgoing message from the day before, he said.

So there we were, a day before the biggest game of our season to date, facing down the best high school basketball player in anyone's memory, a kid who'd probably be a starter in the NBA in less than a year, and two of my best players couldn't even make it to school. This was a problem. A big problem.

The way it works is you have to be in school in order to practice. If you've got a game on a school day, you've got to be in school in order to dress for the game. It's a state law. But on top of that, I have my own law. I take it one step further. I tell my guys that if they don't *practice* the day before a game, they can't play. It's cut-and-dry, plain and simple. Naturally, there are times I want to sit a player during practice, because maybe he's nursing an ankle sprain or he's been out sick and we want to give him one more day of rest, but he's there in the gym and only sitting out on my say-so. If you miss a practice under that scenario, I might not let you start in a game the next day, but I'll bring you off the bench and let you do your thing.

This put us in a tough spot in terms of Rashon and Anthony. It didn't put *me* in a tough spot at all, as a coach, because it was a no-brainer. It was tough only because these two kids had now put their teammates in a tough spot; here they were going up against a once-in-a-generation high school talent like Kobe Bryant without our one and our two. Folks outside our program couldn't understand why Rashon and Anthony weren't dressing for the game. It's not like we called a press conference or anything, but those who knew me understood the deal.

If you don't practice, you don't play.

Like it or not, agree with me or not, no one player was bigger than the team. Heck, no *two* players were bigger than the team. But there was a lesson here that was bigger than any one game, against any one opponent—even if that one opponent was Kobe Bryant.

Even Kobe couldn't help but wonder why Rashon and Anthony weren't dressed for the game. He came over to my guys during warm-ups, saw them out of uniform, and figured out they weren't playing. They knew each other from all these different camps, and they had a good, friendly rivalry going, so he asked them what was up.

Don't misunderstand, I hated like hell that I was in this spot, but at the same time I liked the opportunity I could now give to two other players. One was a guard named Ali Abdullah, who played a lot of meaningful minutes for us, backing up Rashon. He was a talented young player who ended up getting a Division I scholarship to Howard University, even though he never started at St. Anthony. He was stuck behind a bunch of strong players his whole career, but he made things happen when he got into the game, and he was always a key player for us coming off the bench.

The other was a role player named Gary Dunbar, a good, hustling athlete who never really played an impact role for us other than this one game. He started in the frontcourt in place of Anthony, which came with the double-edged assignment of guarding Kobe Bryant. Can you imagine? First game as a starter and you draw Kobe's number? But Gary, to his great credit, didn't shrink from anything. He stepped up his game and went up against Kobe like he was any other player—like he did this sort of thing all the time instead of . . . well, *never*.

The game was back and forth, up and down. We were playing each other close with just a couple seconds left in the first half. On any other night, if we'd been playing at full strength, this would have been a good showing, because I always liked our chances when it came to conditioning and mental toughness. Over a long, hard-fought game, that's what usually wins out, and more times than not we'd pull away in the second half, only here I worried that without two of our key guys the rest of our group might lose focus or run out of gas.

On what should have been the last play of the first half, with Lower Merion up by a point, they inbounded the ball to Kobe Bryant, who started advancing it up the right sideline. Gary Dunbar was playing him tight, and on the third or fourth dribble he noticed Kobe wasn't doing anything to vary his rhythm. He was being careless with the ball, nonchalant, like he didn't think Gary Dunbar, this player he'd never even heard of, would be someone he'd have to worry about.

But Gary was a smart kid. Kobe might have never heard of him, but Gary had heard of Kobe. In his own head at least, this gave Gary a kind of edge. He had something to prove—but even more than that, he knew the kind of player Kobe could be, so he tried to take him out of his game. He saw that Kobe's head was someplace else. He timed out Kobe's first couple dribbles and then reached in for the steal. He caught Kobe completely by surprise—and caught enough of the ball to tip it toward our frontcourt and drive with it toward our basket.

Man, it was something to see.

Now, a play like that, it doesn't mean anything if it doesn't lead to points, and here's where our coaching kicked in. We have a drill we run into the ground during practice where we follow our own guy to the hoop every time there's a breakaway. We call it "covering the backboard." It's one of our rules, to always, always, always cover the backboard—because you never know. What it means is that the closest kid to the play, wherever he is on the court, he has to bust his butt and break for the basket as hard as he can, hopefully in time to grab the ball and tip it back in that one time in a hundred when our guy misses an easy, fast-break layup. It's the same play that beat us in that Miami Senior game, when Rashon went for that steal instead of giving a foul, and here our closest man was Delvon Arrington, who together with Rashon and Anthony was part of our go-to trio of players that season. (Delvon ended up playing at Florida State, where he was team captain—and where he still holds a bunch of school records.) It fell to Delvon to pick up a lot of the scoring for us that night, with Rashon and Anthony on the bench, and here he was out at half-court when Gary Dunbar started his drive.

Delvon broke for the basket without even thinking about it. I expected as much, because we work on that drill every day in practice. We've got a whole sequence of board drills that come from Jerry Wainwright, who used to be the head coach at Richmond and, later on, at DePaul. An excellent college coach. I saw him run these drills at a clinic, and I grabbed at them.

We've been using Jerry's drills for years. In one, we have our guys work just on tipping the ball. The ball comes off the rim, and we have them practice tipping it righty or lefty. Over and over. If the ball falls to the right side of their bodies, they're supposed to use their right hand; if it falls to the left, they go left.

We had run those drills so many times, and hollered at our guys to cover the backboard so many times, that Delvon didn't even have to think about it—and sure enough, Gary Dunbar's shot rimmed out toward the left side of the basket. When it did, Delvon was there to tip it in with his left hand, just as time was running out, and we closed out the half with a one-point lead and all kinds of momentum.

Just on the back of that one play, the game seemed to turn.

Really, our guys were pumped, watching Gary take it to Kobe like that and turning the scoreboard around for us. Everyone in our locker room was excited about it, and I imagine the reaction in the Lower Merion locker room was completely opposite. In fact, when Kobe came out to start the second half, you could see his body language was all off, like he was in a funk. That one play had pushed him off his game, and we took advantage of it, running the lead to seven, eight points in the first minutes of the second half. We kept the lead the whole rest of the way, going on to win the game by about fifteen, and it all goes back to these two kids, two of my stars, having to miss out on one of the biggest games of their careers.

A lot of coaches, they hear how I handled Rashon and Anthony on this, they don't get it. They can't understand how I'd jeopardize a meaningful game or a couple notches in our national ranking just to prove a point—but I wasn't out to prove a point. These kids messed up, that's all. When you mess up, there are consequences. When you mess up, you have to be accountable. Doesn't mean I was throwing in the game, just that I would now give two other kids an opportunity to come up big for us. And they did . . . they surely did.

Our next big test as a team came at the Above the Rim Holiday Classic in San Diego. We'd gotten into the habit of traveling to out-of-town Christmas tournaments, and this one was a particular favorite. Our guys always looked forward to it, for the adventure, but more than that it was a chance for them to see a different type of competition, beyond the Northeast—and a chance for them to be seen by coaches outside the region. A lot of times, close to home, they ended up knowing a lot of the players on the other teams, from camps, clinics, AAU ball, whatever, so it was good for them to match up against an opponent with no shared history.

Our big showdown came in the finals against Crenshaw, a Los Angeles public school with a strong basketball program and a big reputation. It was still somewhat early in the season for us, just a couple weeks after the Lower Merion game; we hadn't really hit our full focus as a team, even though we hadn't lost a game. Still, I thought Crenshaw could give us trouble. They were beating up everybody in the tournament; to hear the other coaches talk, to listen to the fans, they were certainly the favorites. But that was just on paper, and I didn't know that just yet. All I knew at the time was that when you take a bunch of Jersey City high school players all the way to California just to play a couple games, you might as well win the championship. Like I said, I hate to lose, and the only thing I hate worse than losing is traveling a long way to lose a game. Makes the trip home pretty unpleasant. So when we learned we were going up against Crenshaw in the finals, I wanted to be good and ready.

Turned out we were in their heads too, only Crenshaw's strategy was to press us, all game long. Unfortunately for them, we were able to counter it almost every possession, so we had an easy time of it on the scoreboard. Ended up crushing them, actually. Basically, we kept running the same play, pitching it long to our big man, Ajmal Basit, who finished with thirty-six points in the game and was named MVP of the tournament. Ajmal took twenty shots against Crenshaw, all of them layups, and almost all of them on fast breaks to beat the press. It wasn't exactly a typical game for Ajmal, who also grabbed fifteen rebounds, but when your opponent keeps giving you the same opening, you have to take it.

Don't get me wrong, Ajmal was a talented player. He had a lot of big moments for us and filled a big role. He went to the University of Massachusetts–Amherst on a full scholarship and finished his college career at the University of Delaware. After that, he played pro ball in Europe for a good long while, and these days he coaches high school ball in Georgia, so he's clearly made a life in the game. He took a lot of heat from his teammates that day in San Diego, though, despite his MVP honors—or maybe because of them. When we got back to the locker room after the game and the championship ceremonies, Ajmal's teammates started booing him mercilessly. It was just a bunch of good-natured razzing; the entire team was in on it, the coaches too, and I've got to give Ajmal credit because he shouldered it well enough. The whole way home, the guys kept on him about giving back his MVP award, because all he did was score a bunch of layups, and he just smiled and went along with it.

Looking back, that was an important trip, because it helped knit us together as a team, and because it reminded our players that you can't always play to an opponent's reputation. Sometimes you have to play to your strengths and let the other team adjust to you. That Crenshaw team was a perfect example. They'd been running through the competition—not only in that one tournament but all through the season—and the reason we were able to handle them so easily was because we didn't let them take us out of our game. We'd scouted them of course, same way they'd had a bunch of eyes on us. But that didn't mean we had to change things up. We knew they liked to run the press—early in games, all game long. And that was just fine with us. We worked all the time in practice on beating the press. Our guys knew their roles, they knew the situation. We had ball-handlers who could handle that kind of pressure. We had a bunch of plays we could run. And we had a big, athletic player like Ajmal Basit, who was a terrific finisher.

It was a good lesson, going into the postseason tournament. With the Kobe Bryant/Lower Merion game out of the way and the Crenshaw game out of the way, we had a clear path to the Tournament of Champions bracket back home. We'd also managed a couple statement-like wins against two other nationally ranked opponents—St. John's of Prospect Hall, out of Frederick,

Maryland, and St. Raymond's from the Bronx—so it's not like we weren't tested, but it worked out that our tough matchups were spread throughout the season. There were a couple long stretches in there when nobody on the schedule could match up with us, so we tried to keep our guys sharp and give them something to play for.

A lot of times, when you're facing a series of weaker opponents, the challenge for a coach—especially a high school coach—is to get your team up for a game. You don't want your players to become complacent or to disrespect a team on the schedule, because any team can surprise you, at any time. So I try to push these kids by getting them to push each other. I tell them everybody's spot is up for grabs. Nobody's minutes are guaranteed. That's been my approach all along. Even my starters, I want them to feel like they have something to prove, like their teammates are gaining on them. We go at it hard in practice. And in our games too. Doesn't matter if it's a tough opponent that matches up well with us or if we're playing a weaker team that doesn't expect to compete. We play at full speed, full tilt, full volume, all the time. I'll stick to my regular rotation. Part of the reason for that is I don't want to disrespect the other team by easing up, but an even bigger part is I don't want us to develop any bad habits as a team. You take your foot off the gas in one game, it's hard to stomp back down on the pedal when you need to, so I want my guys to play every game like their season depends on it—like we're always, always, always about to be pushed.

Sure enough, we ran through the field in the postseason tournament, ended up winning the state championship, each game by double digits, but then we had to finish off the season with the Tournament of Champions. As always, we were the smallest school in the field, as winners of the Parochial Class B championship—but still, we were the top seed, over the Parochial Class A winners and the winners of the four public school divisions. Shawnee High School in Medford Lakes, a midsized public school, was the second seed, and they had a particularly strong team that year, so it looked like we would square off against each other in the finals.

And in fact, that's just how it shook out.

There was a lot on the line for us. We were the number-one-ranked team in the country going into the Tournament of Champions, so if we ran the table we'd be national champions. It's kind of a mythical title, same way it used to be in college football before the Bowl Championship Series took shape and pitted the top two teams in the country in a true national championship game. But we were the consensus number-one team in all the polls—and had been for most of the season, going all the way back to the preseason—so all we had to do was win out and we'd earn the right to call ourselves state champs, Tournament of Champion winners, and national champs—not a bad way to cap our year.

Plus, there was that unblemished record we had going, so naturally we wanted to keep our perfect season intact.

Like I said, there was a lot on the line, but even though I didn't want my guys to focus on any of that, as we breezed through the state tournament and then the semifinal round of the Tournament of Champions, it became a bigger and bigger deal. I couldn't shut out all those other distractions for trying. It's like we were playing for posterity, when I'd have liked it if we could close the door on all that other stuff and just play for the win. Nothing wrong with posterity, but it's not really something you can shoot for, something you can count on. If it happens, it happens. All you can do is all you can do, and here all we could do was try to control the tempo of the game and play some good solid defense, with intensity. The rest would have to take care of itself. Or not.

Shawnee came out strong and hard in the finals. The game was at the Meadowlands, which was only about half full, but most of the crowd was with Shawnee. They were such a big school compared to St. Anthony—about 1,500 students to our 240 or so—which meant they outnumbered us in the stands in a meaningful way. I think our guys started to feel like the arena was against them. And maybe it was. We were a little flat to start the game. Our passes weren't as crisp as I would have liked. We got some good looks, but our shots weren't falling. We made some stupid mistakes, gave Shawnee some easy second and third chances. Basically, we were playing like underdogs with something to prove, instead of like champions with an undefeated season on the line.

It was a big game for Shawnee too. We'd beaten them in this same game the year before, when they were the number-one seed in the tournament, so I'm sure they wanted some payback. They wanted to spoil our perfect season and knock us down from that number-one spot. Heck, if I was their coach, I would have used all these things to try and motivate my players. I would have made it so our guys felt like giant-killers. Plus, they had a very good team, a very deep team. They were led by a kid named Malik Allen, who went on to play for Villanova and then for a dozen years in the NBA, so it's always tough when you're going up against a singular talent like that—someone who can really dominate.

All game long, I was thinking it was our game to lose, even with the sluggish way we started out, even with the way we kept letting Shawnee stay in the game, but we couldn't pull away. We'd go up by a couple buckets, and they'd come charging back. The game went to overtime, and it was the same thing all over again. They'd take the lead, and we'd tie it right up, but as the clock started to run down in the extra period it started to feel to me like the game was slipping away from us. Ike Williams, one of our star players, fouled out. And then Mike Fry, another one of our key guys, committed a crucial turnover with a little more than a minute to go in the overtime period.

Shawnee was up by one at that point, and the turnover got them started on a two-on-one break. As they advanced the ball to their end of the floor I got a sick, sad feeling in my stomach. I started to think the game would now be out of reach, on the other side of this fast break, and our undefeated season was about to end. It wasn't like me, to give up on a game before the clock ran out, to give up on our season, but the momentum wasn't with us. Everyone in the arena could sense that the momentum wasn't with us.

Shawnee was playing like a team of destiny; we were just playing.

Happily, mercifully, Rashon Burno was our one man back on the play. Like me, he wasn't the type to give up on a game until it was over. Like me, he'd taken the lessons learned over the long arc of our season and put them into practice. But unlike me, he didn't have the flash of a negative thought. He wasn't thinking our perfect season was just about done, or that our national championship was now out of reach . . . all on the back of that one turnover. He just wanted the ball back.

Here's how he got it. Our bench was at the far end of the court, which meant that we could only watch what was happening from the back of the play. I could see the Shawnee player who'd stolen the ball drive down the right side of the court, flanked by his teammate running on the left side. Rashon had gotten himself in position in front of the kid with the ball, and he was trying to get him to commit. Rashon stepped toward him, to challenge him— hoping, I guess, to get him to give up his dribble and pass the ball to his teammate on the other side of the floor, which is just what happened. And as it happened, Rashon seemed to know it ahead of time, because as the kid sent the ball across the court Rashon moved with it. Next, the player on the left took the pass and put the ball on the floor, and we could see he was about to make a move toward the basket. Here again, the entire arena seemed to sense what was coming, but nobody counted on Rashon. Nobody counted on Rashon having the presence of mind *not* to try to take a charge, *not* go up and try to block the shot, or *not* just foul the kid outright and stop the clock. Instead, he simply stripped the ball away from the Shawnee player, almost like you'd see a quarterback on a handoff. One moment the Shawnee player was leaving his feet, scooping the ball up off the bounce and going hard to the hole for an underhanded layup, and the next moment his hands were up in the air, empty, and the ball was going the other way. Rashon just plucked it away, like a magician's sleight of hand, and threw it down to our end of the floor, to Ajmal Basit, who dunked it to put us back up by one.

It was the most unbelievable, unexpected exchange. We went from being down one, with the ball, thinking all we needed was a good look and a stop and the game was ours to win, to the prospect of being down three on the wrong side of a huge momentum shift with a minute to go in our perfect season. But Rashon Burno, the shortest player on the floor, wasn't about to let that happen, so he made an incredible steal to turn things around and give us back the lead. All in the matter of just a few seconds.

And Rashon wasn't done just yet. On the inbound play after Ajmal's dunk, Rashon picked up his man, the Shawnee point guard, who advanced the ball toward midcourt. Rashon, as the last play had just showed, was a terrific, on-the-ball defender—probably the best to ever play for St. Anthony. (Certainly the best to ever play on my watch.) He also had tremendous instincts and an innate understanding of the inner workings of the game. All of that came into play on the next exchange, because Rashon knew the Shawnee guard was thinking about a time-out. He knew the kid would glance over to the Shawnee bench, to see if his coach wanted him to stop the clock and talk things over, so he waited for it, and waited for it. Finally, the kid turned his head ever so slightly toward his coach, and in that same instant Rashon swept in and stole the ball and drove swiftly to our end of the court for an easy layup, putting us ahead by three.

Again, an unbelievable play.

It was still a one-possession game, so it's not like we could breathe any kind of sigh of relief just yet. But Rashon Burno was not about to let up on defense either. Shawnee immediately called a time-out, to get their players to take a deep breath after those two big steals, which was probably what I would have done in that same situation. But then, on the inbound play, they kicked the ball out to the same guard who'd just had his pocket picked by Rashon—and Rashon stole the ball again! Drove it down the length of the floor and laid it in.

Now we were up by five, with less than thirty seconds to go, but by this point Shawnee was defeated. On the scoreboard, it was a six-point swing, but in reality it was an eight-point swing, because after the Mike Fry turnover they had been looking at that two-on-one break and an all-but-sure-thing layup.

A lot of kids, they'd give up on a play like that. Even a top defender like Rashon, you don't expect him to come away with the ball, but he went at it with passion and determination. He would not be denied—and he wasn't. He ended up saving our entire season on just that one play. Turned out to be the biggest, greatest, most memorable play in the history of our program—and it came attached to the biggest, greatest, most memorable lesson: don't quit.

Don't quit on your season.

Don't quit on your teammates.

Don't quit on yourself.

And if you happen to be a coach with a sad, sick feeling in your gut that your team's perfect championship season is about to go up in smoke . . . don't quit on your players.

Rashon turned that game around for us almost single-handedly. He finished with ten steals, for a tournament record that will probably never be broken. Ten steals in one game! I can't imagine anyone ever getting close to that, and here it came from one of the guys who had to sit out the Kobe Bryant game earlier in the season, from a kid who had a lot to learn about accountability—but a lot to teach his coach and his teammates about what it means to keep at it.

We had quite a group that year. In all, eight of our guys went on to play Division I college ball; that's a lot coming from any one high school team, but it just shows you the depth of talent we had on our roster. As I've mentioned, Ajmal Basit went to UMass–Amherst, Rashon Burno to DePaul, Ali Abdullah to Howard University, and Delvon Arrington to Florida State. Anthony Perry went on to star at Georgetown, while Ike Williams played at Fairleigh Dickinson, Mike Fry at Lehigh, and Jamal Ragland at St. Francis. Even Gary Dunbar, who got a chance to shine against Kobe Bryant, earned a scholarship to Felician College, a Division II program in Rutherford, New Jersey, and his career offers a terrific footnote to a terrific season.

Gary was a strong athlete, but not the kind of basketball player

who could touch the talent we had on our team that year. This is
not a knock on Gary so much as it is a point of praise for everyone
else, but when we put Gary in our starting lineup to match up
against Kobe Bryant, he stepped up his game and played like one
of the top recruits in the country.

He played tough. He played smart. He played big. And he got
a chance to do all of these things simply because he *played*.

Without Gary, I don't think we would have gotten out of
Philadelphia with a win that day against Lower Merion. In fact,
I'm sure of it. His tenacity turned that game around for us, and
he wouldn't have even been on the floor if Rashon Burno and
Anthony Perry hadn't screwed up and missed practice for no
good reason. It all tied in. And the great side benefit to Gary's
role was that he got a story to tell his children and grandchildren.
He lifted his team, and what he got back was a moment to remember for the rest of his life.

Gary comes to our games from time to time. He came to one
not too long ago, with his fiancé. He brought her by to say hello,
and all she wanted to talk about was this Lower Merion game.
She'd heard Gary talk about it, of course, and a part of her just
didn't buy it. The story was almost too incredible to believe—that
the guy she was about to marry had once gotten the best of the
legendary Kobe Bryant on a basketball court. That our perfect
season might have gone another way if Gary hadn't stepped up.
That we might not have been national champions after all.

Turned out we just happened to have footage of Gary's steal
on a DVD, which we sometimes sell at home games as a fund-
raiser, so his fiancé bought a copy to see it for herself.

HARD WORK

Opening round of postseason play.

Technically, it's a second-round game for us, after a first-round bye, but it amounts to the same thing.

I'll say this—it never gets old. Each season, while we fight and build and hustle our way into the tournament, it feels like the rest of the world has been put on pause. It's what we play for all season long, and when it finally comes around on the calendar, I can't think of anything else—because, hey, there's nothing like a single-elimination basketball game to get your juices flowing.

I have my game day routines, my superstitions. A hard workout downstairs in the gym. A sauna. A short nap in the afternoon. A peanut butter and jelly sandwich for lunch. (Maybe two if I'm feeling like I'll need the extra fuel.) A couple sports drinks to replace all those fluids I lost at the gym. Then I get my notes ready, get my head around the game, and I'm all set.

Past couple years, we've been running our Senior Night ceremony right before our opening playoff game. A lot of folks, they hear this is how we set it up, they think we're being arrogant or cocky. Like we take the fact that we'll make it to the postseason, with home-court advantage, as a kind of given. I take their point, but it's not like that. It's just that, for a lot of our players, it's tough for their parents to break away from work for an afternoon game. They can't always make it. They get to what they can, when they can. This way, if we tie it to a playoff game, they get a double bonus. We bring more people out, more extended family members, so it's a more meaningful moment for our senior players.

If we're having a lousy season and it doesn't look like we'll make the playoffs, or it doesn't look like we'll get to host our first-round game, we can always switch things up—but that hasn't happened yet.

As it is, not every one of my guys is represented at today's ceremony. My wife, Chris, is on alert to escort any seniors who don't have a parent or a family member in attendance. My daughter, Melissa, too. They'll walk out to half-court with the player, get some flowers, pose for pictures, and it's nice because they all know each other. You play for me, you're like part of the family, so these kids all know Chris and Melissa. It's not like they're being met by some stranger.

Still, it breaks my heart a little bit that some of these kids are on their own for a moment like this. As moments go, this is pretty damn big. It marks the end of their high school careers, the beginning of whatever comes next. Their folks should be here—but all you can do is all you can do. You set it up so nobody notices these few kids are on their own, so they feel like a part of our St. Anthony family, and then you play the game.

We've drawn a scrappy team from Oratory, a prep school from nearby Summit, New Jersey, in just about the same spot we saw them the year before. That's how it goes in the Non-Public B bracket of the state tournament. You see a lot of the same teams one year to the next. Oratory has just beaten Saddle River Day School a couple nights earlier, in a close first-round game, so these kids are pumped. Excited to be here. You can see from the way they're warming up that they have a nothing-to-lose kind of attitude. They're loose. They're laughing.

Our guys, I don't want them loose. I don't want them laughing. Nothing-to-lose is not how I want my guys to approach anything—this game, any game, any assignment. Always, I want them to play like there's something on the line, like their effort matters. I want them laser-focused. There'll be time for loose and laughing at the end of the season.

We still have some work to do.

Oratory puts up a fight, but they're no match for us. We're bigger, stronger, more polished. We storm to an early lead, 23–4 by the end of the first quarter. Kyle Anderson is playing like a man among boys. He runs the floor like he can do whatever he wants. He's come back from his one-game suspension like he's got something to prove—and he does. To me. To himself.

To the coaches at UCLA, where he'll be playing in the fall. Watching him play, I have to remind myself he's still just a kid—and sometimes kids do stupid things. They should know better, but they don't—not always.

A kid who can play like this, like a dream, he should know better. One day he will. And soon.

Past couple games, Kyle's taken his game to a whole other level. A part of me thinks he's playing like this to make up for letting me down. For letting his teammates down. To compensate. If that's the case, he's doing a whole lot of compensating. In our last regular-season game, against Medford Tech, he poured in thirty-five points, a season high. And here against Oratory, he'll finish with thirty-four, in just three quarters. But it's not just that he puts the ball in the basket that sets Kyle's game apart. It's not just that he's physically able to exert his will. It's the way he sees the game. The way he distributes the ball. The way he sets the pace.

Some of the guys, they've taken to calling Kyle "Slo-Mo," because of how he sometimes moves on the court—slow, almost sleepy. It's like watching a great baseball player, a pure hitter, who'll tell you that time seems to stand still when he's at the plate. Who'll tell you he can see the seams on the ball as it leaves the pitcher's hand. Ted Williams. Rod Carew. Tony Gwynn. The ball waits for them to put it in play. That's Kyle. He slows things down so the game comes to him—and then, when it gives him the opening he's looking for, he explodes to the basket or fires off a crisp pass to a teammate cutting across the lane.

These kids from Oratory, they won't back down. They play with a ton of heart. But they can't stop Kyle Anderson. They've never seen a player of his caliber, don't quite know what to do with him. This is nothing new. Kyle's been playing for me nearly two full seasons, and nobody's stopped him yet.

Sixty games into his St. Anthony career, he's yet to lose—and he's playing like he means to keep it that way.

8.

2003–2004: HARDWIRED TO WIN

YOU CAN RUN A LOT OF PLAYS WHEN YOUR X
IS TWICE AS BIG AS THE OTHER GUYS' O. IT
MAKES YOUR Xs AND Os PRETTY GOOD.
—*Paul Westphal*

BASKETBALL IS LIKE WAR IN THAT OFFENSIVE
WEAPONS ARE DEVELOPED FIRST, AND IT ALWAYS
TAKES AWHILE FOR THE DEFENSE TO CATCH UP.
—*Red Auerbach*

Sometimes you find a way to win despite yourself.
Sometimes the whole is way more than the sum of its parts.
And sometimes, as a high school coach, with an ever-changing

lineup, your players keep finding ways to surprise you—good ways, bad ways, and every way in between.

Okay, so that about sums it up when I think back on our 2003–2004 season. Seemed like there was every argument *against* us winning it all that year, and yet we found a way to answer every argument and keep winning. But here's the thing: it wasn't me or any of my assistant coaches who helped this group of players rise above our low expectations. Wasn't like these kids learned anything about mettle or maturity or found a way to grow their games or carry themselves like champions.

No, they were just a bunch of knuckleheads who could play ball. It was in their DNA.

They couldn't get out of their own way, this group—but absolutely, they could play. And it's no wonder. These kids were shot through with talent, but even more than that, they'd come together as a team in the purest sense. Our key guys had all grown up playing with each other, off each other, all the way back to elementary school—in some cases back to their first travel teams with the Jersey City Boys' Club. That kind of familiarity, you don't often see it at any level of the game. Not anymore. In the NBA, it used to be you'd have a nucleus of players who might stay together for a good long run—the Red Auerbach Celtics, say, or the Red Holzman Knicks—but that's disappeared with free agency. These days you might see a couple guys play together over a stretch of winning seasons, but the supporting cast keeps changing. In college you'll see a group make a splash as freshmen and sophomores, until their first whiff of success when they'll go their separate ways in the professional game.

But here in Jersey City, less than ten years ago, there was this one frustratingly special group that came together on our hometown courts and played a frustratingly special brand of basketball.

Trouble was, away from the court, they were a frustratingly special mess. I don't mean to be too hard on these kids—because, after all, they were just kids—but every day was a struggle with this group. Every day there was some new brand of nonsense we'd have to figure out. We never knew what kind of trouble these players would make in the classroom, on the streets of Jersey City, even in the gym.

Only thing we could count on with this cast of characters was that nothing would be trouble-free.

The story of this season has its roots in the seasons that led up to it. That's always the way of it in high school sports. You lay a path one year for your guys to follow the next; you try to carry forward some piece of momentum or turn a disappointment into some kind of positive. Here it happened that our 2004 seniors joined our program just as we were graduating a team of back-to-back champions. The leaders of those teams were about as poised and polished a group as I've ever coached, so there was every reason to think we could keep a good thing going as our younger guys learned to model the positive behavior of their older teammates.

But that's not quite how things shook out.

As juniors, it looked for a moment like this group would have a shot in 2002–2003 to help us "three-peat"—a phrase that had lately burst onto the sporting scene, thanks at first to Pat Riley and the Los Angeles Lakers of the 1980s and then to Phil Jackson, who'd managed to string together *two* back-to-back-to-back championships with his great Jordan-Pippen tandem in Chicago and was now fresh off another back-to-back-to-back run with his Shaq-Kobe Lakers. Our season came down to the final minutes of the North Jersey final against St. Patrick. As it happened, the game turned on what should have been a coachable moment—assuming, of course, that I'd had a group of *coachable* players. In any case, it was a moment I'd love to have back, so I could go at it again. We were led that year by a six-four forward named Obie Nwadike, the blood and guts of our team, but Obie had a bad ankle sprain and could only play limited minutes for us in that game against St. Pat's. Even without Obie at full strength, we were up a point with a little more than a minute left to play, when we sent our opponent to the line. This alone wasn't troubling, but we lined up in a way that came back to bite us—and the way we lined up was an indication of the frustration to come.

When a right-handed shooter misses a free throw, the ball typically comes off the right side of the basket—more than 60 percent of the time. What this means on defense is that you want to play the percentages and line up your big men on the right side of the lane. Basically, you stack to the right. My guys know that, same way the opposing coach usually knows to line up his bigger guys on the right side as well. We drill it into our players in practice to where it's something they don't even have to think about during games—only here it's like they actually *did* stop to think about it, and that's what screwed them up. They were at the other end of the floor, away from our bench, and St. Pat's switched up late, and our guys blindly followed the man they were guarding on defense.

I don't mean to put this entirely on my players, because in the end it's on me as their coach. I could have found a way to signal my guys on the floor, maybe call a time-out to make sure we were set defensively, but in the split second I had to think things through I must have calculated that the odds of the St. Pat's shooter missing the free throw, together with the odds of the ball bouncing in just the wrong way, were still pretty damn long. Already, we were overmatched, because Obie was out of the game at this point, so it ended up we had Marcus Williams, a six-one junior, trying to box out St. Pat's Grant Billmeier, a six-ten presence who went on to play for Seton Hall, and when the missed free throw bounded to the right side, Billmeier simply plucked it out of the air and put back an easy bucket. For good measure, almost like he was gift-wrapping the game for St. Pat's, Marcus fouled the big man in the act of shooting, making it a three-point play and basically putting an end to our season.

Even if I'd thought to call a time-out, I didn't have any left in my bag of tricks because our point guard Derrick Mercer had burned them all. Derrick was only a sophomore, and he was only playing because I'd had to suspend Ahmad Mosby for missing a couple practices, and Derrick was just overmatched, overwhelmed. He was facing a talented guard on his way to play at Villanova, and Derrick just couldn't keep up, so whenever he got into trouble he called time to bail himself out.

One by one, the links in our chain of championships were coming apart, so that now, when we got the ball back, down two, we were unable to stop the clock and set up a play, which against a good, well-coached team like St. Pat's meant we couldn't get off a decent shot.

And that was that—and in the postgame analysis it wasn't hard to see where we broke down.

It wasn't all on Marcus, that one play where we lined up the wrong way on the free throw. It wasn't all on Ahmad, that he'd missed a couple practices and earned a suspension just before the postseason tournament. It wasn't all on Derrick, that he burned all of our time-outs. But I mention all these lapses because, taken together, they represented the kinds of bonehead, knucklehead moves this group would make more often than not. They played with flash, but not a whole lot of sense; they played hard, but not smart. And the most frustrating piece to this loss was that we had a fine group of levelheaded seniors on that 2002–2003 team, guys like Obie and Terence Roberts, who I thought might have been a positive influence on these younger players—but they had no better luck with them than me or my coaching staff.

A lot of coaches will tell you they learn as much from their players as their players learn from them. It's a nice line—but a lot of times it's just that, a line.

And yet here it rang true. Here I learned from my players that poise and polish are not traits you can simply hand down from one group of graduating seniors to the next. Here I learned it didn't matter how much I yelled, how much I threatened, how much I *willed* these kids to carry themselves the right way . . . they'd still find a way to mess up.

This was a shame and a worry. It was a shame because I would have liked to send that group of seniors out on a winning note, and it was a worry because I now had the entire off-season to figure out what the hell I was going to do with these returning kids. I was bringing back a bunch of juniors—Marcus Williams, Otis Campbell, Ahmad Mosby, Lamar Alston, and Shelton Gibbs. Sophomores Derrick Mercer, Sean McCurdy, and Barney Anderson would factor in as well. They'd been around, this group. They'd played with some talented upperclassmen, and even after our last-minute mix-up against St. Pat's, we were still holding out hope that at least *some* of the good habits of the older group would rub off on these younger guys, but it's like they were immune to good habits.

They'd play the game their way or not at all, and as our next season approached I looked up and down our lineup of returning players and didn't see a single guy I could pick out who might lead this team in a positive way.

Not one.

Now, in fairness to these kids, I should point out that almost all of them came from single-parent homes, and it's tough to work against that as a coach, as an educator—heck, as a caring, feeling human being. You see a kid struggling like that, the deck stacked against him, your heart tells you to cut him some slack, give him a couple extra benefits of the doubt. But your head is supposed to know better. Your head is supposed to know that sometimes you need to be hardest of all on the kids who have it tough enough already—and this group certainly had it tough. Marcus Williams was being raised by his mom. Ahmad Mosby was being raised by his mom. And on and on. Make no mistake, these were all good-hearted, hardworking people, but there were very few posi- tive male role models in the lives of these young men. Even worse, my returning players tended to live in some of the worst parts of the city, surrounded by all kinds of negative, even dangerous influences. Marcus lived in the Curries Woods projects, one of the most violent housing projects in the United States. Just to give an idea of his home environment, the Spike Lee movie *Clockers,* based on the Richard Price book of the same name, was set in Curries Woods, and the place was so unsafe, so unwelcoming to outsiders, the film crew had to use another set of buildings in New York for their location shooting.

I knew the area from my time as a probation officer, so I knew Marcus was up against it, which was why I might have been root- ing for him a little more than I was helping him throughout the four years he played for me. That was the great puzzle of this group. They were likable kids, all around. As individuals, one- on-one, it was possible to see all kinds of hopeful potential in each and every one of them. They were a maddening bunch to have to coach, and they were difficult to get under control, but deep down

I believed in these kids. Deep down I knew their actions didn't always match up with their intentions, so that's why I found myself pulling for a kid like Marcus.

Same goes for Otis Campbell, who lived off Fulton Avenue in one of the worst parts of the city, not far from Shelton Gibbs. They went to the Number 34 school growing up. They'd both been living by their wits for so long, darting in and out of trouble, it's a wonder they managed to make it to high school.

(Shelton actually moved out of Jersey City during his senior year after he was mugged at gunpoint; he ran away and held on to his money, but his attacker fired his gun, and that was enough to convince Shelton's parents to leave the area.)

Ahmad Mosby lived in the Hudson Gardens, another rough housing project, across the street from Dickinson High School. Most of the males in his family were either deceased or in jail—and if it wasn't for the positive influence of basketball, Ahmad and his buddies might have turned down a couple wrong roads before they ever made it to high school.

The only returning player with a positive, hard-charging work ethic was a talented junior guard named Sean McCurdy, who came to us from all the way up in Connecticut. Sean was a bit of an outsider among this group. Not because he was white, or from more of a middle-class background, but because he seemed to want it. Basketball, college, opportunity . . . whatever you set out in front of him, he longed for it. Sean was the only kid on this team without any Jersey City roots, one of the only kids with two educated parents (along with Shelton Gibbs), and one of the only kids for whom college was not a reach but a given (again, along with Shelton). Sean saw the game for the tremendous opportunities it offered, and he had the drive and the discipline (and the talent!) to take full advantage. He came to us because he'd met one of my assistant coaches at a basketball camp one summer and drove down from Connecticut with his mom just for the chance to play during one of my open gym sessions. End of the session, Sean's mom came over to me and said, "Coach, Sean has something he wants to say to you."

Now, I'd been on the receiving end of that conversation a hundred times. A kid comes by to run with us, then his parents or his older brother or whoever it was who made the trip with him encourages the player to come by and introduce himself and thank me for the chance to play.

I wanted to save this young man the trouble, so I said, "That's all right, Sean. No need to thank me. Come by whenever you want. Gym's always open."

But Sean had something else in mind. Oh, he was grateful for the opportunity to play, but he wanted to talk about maybe transferring to St. Anthony. He said, "My mom and I have talked about this. We've heard a lot of good things about your program."

I wasn't expecting this. Normally, a kid wants to play for St. Anthony, he's got some sort of connection to the program, to Jersey City. By this point, after I'd been coaching almost thirty years, I was starting to see a lot of kids whose dads used to play for me, or maybe their dads had played against one of my teams. Almost always, there was some kind of link, but here with this kid the only link was basketball. He'd come from a well-known Indiana basketball family. His grandfather was a legendary high school coach back home. His uncles had played college ball. I didn't know any of this at the time, but I learned it soon enough. I also learned Sean and his mom had done their research and decided St. Anthony was a good breeding ground for guards, so that's where he wanted to play, where he thought he'd get the best shot at a college scholarship in a big-time program.

He played with us another time or two, and each time Sean drove down with his mom from Connecticut they looked at places where they might live in Jersey City, in a stopgap sort of way. Their idea was Sean's brother and sister would stay in Connecticut with their father, while Sean and his mother would get an apartment nearby.

At one point, I went to Obie Nwadike and Terence Roberts, who were graduating, wanting their take on how Sean would fit in with our returning group, and they both agreed that this kid, as a sophomore, was way more mature, way more focused, way more *coachable,* than the group of juniors I had playing for me already. This was true enough—only one thing I hadn't counted on was how tough it would be for Sean to fit in with this group away from the court. You have to realize, this was a tight, homegrown bunch, so they tended to ignore Sean in school and around town, but Sean didn't seem to mind—or if he did, he never let on. They worked well enough together in the gym, and that seemed to be Sean's bottom line, so we left it at that, and as our season got under way I didn't quite know what to expect, had no clear idea how things would go.

Our season didn't get off to the most promising start—and this presented a kind of double worry for me and the St. Anthony administration because I'd agreed to allow a sportswriter full access to our comings and goings as a team, in preparation for a book on a season with the St. Anthony Friars. The sportswriter, Adrian Wojnarowski, covered basketball for the *Bergen Record,* and his book, *The Miracle of St. Anthony,* would go on to become a big best-seller, but as he was working on it, hanging around our school, our players, our games, I had no idea what kind of picture he was getting.

Actually, that's not entirely true. I had a very good idea what kind of picture Adrian was getting. What I didn't know was what he'd choose to *see* in that picture, or how that picture might develop. I worried Adrian would take one look at these kids, at the way they wore their do-rags to school or skulked around our hallways and in and out of detention like punks, and come away thinking we were running some sort of reform school for derelicts and no-accounts. Always, when you allow a reporter into your environment to see what he might see, you want to put your best foot forward—and about the only place these kids came close to doing that was on the basketball court. (Even then, I could never be sure!) For our program, it was important that Adrian's book shine some kind of positive light on our school, but I didn't think that was possible with this group.

As it turned out, Adrian got a good story out of the deal, and he even found a way to put a positive, hopeful spin on it. Somehow our guys kept winning and winning, despite digging themselves into all these different holes along the way, and as I write this now I can't help but realize it's almost always worked out to the good whenever there's been a reporter tracking our season for a book or a documentary or some other media project.

Consider: Adrian threw in with us before the season, with no way to know that we'd find a way to scrape past our difficulties and finish with yet another state championship, yet another undefeated season.

A couple years later, I agreed to allow an outfit called Team-Works Media and director Kevin Shaw to bring their cameras

behind the scenes to chronicle our 2007–2008 season. The result-
ing documentary, *The Street Stops Here,* offered an inside glimpse
at what once again turned out to be a magical season. Another
perfect record. Another "mythical" national championship.

It happened again in 2010–2011, when CBS News producers
shadowed us all during the postseason for a *60 Minutes* profile
with reporter Steve Kroft, and we once again finished undefeated,
at the top of the national polls.

And now, for good measure, we've run the table again, after
I decided to write about our 2011–2012 season for the book you
now hold in your hands—and I don't mean to give away the ending or suck the tension from these pages, but it's pretty clear from
the table of contents how our season just ended.

But all of that is getting ahead of the story; it's interesting, but
a little beside the point. First order of business heading into our
2003–2004 season was to get Ahmad Mosby back in line after the
way he'd blown off our practices down the stretch the year before.
I brought him in and told him he had to convince me I could
count on him going forward. Told him he'd let his teammates
down by blowing off those practices down the stretch. I laid it on
thick. I also told Ahmad it was time to make some changes in his
life, that he wasn't a kid any longer, that he had to start acting like
an adult and taking responsibility for his actions.

One way we would do this, I said, was to lose the nickname
Ahmad had carried since childhood. He'd been known as Beanie,
going back as far as anyone could remember. In his family, he
was known as Beanie. In our hallways at school, he was known
as Beanie. On the streets of Jersey City, he was known as Beanie.
At the Jersey City Boys' Club, Beanie.

"Beanie's out," I told him. "Beanie hasn't been doing so well.
From now on, you're Ahmad. Ahmad will do better."

It felt to me like we had a good talk, like we were turning a page and starting fresh, but then Ahmad pulled a Beanie move and found a way to miss our first practicc. Wasn't entirely his fault, but he should have seen it coming, and now he had to accept responsibility for it. What happened was, he was up in Irvington, New Jersey, with his family for Thanksgiving, about forty minutes west of Jersey City, and he woke up on the Friday after the holiday and couldn't get anyone in his family to drive him to practice. Any other kid, these same circumstances, I might have let it go, but with Ahmad it struck me as just the latest version of "more of the same."

Otis Campbell checked back in with me, start of his senior year, and we had a similar talk. He also had a lot to prove, because another sidebar drama of the previous postseason was that he couldn't dress for the state tournament after deciding it was a good idea to glue one of his teachers' possessions to her desk—but then he went and dragged his feet on his physical, had to miss our first week of practice. (Really, it was always something with this group.) This was especially infuriating, because every year a good friend of mine, Dr. Steven Levine, volunteers his time and comes to the school and does the physicals for all of our athletes, so the medical clearance shouldn't be a problem for any of them, but Otis found a way to make things difficult yet again—and here too we were back in "more of the same" territory.

Lamar Alston spent much of his off-season bending so many different rules I had to bounce him from the team before we were even under way, so in my head he wasn't even in the mix as we jump-started the season. More of the same.

That's three guys I'd been counting on to play a big role for us, unable to make it to our first practice—not to mention Shelton Gibbs, who had to miss our entire first weekend due to the death of his grandfather. There were hardly enough bodies to run full-court, so by the time we got going it was already looking like a long season.

And it surely was. All year long, these clowns were like the old Oakland As of the early 1970s, leaving all kinds of disasters in their wake and still finding a way to get it together by game time. Their school days were one problem after another. Their home lives were filled with uncertainty and tension and difficulty, but their basketball lives were all about raw talent, adrenaline, guts, instinct—almost like they'd been hardwired, preprogrammed, for success on the court, even as they couldn't help but screw up off the court.

(Here's a first for our program: Marcus Williams actually fathered a child while he was still in high school. We didn't find out about it until late in the season.)

I had to lay in a curfew to try and keep these kids in line, which in turn meant I had to lay in some kind of system for checking up on them to make sure they kept to their curfew, so it was just one pain in the neck after another. Their moms didn't seem to mind if they came home at night, if they slept out at this one's house or that one's house, if they managed to eat a hot, nutritious meal after a hard practice. In a lot of ways, these kids were on their own, without showing a stitch of the maturity or levelheadedness that might have justified that kind of responsibility.

In addition to being the wildest group I'd ever coached, it was also the smallest—probably one of the shortest teams in the country that year (or any year, for that matter). Barney Anderson was the only kid over six-two on the team—and at six-four, he wasn't exactly a towering center. We had kids at six-one, six-two, matching up against power forwards at six-eight, six-nine. On paper, we went into almost every game overmatched—but athletically, these kids were something to see. "On paper" meant nothing to this group. As dysfunctional as they were, as unreliable as they were, they had a feel for the game like nothing I'd ever seen. Marcus, at six-one, was able to team with Barney and dominate around the basket, and we'd play off of them and usually run a three-guard set with Derrick, Ahmad, Sean, and Shelton sharing time in the backcourt. Individually, they weren't stand-out offensive players, but as a team, as a unit, meshing and gelling and coming together, they were tremendous. They knew each other so well from all those years playing together, I could sit back and imagine they were like the high school version of those great New York Knick championship teams. DeBusschere, Bradley, Frazier, Reed, Monroe, Barnett . . .

In the run of play, each kid could predict what every one of his teammates would do in any given situation, and if you'd ask him about it later, maybe break it down and see if there was anything we could learn from what just happened so we could call on it again, he'd just shrug his shoulders and roll his eyes and wait impatiently for me to finish talking to him. Even Sean McCurdy found a way to knit himself competitively into this group; socially, the others kind of stiff-armed him from whatever was going on at school or on weekends, but that was just as well with Sean. He stuck to himself, to basketball. But on the court he became another key piece of our well-oiled machinery; he fit himself in like he'd been here all along.

As a team, we did get a little bigger midway through our season, when Ahmad Nivins joined our program. Ahmad was a skinny, six-eight transfer from County Prep, a technical school on Montgomery Street in Jersey City—a personnel move that had no business working out but one that worked out just the same. You have to realize, adding a transfer from County Prep was not a whole lot better than adding a kid with only club or intramural experience. Basically, this kid hadn't played any organized ball—certainly not at our level—but he had size, which we desperately needed.

Ahmad Nivins had been a baseball player all his life. That was his focus, his passion. But as he grew, as I saw him on ball fields around town, I kept telling his dad to encourage Ahmad to give basketball a try. His size was too much of an advantage to ignore. I didn't care so much whether he played for us at St. Anthony or for some other school in the city, but I really thought this kid had a better shot at a college scholarship on the court than he did on the diamond—and finally, he came around.

As a late transfer, he wasn't eligible to play for us straightaway, and the way he finally joined us was interesting. The first game he could play for us came midway through our season, against St. Joe's Metuchen, and it just so happened that St. Joe's had its own big man making his debut for them that same game. That big man? Andrew Bynum, who had to sit out the first half of *his* season after transferring from the Solebury School in Pennsylvania. The great revelation that came out of this game was that Ahmad Nivins could play.

As I write this, Ahmad's playing professionally in Spain. He was drafted by the Dallas Mavericks in the second round of the 2009 draft—and if you read between the lines of the Dallas–New York trade that brought Tyson Chandler to the Knicks, you'll note that New York now controls Ahmad's draft rights, so he might yet make an impact in the NBA. But back when he was a skinny teenager, just learning the game, we had no idea what to expect out of Ahmad.

Against a top player like Andrew Bynum, Ahmad Nivins was able to make an impact on the game—and for the first time I started to think this group might have a shot in the tournament. I mean, it was one thing to rack up all these wins in the regular season, even against some talented teams, but I didn't think thcsc kids would do any kind of damage against the top teams in our state. Not with the way they carried on like a bunch of lunatics. Not without any size. But once Ahmad Nivins announced himself as a player for us, that all started to change. Well, maybe not *all* of it. We were still a bunch of uncoachable bozos, but at least we had a guy underneath who could grab a couple rebounds, maybe push some people around.

It's hard to be good. It is. I don't mean just on the basketball court. It's hard to be a good person, to make smart choices, to put yourself in a consistent position to succeed. It takes work. It takes focus, a certain determination. And a lot of times it takes a good deal of help, so that's one of the things we try to do when we see a kid headed for trouble. We surround our young players with older role models, with coaches who keep a constant eye on them, and we give them specific guidelines we mean for them to follow. That's where our "contract" comes from. It steers them through all the different situations that might come up in school, on the street, or on the court.

Probably, the toughest rule we have to instill in our players is to be on time. It's fundamental. We insist that, whatever it is, you have to arrive fifteen minutes ahead of the scheduled time. This way, you're waiting, you're prepared for whatever is going to happen in that class, that practice, or that part-time job. Whatever it is, you're there early and ready to go.

Lately, we've taken to calling this "Tom Coughlin time," in a nod to the New York Giants coach. Every meeting Coach

Coughlin calls, the New York Giants players are expected to be there fifteen minutes early. That's his thing. In his mind, you're late for a 9:00 A.M. meeting if you're not sitting in your seat at 8:45. You're not prepared, and if you've ever heard Coach Coughlin interviewed, you'll know he puts a ton of weight on being prepared. Everything else falls from this right here. He'll even fine his players if they're not there early, to where the NFL Players Association tried to weigh in and complain. But Coughlin wouldn't budge. When I heard that, I thought it was just the greatest thing ever, so we started using "Tom Coughlin time" for our own practices and other team events. We tried to let our kids know that the person who comes rushing in the door for a meeting is invariably unprepared for that meeting. If you're in a school setting and you rush into class just as the bell starts to ring, you're not organized, you're not focused, you're not ready to learn. You won't be able to compete with the other kids in that class who've gotten there early.

Every game we played, our aim was to have these kids ready to play one full hour before tip-off. We never wanted them to arrive as something was getting ready to start, and it was a tough sell for this group—at least at the beginning. They went at things in their own way, on their own time, so it took awhile to get them to adjust their clocks and meet our expectations on this. It was easy enough if we were on a team bus, if they were a captive bunch, but it was sometimes an adventure getting them all to practice on time or to team functions. Unless they were on a basketball court, most of the kids on this team were extremely immature. They weren't ready for college. No one was ready to step up and be any kind of team leader.

Meanwhile, off the court, there was an endless series of headaches and heartaches. The biggest of these had nothing at all to do with basketball—at least, nothing *directly* to do with basketball—although it set in motion an agonizing, emotional few years when a lot of us at St. Anthony took turns wondering about the future of our basketball program, even the future of our school. Everything turned on the sad news that Sister Alan Barczewski had been diagnosed with liver cancer. For years she'd been such a force, such a presence in our building, and such a powerful, positive influence in the lives of our players—only here we were all forced to start thinking about what our lives would be without her. This year, for the first time, Sister Alan couldn't be in our building every day, and even when she was present, she was less and less available to our kids. You'd think the fact that she was battling cancer might have been enough to inspire a group of high school kids—but this was a group that needed Sister Alan's sure, guiding touch more than any other group of kids ever had, so they were even more restless, more distracted than usual. They didn't always make it to their classes or to practice or to whatever it was that was expected of them. Sister Alan had always been great at cracking the whip, keeping our most difficult kids in line, but that year her focus was elsewhere.

Our focus was elsewhere.

Happily, mercifully, Sister Alan wasn't going anywhere just yet, and in fact her doctors gave her a good fighting chance, but nobody quite knew what course her illness might take. Nobody quite knew what would happen to our fund-raising efforts without Sister Alan's full support and enthusiasm. Nobody quite knew how we'd coordinate our basketball program without Sister Alan on top of things. Nobody quite knew how to motivate these kids, to make sure they'd be able to graduate with their class and remain NCAA-eligible.

Most years college coaches lined up to recruit our graduating players, but this group was a tough sell. It's not like they weren't capable of playing at a top-tier college program, but a lot of these top-tier coaches just weren't interested in taking on the hassle. I had to be honest with them. I had to let them know what they were getting into—for their sake *and* for the sake of my players. I knew my guys needed to be in a structured, supervised environment, but then I'd arrange college visits for them and they would find a way to blow them off. A couple times I even drove to their apartments to pick them up to visit a junior college coach, and the kid would be a no-show.

My one hope for this group, in terms of college ball, was to get them out of Jersey City. None of them had the grades or the credits to play Division I ball, even though they all had the talent. But that didn't mean they couldn't play Division II ball or maybe go to community college for a while, so I looked long and hard for programs that might be a good fit. I finally found what I thought was the perfect environment—in Florida, at Pensacola Junior College. I went to visit the school myself when I was down there for a clinic and talked for a bit with the coach, who used to be an assistant at Northwestern. I gave it to him straight, and he was very encouraging. We worked it out so that I could send Marcus, Otis, and Ahmad Mosby down to see him for a campus visit at the end of the season—and if everything worked out, he'd offer them scholarships, and after two years they'd each have their associate's degree and some good basketball under their belts and be able to transfer to Division I schools.

Other than that, though, there wasn't a whole lot of recruiting activity going on with this group during the season—another way this team stood apart from most of the other teams I'd coached. At times we were more concerned about making sure these kids graduated from high school than where they'd go to college, so we took a "first things first" approach.

It was maddening, dealing with these kids—and yet they kept winning. To this day I'm convinced that the main reason we did so well on the scoreboard was that other teams just couldn't figure us out. We played a willy-nilly style of ball—more like street basketball than organized basketball—and we just ran through the field in the state tournament and the Tournament of Champions. We played big when it counted, and there'd be times when I was watching these kids run up the score with such joy and abandon that I realized what was so special about this group. They thrived on the court, I think, because their lives were so difficult away from the court. The gym was the only place where they could have any kind of peace of mind, any kind of assurance that things would shake out to the good; during our games they could feel like they were in control.

The kicker to that Pensacola Junior College story was that we did manage to get these three knuckleheads down there for a visit. My hope as they left on their trip was that at least two of them would decide to attend. It seemed perfect. The basketball team played at a high level for a junior college program. The school wasn't too far from the beach. There were shuttle buses available to take students to the beach, to the airport, to the mall, so it's not like our guys would need a car. And the best part? It was far, far away from the long list of negative influences they'd learned to attract in and around Jersey City. So what happened? They came back complaining that there wasn't anything to do down in Florida, so we were back at square one.

Basically, I think these kids were afraid to take the next step in life. They desperately needed to get out of Jersey City, to start surrounding themselves with a more positive, more purposeful group of friends, but it was hard for them to pull the plug on what they knew.

Turned out these kids knew better than I did what was best for them. Yeah, they needed to get out of Jersey City, but they also needed to separate from each other. They'd been joined at the hip for so long—on the court, off the court—that they brought out the best and worst in each other. The best came when they were playing basketball; the worst came when they were doing anything else. So they went their separate ways and found ways to thrive. It's like all that good hardwiring finally had a chance to kick in. In the end, Otis went to a junior college in Hutchinson, Kansas; Marcus went to the Globe Institute in Manhattan; Ahmad Mosby went to Ramapo College, a Division III school in northern New Jersey; and Shelton went to Dominican College in upstate New York. They all continued to play ball. They all found a way to graduate. They all grew as young men. They still get together back in Jersey City, and when they do I imagine there's a whole lot of "more of the same" as they grab at some of their old habits, but it's when they're off on their own, doing their own thing, that we're able to see that anything is possible.

9.

2007–2008: AT LAST

YOU CAN'T GET MUCH DONE IN LIFE IF YOU ONLY
WORK ON THE DAYS WHEN YOU FEEL GOOD.

—Jerry West

A BASKETBALL TEAM IS LIKE THE FIVE FINGERS ON
YOUR HAND. IF YOU CAN GET THEM ALL TOGETHER,
YOU HAVE A FIST. THAT'S HOW I WANT YOU TO PLAY.

—Mike Krzyzewski

Every winning streak starts with a loss—and for the 2007–2008 group that loss came the year before in the North Jersey final, to St. Patrick. It wasn't just a simple loss to end our season; it was a no-doubt-about-it, hang-your-head kind of defeat. We hadn't lost a game the whole year, we were liking our chances, but St. Pat's just took it to us. They were bigger, better, tougher. They ended up beating us by double figures, controlling the game the whole way, so it sent us into our off-season with a lot of things to think about, a lot of things to work on.

The only good thing to come out of that game was that there was nothing to second-guess. It wasn't like our guys could kick themselves over this play or that decision. Wasn't like I could have taken a different approach. We just got beat was all. Crushed. St. Pat's was a deep, talented team. They had a kid going off to North Carolina (Dexter Strickland), a kid going to Memphis (Jeff Robinson), a kid going to Villanova (Corey Fisher). Physically, we couldn't compete. Chris Gaston, our best all-around player, was coming back from a knee injury. He was our go-to big guy, and it looked like he'd miss the entire postseason, but he got himself back for this one game, managed to limp through and put up some numbers. Still, it wasn't enough to turn things our way.

Out of this one loss, we found our focus for the coming season: St. Pat's. They were in our sights, we knew we'd see them again, and we were determined to be ready for them, but Chris Gaston was graduating and we were returning a team of mostly guards, so it's not like we would be any bigger or stronger. It's not like we could prepare for St. Pat's the same way and expect a different outcome. People always say that's the definition of insanity—to do the same thing over and over and expect a different result. It's not like St. Pat's was looking to downsize, to play at our level. They'd be bringing back a lot of strength, including another big man who'd go on to play at Kansas (Quintrell Thomas). On top of that they were adding Michael Kidd-Gilchrist, probably one of the most highly rated, most talked about freshmen in the country (who four years later would lead Kentucky to the national championship, again as one of the most highly rated, most talked about freshmen in the country), so they would be a test all over again.

True, we could have just as easily placed our focus on Paterson Catholic, because they also had a very strong, very physical team. We knew the road to the state championship would go through one of these two programs, but on paper at least, St. Pat's looked like the team to beat. Plus, telling our kids we were gunning for the team that ended our season the year before made it a whole lot easier to rally the troops; our guys didn't like the way St. Pat's had pushed them around, so they were eager for another shot at them.

That was our goal—to take it to St. Pat's the same way they'd taken it to us. That said, it was one thing to have St. Pat's in our sights, but quite another to reel them in. We couldn't just set it out there and will it so. We couldn't match up with them in length and size. We needed a game plan, so we hit the weight room, hard. I gave our guys a couple weeks to recharge, refocus, and then we started getting together to work on our strength and conditioning—a couple days a week at the beginning, and then we kicked it up over the summer and into the fall. Back then, we were working with a personal trainer named Joe Paglia. I'd met Joe at a gym where I used to work out, and I admired the way he worked with young athletes. He was a tremendous motivator. He'd come by to see us play a couple times, to see us practice, and he had some good ideas on how to help our guys play a more physical, more punishing type of game.

So we set about it.

Outside of Chris Gaston, the team that lost to St. Pat's in the North Jersey final was made up predominantly of juniors. We'd been expecting big things out of this core group—Jio Fontan, Mike Rosario, Tyshawn Taylor, and Travon Woodall—and even though they'd yet to put it together to win it all, they'd made a couple dazzling runs. They made a big splash right out of the gate, as sophomores. You don't normally see a group of sophomores run the table, but these guys led us to a terrific season—finishing at 26-3, after losing to St. Pat's in the North Jersey final. And then, as juniors, this same core group very nearly delivered, going undefeated until they ran into the brick wall of St. Pat's to end our season.

With Chris Gaston gone, six-five A. J. Rogers would step into an increased role. With his height, I figured on him to get a lot of inside minutes for us. Dominic Cheek was coming up from the junior varsity, and even though he was also six-five, he was more of a perimeter-type player. They'd both play huge minutes for us, but A.J.'s game was big, while Dominic's game was small; together, they'd give us some nice balance to go along with our core group of four. They'd be joined by Alberto Estwick, another guard, and Medut Bol—who at six-eight, rail-thin, maybe 160 pounds, was a much smaller, much skinnier version of his dad, Manut Bol, one of the tallest players in NBA history.

Other than Tyshawn Taylor and Medut Bol, they were a mostly local, mostly ground-level bunch—meaning, they'd been a part of our program since freshman year, and some of them we'd seen in camps and rec leagues since they were in middle school. Ty was originally from the area, but he'd moved to Florida as a kid—had a rough road for a stretch. At one point he was living with his mom and his sisters in a shelter. His father was out of the picture, and Ty and his sisters were getting the short end of it. Luckily, Ty joined the Boys' and Girls' Club in Clearwater, Florida, and found a mentor who encouraged him to play ball, and soon enough he was playing on a local AAU team and turning heads. This alone was something to celebrate. A lot of kids in that

kind of circumstance, without a positive male role model, with
so much struggle and sadness, they might channel their energies
and frustrations in a negative way, but Ty put it all into basketball.
He turned himself into a very good street player. Undisciplined,
but enormously talented—and the more he played, the more he
started to realize that playing ball might be his ticket up and out
of a difficult situation.

Ty came by our gym one summer, just before his sophomore
year. He was in Jersey City, visiting family. His cousin, Eddie Cas-
tellanos, a kid from Hoboken who went on to play at Stony Brook,
brought him to an open gym session at the rec center. At the end
of the session, Ty came over and thanked me for letting him run
with us and asked if he could maybe come by again. Whenever we
opened the gym, those two were there, and at the end of the week
Ty came over again, told me how much he loved playing with our
guys, how much he loved being back in Jersey City. We got to
talking. Ty told me a little about his background, about what was
going on with his family. His cousin Eddie told me a little more.
By the end of the week, Ty was telling me he wanted to find a way
to stay in the area, said he would talk to his mother about it. Said
he thought he could stay with an aunt in Jersey City, maybe find a
way to attend St. Anthony in the fall.

In the end, that's just how it shook out, and the way Ty came
to our program is a good example of how a lot of our guys fall into
the mix. We don't go looking for players, but sometimes players
come looking for us. They'll run with us a time or two, sit in on
a couple practices, and they'll want in. Maybe they're not happy
with where they're playing or how they're being used. Maybe
they've had some kind of falling out with their coach or with a key
teammate. Maybe they want to be challenged a little more in the
classroom and figure they'll get a better education in a smaller,

parochial school setting. Or maybe they think we have some kind of direct pipeline to a college scholarship, because we end up placing so many of our players in good spots at good schools. Usually, the kids who drift toward our program during their high school careers come from the Jersey City area, but from time to time they'll find enough to like about St. Anthony that they'll change things up in their own lives just to play here. They'll commute if that's what it takes—and in a case like Ty's, they'll work it out so they can stay with family in the area.

I couldn't offer a kid like Ty any kind of guarantee in terms of playing time or what kind of role he'd fill for us or even if he'd see any kind of time on the floor. What I could offer him—what I *did* offer him—was an opportunity to become a better player and to surround himself with a community of adults who would enter his life and help him become more and more conscious of the choices he was making, on and off the court. That's all. For some kids, that's everything—for others, that's not nearly enough. They want some kind of assurance that they'll play. They want a scholarship, or a commuting allowance, or a promise that I'll be able to introduce them to a specific college coach or program . . . some way to convince themselves the move will be worth their while.

But all I can promise is a shot—and that was all Ty wanted.

As a basketball player, Ty was a work in progress. He came to us as a hustling, athletic street player. He'd never been coached in any kind of formal way. His shooting form was terrible, so first thing we did was restructure his shot. Also, he didn't really have a position, so we had to get him to think like a ball-handling guard, which was where I thought he'd realize his full potential. But when he first came to us, he was just a bundle of energy—a terrific athlete with enormous potential. And on top of that potential, he wanted to play. You could see it in his eyes.

Ty joined us for his sophomore year and teamed with Jio Fontan, Mike Rosario, and Travon Woodall to form a dynamic nucleus, and it was this group that would now set the tone for our coming season. We were an individually talented, guard-heavy team, but I figured we could run all these other teams into the ground. Anyway, that was the plan, and it all came together on signing day, November of their senior year, when six of our guys—our four returning starters plus A. J. Rogers and Alberto Estwick—formally announced where they'd be playing college ball.

It's always a big deal at a school like St. Anthony when a player can share such exciting news with our students and faculty. It's like our whole building is bursting with pride and excitement—because, really, it represents such a landmark achievement in the lives of these young men. It's a validating moment—for these kids as individuals, for their families, and for our program at large—and a powerful symbol to *all* of our students that with hard work and discipline, anything is possible. And here, to be able to celebrate the accomplishments of six students all at once . . . well, it was a great, great day for the entire St. Anthony community. Six students! Six full scholarships! Looking back, that had to be one of the proudest, finest, sweetest moments for our basketball program. Doesn't usually happen that you have almost your entire senior class ready to commit ahead of the season like that, but when it does, it's truly special. Doesn't just mean that you and your assistant coaches are doing something right—it means those six players have been doing something right all along.

Here's how it shook out on signing day . . . how it's shaking out still . . .

Travon Woodall announced he'd be going to Pitt—and after redshirting a year due to injury, he's looking ahead to his senior season as captain.

Jio Fontan would be going to Fordham, where he played for a year and made the all-rookie conference team. After that, he transferred to the University of Southern California, where he's going into his senior season.

Tyshawn Taylor committed initially to Marquette, but when Marquette coach Tom Crean announced a couple months later, right after the NCAA tournament, that he'd be leaving to coach Indiana, we worked on Marquette to release Ty from his scholarship commitment so we could help him explore other opportunities. It wasn't clear just yet that Ty could find a better situation elsewhere, but we wanted him to be able to seek one out. Out of that, he decided to go to Kansas, where he's just capped an outstanding four-year career by helping the Jayhawks make it to the NCAA Finals. And now he's looking ahead to his rookie season in the NBA, playing just across the Hudson River from Jersey City for the Brooklyn Nets.

Mike Rosario was on his way to Rutgers, where he'd play for two years before transferring to Florida—and as I write this, Mike is looking to re-up with his Friars teammates Jio Fontan and Chris Gaston, as all three have been invited to try out for the Puerto Rican national team looking to qualify for the 2012 Olympics. If it works out, they'll be the first St. Anthony players to play in the Olympics—and if it works out that all three players are somehow reunited on the same team, after playing college ball at different schools, in three different conferences, it'll be one of the great storylines of the summer games.

(A footnote: Mike Rosario was the only one of the three to make the team. Jio might have joined him, but in the end the team doctors at USC decided he'd be better off sitting out the Olympics to get ready for the season, after an injury to his knee the year before. And Chris Gaston made the first couple cuts, but didn't make it to the final round.)

A. J. Rogers signed with St. Joe's, although he ultimately switched to Norfolk State, where, after sitting out a year, he was on the team that stunned number-two seed Missouri in the first round of the 2012 NCAA tournament.

Alberto Estwick, who'd come off the bench for us in most games, would join his Friars teammate Chris Gaston at Fordham.

Medut Bol was also a senior on that 2007–2008 team, and after going to prep school for a year to shore up his academics, he earned a scholarship to Southern University, where he'd fill out and add a little power and presence to his inside game.

Keep in mind, this was also a team that would feature Dominic Cheek, who declared for the NBA draft following his junior year at Villanova, so we had a potentially dominant collection of players, except for one thing—we hadn't won anything yet.

The fact that they'd yet to put it all together to win a championship began to mean something to this group, and I played it up as the season got under way. We already had a focus for our season, preparing to turn things around against St. Pat's in the state tournament, but now we had a theme to go along with it. Coming off the high of signing day at our school, I kept telling our seniors they'd accomplished just about everything they'd set out to accomplish when they started their high school careers. They'd established themselves as players. They'd taken care of their educations. They knew (at least a little bit) what their futures might look like. But they'd yet to win it all. They'd had that great sophomore season, falling just short of a championship. They'd had that great junior season, falling just short of a championship. And now they were looking ahead to a senior season that would be their last shot at winning it all. This was no small thing, because in all the years I'd been coaching at St. Anthony, no senior class had ever graduated without winning at least one state title—so I put it to them straight.

"That's a helluva legacy," I said during our first official practice of the season. "Can't imagine you guys want to be the first group to graduate from St. Anthony without at least one ring. Just one lousy ring. Some of our guys have graduated with *four*. You guys don't have any. So what are you gonna do about it?"

I wasn't particularly nice or nurturing about it—but "nice" and "nurturing" don't win championships.

It happened only one other time on my watch as head coach that a group of seniors was facing the prospect of graduating without a title. Our 2001 class had been in the same boat. We hadn't won in 1998, 1999, or 2000, so there was a ton of pressure on that team. Nobody wanted to be the first to leave St. Anthony without a ring, and those seniors still talk about being overwhelmed by a powerful combination of joy and relief when they beat St. Augustine's to win their one and only championship. They sat in the Elizabeth High School locker room at the end of that game, crying. They were all just beside themselves, excited that they'd finally won, but at the same time overcome by all these bottled-up emotions. The seniors on that team were Pete Cipriano, Juan Baquero, Carmine Charles, John-Paul Kobryn, and Isaac Ross, and whenever I hear from one of those guys, they take me back to that locker room after that game. They carry that moment with them still, so I made sure this 2008 group was carrying it with them as well. I even had Carmine Charles come back and visit with this current team, so they could hear it firsthand. Carmine had been a substitute for us on that 2001 team, but he was just as caught up in the moment as any of our starters. He talked about how important it was to all of them to be able to call themselves champions at long last. He talked about how they could finally feel they were a part of the great history of championship basketball at St. Anthony.

We kept talking about it and talking about it . . . all season long. Not to put pressure on these kids, but to give them something to shoot for. Something to play for. After all, they were all college-ready; more than that, they all knew where they'd be playing next year—they'd all proven themselves individually. But as a group, they'd yet to put it all together—so we put it on them.

As I mentioned, we were a guard-heavy team, which meant we had to work as a finely tuned unit on the floor. Some years it could be the polar opposite. You could have a group of long, lanky guys, so you'd have to play a certain way. In basketball, you can make up for a lot of deficits with height and length. But this team was all about quickness and athletic ability and stamina and skill level. We didn't really have any strength or size around the basket, so that limited some of the things we were able to do.

And yet, somehow, we managed to win. Consistently, and sometimes even surprisingly, we managed to win. All we had to do, I kept telling my guys, was keep getting better. Each game we tried to push it to a new level. That wasn't unique to this one team, to this one season. Always, you want to grow your game every time you take the floor. You want to set it up so that if an opposing coach sees you play in December, he'll think one way about your team, but then, if you come up against that same coach in February, he'll think a whole other way. You figure it out as you go along, what each group is good at, where their strengths lie, where they can improve. You start to see what weapons you have, and you find a way to use them all—at just the right time, in just the right way—so by the time you reach the latter part of your season, you know who you are as a team. You know your players, right down to their bones. You know their tics, their tendencies. You're happy with your development as a team. And then you reach a kind of pinnacle and try to stay at that level the rest of the way. Peak too soon, and you'll probably fade down the stretch. Peak too late, and you'll have a tough time against the very best teams when the games matter most. The timing has to be just right.

It worked out that year that we were asked to represent the state of New Jersey at a Christmas tournament in Albuquerque, New Mexico, so this was our first true challenge—and our season had *just* started. Back of my mind, we were a long way from peaking, but I knew we'd have to get up for these games. I knew that if we played well here, it would set our entire season in motion; if we stumbled, we'd start to doubt ourselves before we even had any idea what we were about. We opened the tournament against the host team, La Cueva, and handled them pretty well, but the real test came in the final against a powerhouse Lone Peak team from Utah. They grow them big in the Rocky Mountains, I guess, because this team had a couple feet on us, all told. Their starters were six-ten, six-eight, six-seven, and six-five, with one "little" guy, at six-one, running the point.

Mike Rosario had emerged as our best outside shooter over the previous couple seasons, but he couldn't find the basket. He was 0-7 from the field, but we found other ways to score. We played a solid, swarming defense and won by eleven points, and as we left New Mexico I was pleased with our performance. Mike hadn't made a field goal, and we still managed to win, which got me thinking we'd match up okay against the other "big" teams on our schedule.

Turned out there was only one game in the entire regular season where we trailed in the second half—and it came against another "big" team, American Christian Academy from Aston, Pennsylvania. American Christian has since closed its doors, but at the time it was a top-ranked, basketball-focused program, almost like a finishing school for the nation's best prospects, so this team was loaded. They were led that year by Tyreke Evans, who now plays for the Sacramento Kings, and MoMo Jones, who'd lead Arizona to the Elite Eight in the NCAA tournament before transferring to Iona, where he joined his American Christian teammate Michael Glover. Up and down the bench, this group was strong, with about eight or nine kids who'd go on to start for top Division I programs, so we knew they'd be one of the best teams we'd see all year.

And they were. Turned out *we* were also one of the best teams *they* would face all year, so it was a stalemate-type matchup on both sides of the ball.

The game started out as a defensive battle. We were up at halftime by three or four baskets, but it was one of those close games; we couldn't get any kind of separation on the scoreboard, and Tyreke Evans was a first-team All-American, capable of taking over a game on his own, and that's what he did to start the third quarter. American Christian went on a bit of a tear, pushed the tempo, and took back the lead. On the back of this, we started rushing our shots, missing some opportunities, relaxing on defense. Basically, the game was starting to slip away from us, so I did what all coaches do in that situation: I called a time-out.

Now, the time-out is one of the great weapons in a coach's bag of tricks. It's one of the few maneuvers in team sports that allows a coach to directly impact the flow of a game, but a lot of folks outside of basketball don't fully appreciate the tactic. These days, when the networks cover college and pro games on television, they stick a microphone in the huddle and listen in during time-outs, and the announcers make a big deal out of analyzing each coach's strategy or style with his players, but I've never believed that what you actually *say* as a coach matters as much as the time-out itself. In these middle quarters, in the game's middle moments, it's a point of pause in a game that might be running away from you, a chance to stop the other team's momentum and tilt it back in your favor. Yeah, you want to use the time to fill your players' heads with whatever it is you want them to be thinking about, but mostly you want to slow things down, change things up. It's a whole different story when you're running out of time and you need to stop the clock to run a play or to set your defense—those time-outs are all about strategy. These momentum-stalling time-outs are more of a stopgap move—because, hey, sometimes you just need to catch your breath. You're like a fighter getting pummeled against the ropes who looks to tie up his opponent, to get the ref to separate them and send each man to his own corner to regroup.

Typically, when I'm out to slow another team's run, first thing I'll do when we huddle is give our opponent credit for whatever's been going on out there on the floor. I'd rather start out by praising the other guys for doing something right than by ripping into my own guys for doing something wrong, so that's what I did here soon as American Christian took the lead. I told my guys they needed to pay better attention to Evans, who was just killing us off the dribble. I reminded them of that line from Coach K I used to open this chapter, the one about five fingers working together to form a fist. It's a quote my guys hear all the time in practice, and here I thought it would be useful to put it back in their heads that we needed to work as a unit.

There's a tendency during a time-out to fill your players' heads with as much information as possible, but this can be a dangerous thing, because you don't have a whole lot of time. As a coach you might find yourself running through a whole bunch of stuff, almost like you're reading off a list. You never know what your players will hear, what will stick, but I'm as guilty as every other coach in these moments. I might have some ideas on how to fill the time in theory, how to squeeze the most out of every time-out, but when I'm caught in the moment, I catch myself trying to download every single thought I've had since the last huddle.

Here I'd noticed that my guys were trying to take control of the game on a single possession. We were looking to go up by fifteen points, just on one shot, doing it all at once, rushing, so I told them all to calm down, to look for the open man, to swing the tempo back in our direction. I had to give American Catholic credit—they were good, they had us on our heels. But we were good too. We just needed to push back.

Basically, we needed to play *our* game—not theirs.

Time of possession in basketball is a lot like time of possession in football. If you can keep a team playing defense for a period of time, they break down. They start to tire. So it follows that if you work the clock each time down the floor, you'll get better shots. Maybe not the first time, maybe not the second time, but over time, over the course of a game, you'll find more and more openings, better and better looks. This is especially so in New Jersey, where we don't play with a shot clock, so it pays to be patient with the basketball. Obviously, you can't do this late in the game, when the clock starts to work against you, but we were only down by a couple points, still in the third quarter, so we needed to slow the pace. And it worked out that we were able to do just that—we ended up reestablishing control and winning the game by eleven points. It was an important win for us, because it was the second-to-last game on our regular-season schedule, so it set us up nicely for a postseason run.

That peak I mentioned earlier in this chapter? Well . . . we were just about there.

Long as I'm on the subject, let me just slip in another few words on time-outs. In high school ball, you're allowed four each game, and I always try to leave two on the board for the end of the fourth quarter. Doesn't always work out that way, but that's my game plan. I've never been big into calling time to chew a player out or to make an immediate correction; I like to see my guys play through their mistakes—or if they can't, I'll find a way to communicate with them during the run of play. In this one respect, I've looked to a coach like John Wooden as a model. Coach Wooden was famous for letting his players figure things out on the floor. His job, he always said, was to work with them in practice, to prepare them for each and every situation, not to sit on their shoulders and micromanage the game as it developed, so I've tried to follow his lead, especially with respect to the careful spending of my four time-outs.

Of course, this approach is subject to change at different points in the season. Early on, when each individual game only matters for what it can teach your players, for what you're building toward, I'll sit on my time-outs as long as possible. I'll let my guys play through pressure or try to withstand a momentum run on their own. But once you get to the postseason, when each game matters most of all, you have to play it a little differently. You have to break a momentum run before you're stuck behind a big deficit, because you don't have the luxury of playing through your mistakes.

It's win or go home—and at St. Anthony, we're never ready to go home, not when winning is an option. Here against American Christian, it didn't much matter if we won or lost. It only mattered later, in the final accounting, when we'd strung together a season full of wins and found ourselves looking at another undefeated season. And so at that point, absolutely, this game against American Christian was critical, but when we were in the middle of it, it was just a chance for our guys to respond to the kind of pressure they'd yet to see all season.

The kind of pressure they'd surely see again.

Back at school, away from the court, Sister Alan was struggling—and her St. Anthony family was struggling right along with her. She'd been a fixture at our games for nearly thirty years, but even more than that, she'd been the heart and soul and spirit of our school. Remember, she came to our school as a young nun, on her first open-ended teaching assignment. And now, to see her in such declining health, to think she might be losing her long battle with cancer . . . well, it was a deepening sadness for our entire community.

We all felt it among the faculty and staff. But the students felt it too—my players especially. Ever since Sister Alan connected with Ben Gamble's group back when he played for me in the early 1980s, she'd formed a special bond with each and every team. She became like a surrogate mom to a lot of my players—making sure they ate properly, stayed on top of their homework, dressed warmly in winter, whatever. She worked the crowd at our games, talking to the refs, talking to our players, like a homegrown, sanctified version of Spike Lee. She was our biggest, loudest, proudest cheerleader, but even more than that, she had our backs. As athletic director, she worked closely with all of our student-athletes, but with our basketball players in particular she was the one who helped to make sure their transcripts were all in order, that they were NCAA-eligible, that they had what they needed at home in order to do their thing in the classroom and on the court.

Even when she left the classroom to take on a more administrative role, she found a way to teach, to inspire.

Meanwhile, Sister Alan struggled. Her presence continued to be felt in our building, but she herself couldn't always be there, and we started to notice a whole bunch of gaps. I suppose we might have anticipated this, on one level. She'd had her fingerprints on just about everything at our school. She ran our Ring Day ceremony for the junior class; she led the programming for all of the religious holidays; she upheld all of the traditions that had become a part of the fabric of our school—and in some cases, she started new ones if she felt they might knit us together as a community. And then, all of a sudden, when she couldn't be in our building every day, we began to see the spaces she'd filled for us.

Left us wondering how we'd get along without her.

Sister Alan hated that she had cancer, and she fought like crazy to beat it. For one thing, she didn't like to lose. (She got that from us, I liked to think.) But for another, she didn't want to miss out. Her life had become so fundamentally intertwined with the life of our high school, with the lives of our students, that she wanted to stick around to see how it all would turn out. She worried about this or that student. She worried about our budget. She worried over both the big picture and every last detail.

Over the last years of her life, we all took our cues from Sister Alan and started worrying about *her*. She had a doctor over at Sloan-Kettering who had her on all kinds of exploratory drugs. Some of them worked, some of them didn't. She had good days and bad days. On the good days, she'd make it into school, and the whole place would be lifted, but then there'd be a stretch of bad days when Sister Alan literally couldn't lift herself out of bed, and her absence would be felt throughout our building. I'd sit with her sometimes as she ran through her laundry list of side effects and weird reactions to all the different drugs and treatments she was taking—like the one that burned the bottoms of her feet—but she was quick to turn the conversation to some other topic.

She hated that she had cancer, yeah, but she also hated talking about it. She would have much preferred to talk about how our season was going, how I thought we'd do in the tournament, how she wanted nothing more than to see this group of seniors finally get their rings. And she did. It would be the last group she'd have a chance to cheer, and I think we all knew it, so it was a bittersweet moment for the St. Anthony community.

Sister Alan died the following year, and one of the great tributes to her life and legacy was that almost every one of my players, past and present, found their way to her wake at Felician College. The place was filled to overflowing with former students—not just my guys, of course, but I noticed my guys most of all. Wherever they were, whatever they were doing, they found a way to make it back to Jersey to remember Sister Alan, and it was a wonderful thing to see. As I sat with my wife, Chris, and took in the scene I realized that a lot of these kids hadn't had any kind of organized religion in their lives when they came to the school. Whatever faith and focus they'd taken away from their time at St. Anthony—that is, the faith and focus that had nothing to do with basketball—was mostly due to this wonderful woman. A nun from Philadelphia who knew as much about the 76ers and the Eagles and Villanova and LaSalle as they all knew about the

Giants and the Knicks and Fordham and St. John's. Who made religion accessible to a group of hardscrabble, hard-charging kids who all needed a little direction in their lives.

She would be missed, that was for sure, but I realized, looking at all these kids filing in and out of Felician College, filling the chapel for her funeral, seeking me out to talk about some conversation or other they might have had with Sister Alan over the years, that she'd continue to be a big part of St. Anthony basketball. That she'd be with us always.

For all our worries over whether we'd see *either* Paterson Catholic or St. Pat's in the state tournament, it worked out that we had to fight our way through *both* teams. We drew Paterson Catholic in the North Jersey semifinal, but we were prepared for them. They were bigger, but we were stronger. Despite our size, we played a power game, but we did it with quickness and skill and efficiency. We won 84–71, which was hardly a one-sided score, but it felt to me like we were in control the entire way. Felt that way to my guys too, because they came off the floor with a ton of confidence, which is what you want to see in the postseason, especially when you know your next opponent is watching.

The North Jersey final, against St. Pat's, was a whole other story. For this game, we came out tight, tight, tight. The contrast was startling. We'd played Paterson Catholic on our own terms, in our own way—meaning we were extremely patient with the ball—but all of that went out the window here. In fact, it looked early on like we were reverting to some of the bad habits that had nearly cost us that game against American Christian. Once again, we were rushing our shots. We weren't making them guard us. We were trying too hard individually.

Ty hit a shot to tie the game at the end of the first half, and I headed into the locker room thinking we were lucky to have kept it this close. Defensively, I thought we'd done a good job in the first half. We'd bothered their big man, kept them from easy shots. Overall, I thought we'd matched up well against St. Pat's. Their size wasn't bothering us. We were doing okay on the boards. But we were playing a kind of hurry-up offense that was taking us out of the game, so I sat my players down and got them thinking back to that time-out against American Christian. Got them thinking about taking control of the game, setting a new tempo. Basically, I wanted them to relax, spread the floor on offense, move the ball a bit better, find better looks at the basket.

At that time, the offense we were running was called a "dribble-drive," which basically meant that, with all those ball-handling, perimeter-type players—five Division 1–bound guards —featured in our rotation, sometimes all at the same time, we were constantly looking to drive the gaps, penetrate, maybe kick it back out to a shooter with an open look. Most high school teams would have a tough time matching up with four or five ball-handlers who could all hurt them off the dribble. However, in running that kind of offense, our guys would sometimes go rogue and play more of an individual style of game and maybe start to rush their shots.

Our biggest problem, first half of this game, was that we weren't working together. Our defense was fine. We'd had some turnovers that led to some points. But our biggest problem was we were too quick trying to make plays when we had the ball. We weren't patient enough—same way we hadn't been patient enough in the early going in that American Christian game. And so I hit those same notes in my talk. It's a lot like in football, I reminded my guys, where time of possession is all important; the same principle applies. You need to make your opponents play defense. You want to make them work, make them spend at least as much time guarding you as they spend attacking at the other end.

One of the things I try to get my guys to do is reverse the ball from one side to the other on offense, to make our opponents play both sides of the court, which allows us to attack the basket a little more aggressively after the ball's been reversed. But that doesn't happen if the first guy who touches the ball tries to make a play.

We were in the home locker room at the Rutgers University Athletic Center. It was like a hundred other halftime talks. These kids had heard it all, but they needed to hear it again. I told them they were a little hyper, told them to slow things down, move the ball around, weaken the defense. And as I spoke I tried to model this behavior in my demeanor. I tried to keep calm myself, which is how I usually play it during big games. Really, I don't think I've ever yelled in a state tournament locker room. There's no reason to. Our kids are so well prepared, so zoned in to their performance, that the flaws in our game almost always have to do with them trying too hard. Trying to do too much, too quickly. So my tone, my delivery, is meant to counter that. Yeah, during the season I'll yell like crazy. During practice I'll yell like crazy. But halftime in a state tournament locker room, that's not the time or the place for me to yell like crazy. It puts out the wrong message. Yelling is for when you're not a team yet, when you're trying to get everyone's attention. Yelling is for when you need to motivate an individual player in practice. But by the time you finish a twenty-six-game regular season, you should have solved all of these problems and the focus needs to be on the game situation, so yelling goes out the door. The thing to do is keep calm, help your players take in the big picture. Make your adjustments.

Second half of the game, we turned it around. We were dominant, but it was a patient, painstaking kind of dominance. By that
I mean we didn't do anything too terribly different on defense,
but we started to take our time with the ball. Didn't happen all at
once, but we started to have better possessions, make fewer mistakes, and the scoreboard reflected that soon enough.

The turning point of the game came on a remarkable three-
point play by Tyshawn Taylor in the fourth quarter. It was one of
those electric, highlight-film plays that can really stamp a game.
Ty took the ball down low and drove baseline, and as he did one
of the St. Pat's big men came across the lane to block the shot. Ty
was somehow able to just hang in the air for the longest time. It
looked for a beat or two like he was levitating, but that's the kind
of natural athlete he was—he could get his body to do all sorts
of incredible things, and here he pulled the ball down just as he
was getting whacked, and then laid it back up again for a not-so-
easy basket. The foul itself was huge, because it was the big man's
fourth foul, and it effectively took him out of the game the rest of
the way, but the fact that Ty was able to stay with the play and
somehow make the shot really lit something in our guys.

It put it out there that we were a different team than we'd been
just the year before. Same guys essentially, but a different team. A
championship team.

At last.

10.

2010–2011: CHAMPIONSHIP HABITS

FATIGUE MAKES COWARDS OF US ALL.
—Vince Lombardi

YOU'RE NEVER A LOSER UNTIL YOU QUIT TRYING.
—Mike Ditka

The story of our 2010–2011 season started to write itself a couple years earlier, with the economic downturn that cut spending and confidence all across the country—in our inner cities most of all. Parochial schools in our area were closing left and right. Families were hurting.

What this meant in basketball terms was that the balance of power kept shifting. All of a sudden, there was all kinds of talent, bouncing around different schools. And it wasn't just a Jersey City phenomenon. It was happening all over. Kids would begin their high school careers in one program, and then that program would shut its doors and those kids would have to scramble.

At Paterson Catholic, money was tight. Enrollment was down. School administrators weren't sure they could keep the place open. We'd had similar worries at St. Anthony, but we'd always managed to raise just enough money at the last possible moment to meet our expenses. One of our biggest challenges each year, apart from trying to raise the money we desperately needed, was keeping all this talk away from the students. It would get in the way of what we were trying to do, what we were trying to build—not just among our student-athletes but across the board—because it's tough enough to teach young people without having them think the rug is about to be pulled out from under them. It's tough to give them a sense of place and purpose if they can't even count on their school being open the next year.

And yet, despite its money troubles and enrollment concerns, the Paterson Catholic boys' basketball team was having an outstanding 2009–2010 season—a season that would turn out to be the school's last. They finished the regular season as the third-ranked team in the country. A big reason for that was that they had one of the region's top sophomores, Kyle Anderson, probably the best pure talent to emerge out of our area in a generation, and an outstanding junior named Myles Mack, a terrific point guard. Their starting lineup also featured Fuquan Edwin, who'd go on to lead the nation in steals the following year at Seton Hall; Derrick Randall, a six-eight junior signed to play for Rutgers; and Jayon James, a playmaking small forward on his way to Iona. That's five starters destined to make an impact in top-level Division I college programs just from this one team, and when we drew each other in the state semifinals that year, it was as if we were playing for the state championship. Paterson Catholic was undefeated, at 28-0; we came in at 25-2. The winner of the game would take the North Jersey championship and face off against the South Jersey champion, Trenton Catholic. Our game was on a Thursday night; Trenton Catholic had won its game on Tuesday, which meant they'd have a couple extra days to rest and prepare for the finals on Saturday.

No disrespect to Trenton Catholic, but our side of the draw was a little tougher that year, our climb a little steeper. Paterson Catholic and St. Anthony were both nationally ranked, so it was generally assumed that the winner of the North Jersey final would go on to take the state title.

Didn't exactly work out that way.

We played great in our game against Paterson Catholic, ended up winning 63–49, leading the whole way. Not a dominant performance, but a strong, gutsy performance, and as we left the building that Thursday night our guys were feeling pretty confident about our chances. It was a big win, a big night—but it was also late for a school night. The game had started at eight o'clock, and I don't think we left the gym until ten, ten-thirty, so it was after midnight before most of our guys got back home. We couldn't really do much more than a light workout the next afternoon at practice, so I just kept them for about an hour. Normally, we'd have gone over our scouting report the day before a big game, but these kids were fried and frazzled, so I sent them home and figured we could do it the next morning before heading out to the Ritacco Center in Toms River for the game.

Didn't exactly work out that way either.

What happened instead was, we brought the guys to the gym that Saturday morning about an hour before the buses were scheduled to take off, went over the scouting report, had a forty-five-minute walk-through, and thought we were all set. I didn't stick around to wait for the bus to show up. Short-hop trips like the drive to Toms River, I like to take my own car, so I left the gym ahead of the team and hit the road. Eric Harrield, one of our assistants, stayed back to ride the bus with the team, along with a couple other coaches, but I like to get where I'm going as soon as I can. On this day in particular. The weather was lousy. A giant nor'easter had been forecast for our region, and the rain was coming down hard, but Chris and I made decent time to the facility. Ben Gamble was in his own car as well, and he also made good time. But there was no sign of the team bus, so we called one of the coaches to get an estimated time of arrival.

Turned out the bus was on the Jersey Turnpike, just passing exit 11, which meant they were headed in the completely wrong direction. Somehow the driver had it in his head that the game was being played at the RAC, on the Rutgers University campus, instead of at the Ritacco Center in Toms River.

I don't think I've ever been more embarrassed as a coach, waiting for our team bus to arrive. I mean, this was the state finals. Talk to people in basketball, talk to guys who've played in NBA championships, NCAA championships, and a lot of them will tell you that the biggest game of their careers was when they played for their high school team in the state championship back home. It's huge. And here we were, ridiculously late, keeping the tournament organizers waiting, keeping the fans waiting, keeping our opponents waiting. There were games scheduled behind us all afternoon, so there would soon be other teams, other fans, waiting too. It felt to me like the whole state was watching. I was furious, frustrated, frantic, fidgety . . . but there was no sense fuming. Mostly, I just paced the gym, trying to get my head around the fact that my guys were due to play the biggest game of their careers in just a few minutes and they were still on the bus, driving through a ridiculous storm.

I was on and off the phone to Eric, trying to figure out the mood of our players, but Eric said most of the guys were asleep. They were so flat-out tired, they didn't even know they were running late, which I took as a good thing. It'd be tough enough getting them dressed and stretched without having them all stressed and anxious about the time, especially considering that the Trenton Catholic players had been ready to go for over an hour.

The game was scheduled for two o'clock that afternoon, and now that I had all this extra time to worry and overthink, this struck me as outrageous. We'd just played a tough semifinal game on Thursday night. Our guys didn't get home until after midnight. Meanwhile, Trenton Catholic had played its semifinal game on Tuesday, so their guys were rested, recharged. I'm never one to make excuses, and I would probably have never focused on it if we hadn't had this screwup with our team bus, but the turnaround time made no sense. You shouldn't ask a team to play a late game on Thursday and then to move on to a state championship game on Saturday afternoon, unless their opponent is going through the same thing.

I only mention it here to show the kinds of thoughts that were bouncing around in my head as I waited for the bus to double back and make it to Toms River. I should have been thinking about the matchup with Trenton Catholic, the few words I'd have a chance to say to my guys as they'd hurriedly dress and get warm, but my focus was off. I was stuck on what might have been, what should have been . . . instead of on what was.

Our guys got to the Ritacco Center . . . eventually. That "Tom Coughlin time" I talked about earlier? That full hour I liked to give my guys to relax and stretch and get themselves mentally prepared for the game? Well . . . that just wasn't happening. Biggest game of the year for us, and it just wasn't happening.

The game finally got going at about 2:45. We went out to a nice lead, and we were up by twelve with time running out in the second quarter, but then Trenton Catholic hit a long three at the buzzer to close it to nine points heading into the half. They left the floor with all kinds of momentum, while our guys kind of shuffled their feet as they went into the locker room, and I turned to Ben Gamble and said, "I think that's gonna come back and hurt us."

And it did. Trenton Catholic came out sharp in the second half, cut the lead to four points going into the fourth quarter.

Then they tied the game at the end of regulation, so we went into overtime.

At the end of overtime, the score was still knotted up.

Second overtime, same thing.

Third overtime, Trenton Catholic had edged out in front, 57–56, to win the state title.

Just like that, we were done.

Paterson Catholic announced a couple weeks after the state tournament that the school was shutting its doors—the latest closing in a troubling trend. It was the third season in a row that a school we'd played during the season had to close the next year, following St. Joe's of West New York and St. Al's of Jersey City.

(The year after that it would be St. Mary's in Jersey City—and the year after that St. Pat's of Elizabeth.)

I hear a piece of news like that, my first thought is for our own program, our own school—but at St. Anthony's we keep dodging that bullet. We keep finding ways to make our enrollment and hit our budget numbers. Just a couple years ago, for example, the former football coach Bill Parcells, who's been a great friend and supporter of St. Anthony High School, stepped up with an eleventh-hour donation of $100,000 to keep the place running, but there was no guardian angel to save Paterson Catholic—and as a Jersey City native, I hated to lose another big-time rival. You grow up playing high school basketball in the area, you go on to coach high school basketball in the area, it's not just a headline to you when you read about these school closings. It scratches at the memories of all the times you went up against those guys in a big game—and it tears at the heart of the city.

My second thought was for the returning basketball players on that team, hoping they all would find a place to play. It's like one big game of musical chairs, but each year, with more and more schools closing, there are fewer and fewer roster spots to go around. At St. Anthony, we don't look at these school closings as any kind of windfall for our program, a chance to add some top talent, because we don't recruit. We don't dream of this or that player who may or may not join our program. However, a lot of families might look to us to see if we might offer a good opportunity for their son, and when that happens, we might get excited about adding a particular player to our program, and that's just what happened here.

Ben Gamble got a call from Kyle Anderson's father, Kyle Sr., just a day or two after the news broke about Paterson Catholic, telling him he wanted to consider St. Anthony for Kyle. School was still in session, but Kyle's dad wanted him to start doing some weight training with our group so he could catch up to what we were doing and hit the ground running if and when he enrolled.

Kyle's decision on where to finish out his high school career was a big developing story in the area because he was such a prominent player, and when folks learned Kyle was leaning toward St. Anthony, a lot of the coverage gave the story an "if you can't beat 'em join 'em" spin. After all, Kyle's team had been undefeated until they met up with St. Anthony in the North Jersey final, so it was an easy hook to suggest he was hopping to the one team that had his number. But it wasn't like that. Kyle was from North Bergen; he knew every player on my team; he'd been to my camps, my clinics; I knew his parents, and they knew me. There was a good fit all around. It made sense, so I was thrilled when he decided to throw in with us—not just because it gave us another big-time player, but because I truly thought it was the right place for Kyle, a place where he could thrive.

From a purely competitive standpoint, we were extremely fortunate to be able to add a player of Kyle's caliber to our roster. Even at fourteen, fifteen years old, you could see this kid had all the tools. Forget that he was six-seven and growing. Forget that he could handle the ball like a point guard and go strong to the basket like a power forward. Forget that he played with an extremely high basketball IQ. Just his ability to pass alone drew your attention. He'd be a real game-changer for us, no question.

Already, we were a little concerned about our returning core from that 2010 team. Jordan Quick and Lucious "Lucky" Jones were still juniors, but they'd struggled down the stretch, and I worried if they could be the cornerstone players we'd need to make it back to the state finals, and if they could lead us back to the state finals as seniors. With Kyle in the mix, though, Jordan and Lucky wouldn't have to be franchise-type players for us—just important pieces to our puzzle. It would take a lot of the pressure off of them.

Some players (even some great players) perform a whole lot

better when you're not looking to them to carry the team, when there are teammates to help with the heavy lifting—and here I'd started to think Jordan and Lucky fit into this category.

A week or so later, I started hearing that Myles Mack might be looking to St. Anthony as well. This was no sure thing, however; Myles was looking at a bunch of schools, and his folks were worried about the transition to our program. Myles was from Paterson, which meant he'd have to take the train to Hoboken each morning, and then switch to the light rail to Jersey City; all told, it would take him about an hour each way, which was a whole lot different than how things were at Paterson Catholic, where his mom dropped him off at school. He didn't really know any of my players; he didn't know me. Yeah, he knew Kyle, so that was a big plus in St. Anthony's favor, but he was also looking at schools closer to home—and as much as we might have wanted to see him in a Friars uniform, I really couldn't say that our school was the best fit for him.

That was for Myles to decide—but happily, he did join our program.

We usually start our spring weight training a couple weeks after the season. That's how it goes in high school basketball these days—it's become a year-round sport, but the emphasis changes at different points in the year. I tell my guys that from April to November is when individual players develop. Our goal as a team— always, always, always—is to make it to the postseason and win the state title, but their goal as individuals is to earn a scholarship to college, to lift their own game to the highest level, and to work themselves into the best possible shape. So we didn't really have to think about integrating Kyle or Myles into our program just yet. Everybody was moving at his own pace, and it worked out that Kyle and Myles were busy playing on their own AAU teams the first part of that summer, so our focus was on our returning play-ers and plugging the holes left by our graduating seniors—Der-rick Williams, who was off to play at Richmond; Elijah Carter, who'd lead Rutgers in scoring as a freshman the following sea-son; Devon Collier, who committed to Oregon State; and Ashton Pankey, who'd sat out his entire senior year with an injury but still earned his way to a scholarship at Maryland. That's a lot of talent, but there was a lot of talent left; we were bringing back Jordan Quick and Lucky Jones and expecting them to grow their games and emerge as team leaders. We were bringing back Je-rome Frink, who'd played a lot for us as a sophomore. Jimmy Hall was stepping up from the junior varsity, along with Rashad An-drews, and I was counting on each of them to take on a big role. And then there was Tyon Williams, who'd suffered a knee injury and had rehabbed as a junior, but we were expecting him back as a senior and figuring on him to be an important player for us.

In June we attended a team camp at Linden High School. Myles and Kyle weren't able to play with us just yet. The Paterson Catholic coaches hadn't placed a whole lot of emphasis on the team camp program, and their players were doing a bunch of different things in the off-season—USA Basketball, AAU, NBA Players Association camp, and on and on. This meant that Myles and Kyle had other commitments they needed to honor, which was just as well because I wanted to see how our returning group might come together as a unit. The Linden camp was the perfect opportunity to do just that. We'd play two-a-day games over a stretch of four days, so in a short time we'd find out a whole lot about our team.

Lately, the way it works is, I hang back during our summer sessions. I want my assistants to get the experience of running our practices and working our sidelines, but I'm there the whole time. I'm taking notes, thinking ahead, looking at the ways we're coming together as a unit. I'm like Red Auerbach toward the end of his career with the Boston Celtics, when he was the general manager. I might huddle with my coaches away from the floor, tell them some of the things I want them to work on, but I try to leave them alone in the gym. I give them the whistle and let them coach—and to judge from this first team camp, they had a lot to work with.

The way it's set up at Linden, it's like a workshop tournament: you play your games at five o'clock and seven o'clock in the evening, or at four o'clock and six o'clock. You stick around and watch the other teams play—not to scout so much as to take everyone else's pulse.

The outcome of each game is not nearly as important as what you take away from each game, what you learn about your players. But there's a clock, and a couple refs, and a scoreboard . . . so at the same time we're playing to win. Here we won our first seven games that week, which put us up against St. Patrick in the last game of the tournament. St. Pat's was a local power, led by star forward Michael Kidd-Gilchrist. Folks around the country now know Michael as one of the major pieces of Kentucky's 2012 NCAA championship team. As I write this, he's just declared for the NBA draft, following his standout freshman season under John Calipari, and a lot of basketball analysts project him as a high-end first-round draft pick, but back in the summer of 2010, Michael was merely one of the best high school players in the country.

Oh, man, this kid could play—but here in this preseason matchup at Linden High School, we shut him down. We put Tyon Williams on him, and Tyon did a good job taking Michael out of his game, which gave our guys a tremendous boost heading into the summer season. We'd run the table at Linden, winning eight games in a row, and we did it without the two big-time players who'd be joining us in the weeks ahead, so I started to think we might be building a special, special team.

We were already good. And we were about to get better.

Transitions are always difficult. It's especially tough on your returning juniors and seniors when you bring in a couple former opponents who can really play. You set it up so they're competing for minutes, competing for certain roles, and even though on the surface that kind of competition can be a healthy thing, it's never easy. There are hurt feelings, bruised egos, but as a coach, you can't really spend too much time on that sort of thing. You're aware of it, absolutely. You talk about it, remind your guys that nobody's job is safe, and then you go about your business and try to get your players to go about their business too.

As good as we'd been the year before—losing in the state championship game after an otherwise successful season—and as good as we expected to be this year, we were definitely a team in transition. That's not a phrase you hear kicked around all that much about a team expecting to win, but in high school basketball, one season to the next, you're almost always looking at ways of bringing new players into the mix and filling in the gaps left by your departing players. There's a revolving door of talent, same way there is in college basketball, so you've got to find the balance between the coming and the going—and here it just so happened that two of our most important pieces were transfers who'd already established themselves among the top players in the state.

One of the ways I tried to bring the team together once Kyle and Myles were able to start playing with us toward the end of the summer was to take a split-squad approach. I had the two new guys play with half the team one game, and then the other half of the team the next game—not because I wanted to high-light their games or put it out that they were now our superstar go-to players, but because I wanted to see how they worked with each and every combination, in each and every role. With two big talents like Kyle and Myles, I needed the integration to cut both ways—I needed my returning players to be thinking how to adapt their games to what their new teammates could bring, same way I needed Kyle and Myles to adapt what they were capable of to *their* new teammates.

By the time the season started, we were beginning to mesh. We struggled in an early-season contest against Gill St. Bernard's when we were outplayed, out-hustled . . . out-coached, probably. But we held on to win. And then, a couple weeks later, we were tested by a strong Massachusetts team, Catholic Memorial, in our holiday tournament up in Boston. We pulled away at the end, but it was close in the first half. They were a well-coached team—and frankly, we weren't hard to defend. We were slow, predictable.

It was while we were away at that tournament that our guys picked up on a rallying cry that would stamp our season. They were watching a Miami Heat game at our hotel, and Dwayne Wade came on for an interview after the game to talk about how the team was still finding its way. Remember, this was just a month or so into the Big Three era in Miami, the first season Wade was playing with LeBron James and Chris Bosh, and Wade said, "We're not a championship team, but we're trying to de-velop championship habits."

I heard that and thought, *That's what our kids need to hear.* So I made sure they heard it. Over and over. Everything we did from that point on, it was all about developing championship habits. Finding ways to get our new players comfortable playing with our returning players—and our returning guys playing with our new guys. We were still integrating, still getting to know each other, just like a Jersey City version of the Heat.

No question, we had all the pieces.

No question, we had a ton of upside potential.

All we had to do was put those pieces together and reach that potential.

Ben Gamble came up to me after that holiday tournament and said, "We'll be able to beat anybody in the state by the end of the season. We just need to keep working."

I didn't see it just yet. I saw us getting better, but I thought the adjustment period might stretch out for a while; I thought there'd be some bumps. Turned out I was wrong. After Boston, we started to gel on the floor. Kyle and Myles worked beautifully together—they were both exceptional passers, with a natural feel for the game—but soon Jerome Frink stepped up and started working off of Kyle as well. All of a sudden, we were looking more and more fluid, more and more focused. It was like our guys had been playing together their whole lives instead of just a few months.

The defining moment of the first half of our season came at the Hoophall Classic in Springfield, Massachusetts, on national television. We were going up against DeMatha, one of our great rivals on the national stage. Morgan Wootten had stepped down as head coach in 2002, but DeMatha was still a power. They were the number-six team in the country at the time of our meeting in January, with five major college-bound players in their starting lineup. By every measure, it should have been a real test, a chance for our guys to add a couple more championship habits to their gear bags, but the game was a blowout. We won by fifty points. Our guys were just outstanding—and here I don't think we can put this on the coach. DeMatha was prepared, same way we were prepared. It's just that we did everything right, played thirty-two minutes of perfect, perfect basketball. No turnovers, no lapses.

Myles Mack wound up outscoring DeMatha all by himself—with twenty-eight points to the other team's twenty-five—and that was with coming out of the game with about three minutes left in the third quarter. He had a tremendous game, but now that I look back on it, all our guys had tremendous games, and I think what happened was we kind of caught DeMatha by surprise. They knew all about our two big-time transfers, so I think they focused a little too much on Kyle and Myles; they seemed to overlook our homegrown guys like Jordan, Jerome, and Lucky, and those three just killed them. And as we put the game away I started to think I'd been guilty of the same thing. Without really realizing it, I'd overlooked the guys who'd been with us all along. I was so laser-focused on getting Kyle and Myles into the flow of what we were doing, I'd lost sight for a moment at *what we were doing*. At what we'd done all last season.

For the first time, in that DeMatha game, I saw what we were capable of. I saw that even though we were a small team, our skill level was way up. We had some deadly outside shooters. Jerome was our big man, at six-five, and Lucky and Kyle were six-five and six-seven, so we had decent size up front, but we were small in the backcourt. Jordan was five-eleven; Myles was five-nine. But Jordan, Myles, and Lucky were all terrific three-point shooters; Kyle could score from anywhere in our end; and Jerome was capable of doing a lot of dirty work for us around the basket—and he could hit a jumper too.

Basically, it was ten games into the season before I figured this team out.

———

We played some really good teams the rest of the way. Friends Central, out of the Philadelphia area. Mount Vernon, who went on to win a state championship. Boys and Girls, who went on to win the city championship—and those two games came on back-to-back nights, so that was an important marker for our season. And yet, as well as we played, as good as we were showing ourselves to be, the consensus in Jersey basketball was that St. Patrick was the team to beat. They'd been the number-one team in the country for most of the season. We'd been in and out of the top ten in a lot of the polls, but never really made a case for the top spot. We were peaking, playing good, solid ball, but most folks seemed to think St. Pat's was at a whole other level. Me and my assistant coaches, we didn't necessarily agree. Our players, we certainly didn't want them thinking that way either. But we kept our opinions to ourselves.

First game of the state tournament, against Hudson Catholic, our guys grabbed an early lead and kept building on it. Ended up winning that game by over thirty points.

Second game of the tournament, the North Jersey semifinal, it was like a repeat of the game before—we jumped out to an early lead, which got bigger and bigger. This game, we ended up winning by over fifty points, so we were feeling pretty good.

St. Pat's had already beaten Gill St. Bernard's by over twenty points in their own North Jersey semifinal game the day before, but I thought it was interesting that they didn't send anyone to scout our game against Oratory. I try to pay attention to stuff like this, and when the game is in your own gym, it's easy to track who's walking in the door. If there are scouts in attendance, coaches or assistant coaches we're about to face, I'll have my guys play a certain way. I'll hold back on some of the things we like to do in certain situations—or I'll put in a new offensive set just for this one game, just to maybe get them thinking in some other direction. We'll play to win, but I'll make sure to leave some of our championship habits in the locker room, and throw a few wrinkles into the mix to keep things interesting.

Soon as I noticed there was no one from St. Pat's eyeballing what we were doing, I decided to break out the entire playbook— and once the game against Oratory was in hand, I had my guys work on everything we might want to use against St. Pat's. That's one of the reasons we ran up such a big score, because I stuck to my rotation the first three quarters and because I told my guys to keep playing hard. Wasn't a question of sportsmanship or playing fair; we were working toward something bigger than just this one game.

All year long, we knew we'd have to beat St. Patrick to take the state title. We'd built our entire season just to get to this one game, and now that it was upon us, I didn't want our guys to still be going up the ladder, still reaching, still striving, hoping to get to some next level. I wanted them to *be* at that level. I wanted them at their best, so I had them run through every conceivable scenario, every inbounds play, every defensive scheme.

That Oratory game was on a Monday night, at home. The North Jersey final was set for Wednesday, two nights later, at Rutgers. It didn't give us a whole lot of time to prepare, but we were ready. Felt to me like the whole world was watching, because it was shaping up to be one of the most talked about games I'd ever been involved in. At this point, we were the second-ranked team in the country, so to have the top two teams squaring off in a game that wasn't even a state championship game . . . well, it was almost monumental. Two tiny Catholic schools, and it was like the clash of the titans. The Rutgers arena was sold out, and there must have been about twenty different camera crews in attendance, along with over eight thousand fans.

It was a media circus, and each team had its own piece of spotlight. A crew from *60 Minutes* had been following us for the past month, led by CBS News reporter Steve Kroft, so they had me wired with a power pack and a hidden microphone. I was also hooked up with the Madison Square Garden Varsity network, so there was a second mike on me as well—and as these young technicians ran the wires from my belt and set me up, I had time to think, *Not bad, Hurley. You're a television star.* On the other bench, St. Patrick coach Kevin Boyle was plugged in to an HBO crew, for a documentary called *Prayer for a Perfect Season,* so when the two of us met at half-court to shake hands before the game, underneath all these lights and flashes, it reminded me of Bobby Fischer meeting Boris Spassky before the start of the World Chess Championship in Iceland.

Okay, so maybe that's overstating things a bit, but in our little corner of the world it was epic—probably the biggest high school basketball game ever played in New Jersey, a state with a rich basketball history.

There was a whole lot riding on this one game for each team. As the top two teams in the country, it meant the winner would have a chance to finish the season as the consensus national champion—while the loser wouldn't even make it to the state finals. In a lot of ways, it was the ultimate win-or-go-home game, because it would put a sudden end to what had been a storybook-type season on each side of the floor.

Let me just pull back a bit and reset the scene. Our team bus couldn't even get into the lot adjacent to the arena. We had to park way away from the facility, and as we walked toward the front doors we could see lines of people trying to push their way inside. Fans were scalping tickets, snapping pictures, asking our guys for autographs. It was unreal, surreal. Soon as we got inside and settled, I sat my guys down and told them to soak it all in. I said, "Look around. This is gonna be some experience. Enjoy this."

But then I tried to get them to shut out all the noise and commotion. My idea was to acknowledge it, maybe even celebrate it, and then set it aside, because I didn't want it to cloud our focus. In our pregame talk, I tried to get our guys to concentrate on our opponent, not the atmosphere. That's why I thought it was important to talk about the crowd and the media straightaway, so we could get past it.

As I spoke, I saw Caroline Kennedy sitting in one of the front rows. Her daughter was an intern on the HBO project, I learned later, so she'd come to show her support, but it was a strange thing to see, a strange thing to have to think about—Caroline Kennedy, out of the corner of my eye, in a packed arena to watch us play. The fact that I noticed her at all in the middle of such a big moment meant I wasn't doing such a good job tuning out all the distractions myself.

Going into the game, I was back and forth with my assistants on how to match up against Michael Kidd-Gilchrist, whose game had only gotten better since we saw him at the Linden camp over the summer. I'll say it again: this kid could play—one of those singular talents who could destroy an opponent all on his own. My first thought was to put Jerome on Gilchrist, but St. Patrick had two other big men Kevin Boyle tended to alternate in and out of his lineup, and I thought I'd need Jerome to neutralize their size. My next thought was to have Kyle guard Gilchrist, but I worried this would put Kyle into foul trouble; Gilchrist was a smart player, and he might look to attack the rim more than usual, which would have left Kyle vulnerable.

Last time we played St. Pat's, we had Tyon Williams on Gil-christ, but Tyon was hurt, so I looked finally to Lucious Jones. This was no easy decision. Last year, down the stretch, Lucky hadn't been so lucky for us—he couldn't guard anybody, which was why I'd been worried about him heading into this season; I worried how he'd respond to the pressures of leading the team in big games as a senior. But guess what? He'd really turned things around on the defensive end. Jordan Quick too. I think having guys like Kyle and Myles around really took some of the pressure off my two returning seniors, so Lucky got the assignment, and I knew he was up to it.

Our warm-up was crazy. The crowd noise was unbelievable. The arena had a real NCAA tournament atmosphere to it—didn't feel like a high school game by any stretch. I'd coached over 1,100 games at that point, and I'd never seen anything like it, and as our guys tried to get loose I worried that the size of the crowd and the moment would go to their heads.

St. Pat's won the opening tip and pushed the ball down the court for an easy layup to start the game. Three seconds in, and we were already down 2–0, and that set the tone for the first quar-ter. St. Patrick put nineteen points on the board, but somehow we managed to score thirteen, so it was only a two-possession game. Trouble was, it felt to me like the St. Patrick points came easy and our points were a struggle.

Second quarter, our guys tightened things up on defense. Whatever nerves or jitters they'd been feeling as the game got under way appeared to settle, and we started to play much better. We ended up outscoring St. Pat's in the quarter by a point, which made it a five-point game, only here we were better able to dictate the pace and flow. Now the St. Patrick points were a little harder to come by, and the St. Anthony points were a little less of a struggle.

At halftime, I huddled with my guys and put it on them to analyze our first-half performance. I said, "What's holding us back? What did you feel like out there?"

I went up and down the bench, polling every single player, and each one talked about how nervous he'd been. I'd expected nerves to play a factor, but not to this extent. A couple of my players said they'd never been more nervous in their lives, so right away I thought this was something we could use. I thought if I could get them to see that once they got into it, once they adjusted to the crowd and the noise and the magnitude of the game, they played better. Whatever jitters they'd been feeling when the game started, they'd managed to set them aside.

I said, "Relax."

Just one word . . . *relax*.

And here again, I tried to match my demeanor to the message. My insides were churning, but I knew I had to appear relaxed to these kids if I wanted to put my point across.

I let it sink in, then I reminded everyone that we were the underdogs in this game. It wasn't a role we were used to playing. Wasn't even a role I liked. But it helped to have the crowd pulling for us. We'd survived the first few minutes of the game, after being down by as many as ten points. We'd cut it to a five-point lead. We'd been having good possessions. And now the crowd was pulling for us even more.

I said, "Let's go out in the second half and try to be a little more relaxed on the offensive end. If you have an open shot, take it. Look for the open man. Do the things you've done all season long just to get here. Don't let these guys take you out of your game."

The third quarter tilted our way at first. We went on a nice run to take the lead, but then St. Pat's answered with a run of its own, to go back up by five. We were back and forth, up and down, but when St. Pat's pushed the lead back to five, I thought I had to do something to put a kind of stamp on the quarter, so with about three minutes to go in the third I called for a time-out as we brought the ball across half-court.

I called a play we'd put in just for this game—for a spot just like this. A standard side-out inbounds play, with a few extra twists. Kyle Anderson would take the ball out of bounds, right in front of our bench, which was on our end of the floor. Our guys would line up in a kind of diamond formation, with Myles Mack up top, Jerome Frank and Lucious Jones at the foul line, and Jordan Quick underneath the rim. At the slap of the ball, Jordan was supposed to cut to the corner off a screen set by Jerome. He was our first option, but there were a series of other options off of that. If Jordan didn't have a good look, he would cut to the opposite corner, setting a screen on Jerome's man on the way, and Jerome would roll toward the rim off of that, looking for a lob. If the lob wasn't there, Lucky would cut toward Kyle for a straight inbounds pass—and this turned out to be the option we used.

Kyle hit Lucky; Lucky dribbled back to Kyle and kind of handed the ball off to Kyle on a dribble exchange; Kyle then moved to the middle of the court just as Jordan set a screen on Lucky's man. Lucky cut to the basket, and Kyle found him for an easy layup.

It was a dazzling play. We called it "Diamond," and we ran it three or four times a year, only in big spots, only in big games at the end of the season. When it worked, it was a thing of beauty— and we spent a lot of time on it in practice, so it usually worked. We'd even worked on it during that North Jersey semifinal against

Oratory, so it had been game-tested just two nights earlier. It was fresh. There are so many moving parts to the play, so many cuts to the basket, it starts to look like a piece of choreography, but our guys had all the movements down.

It takes much longer to describe than to run—in all, it took just a couple seconds.

We got a lot more than two points off of that layup. Sometimes a successful play does a lot of extra business for your team, beyond the result on the scoreboard. It can change the flow of a game, or get your opponents thinking in a whole new way. Here, it put the crowd on our side. They'd been with us all along, but now they were really pulling for us. The arena was filled with die-hard basketball fans, and they appreciated the movement, the second- and third-look options, the simplicity of the play. You could actually hear the crowd kind of ooh and aah as Lucky went up for the finish, and you could see the St. Patrick players looking a little dazed and defeated on the back of it.

They weren't on their heels just yet, but we'd turned the game around.

Last couple minutes of the third quarter, it's like the energy in the gym shifted completely to our side. We started finding every loose ball, hitting every open shot. We were up. They were down. And the crowd was completely with us. Basketball fans, they always like to root for the underdog, and we weren't used to thinking of ourselves in just this way—but we were happy to be the underdog if it put the crowd behind us.

We were down by just one point at the end of the third quarter, so I reached deep into our playbook and told our guys to be prepared to switch to a zone defense we'd been working on all season. I wanted to throw a whole other look at St. Pat's as they came down the floor, maybe push them off their game plan a little bit more, and this zone seemed like just the thing. The zone was called "the Amoeba," and I'd accepted an offer to speak at a clinic in Fresno, California, just before the start of the season for the express purpose of learning it. Essentially, the Amoeba is a 1-1-3 zone used by a lot of coaches on the West Coast. You don't see it a whole lot in our part of the world, although we'd used it a couple times during the season in small doses—just to give our guys a feel for it. And so, in the huddle between quarters, I said we'd switch to it if we could go up by a couple points, maybe use it to get a little separation and put the game away.

St. Pat's came out tired to start the fourth quarter. This alone wasn't so remarkable. A lot of times teams had trouble keeping up with us for an entire game. They might get off to a strong start, but we were so fit and focused, they couldn't run with us the whole way, and that's just what happened here. It was only remarkable, though, if we could find a way to turn the other team's fatigue into some kind of advantage.

We started the fourth playing man-to-man, extremely physical. Started forcing St. Pat's into taking quick shots. On offense, we were able to run the ball, get Myles out in the open court. We really picked up the pace of the game, and as soon as we managed to push the lead to four or five points I had our guys switch to the Amoeba zone.

The great thing about the Amoeba is that it's deceptive. It looks like you're playing man-to-man. You pick up the other team's ball-handler at half-court, with just one defender. Your other guard is positioned back near the foul line, and he'll start to defend off the first pass, and here again it looks like man-to-man. But then what happens is that the initial defender who'd been up top drops back toward the lane, and you're able to play much more aggressively than you would in a typical zone. It's a very

confusing zone to go up against if you've never seen it before—
and even if you've seen it a time or two, it can be unsettling.

St. Pat's didn't really recognize what we were doing, couldn't
really respond to it, and we got a couple big stops to really put the
game away. At one point we shut them down for almost four full
minutes, and by the time they figured out what we were doing
the game was out of reach. We outscored them 23–5 in the final
quarter, to win 62–45, and as I left the arena that night, after
the excitement and the hoopla died down, I reminded myself that
momentum can be a powerful force in a basketball game. We'd
pushed all the right buttons, at all the right moments, and managed to turn a great team into a team that did not play like a
great team. Michael Kidd-Gilchrist, a great player who did not
play like a great player, couldn't solve our defense or turn things
around. He scored only seven points—none in the second half—
and I had to think it was all about using momentum to advantage.

We went at it hard, all game long, and once the game swung
our way, we went at it even harder.

The win vaulted us into the number-one spot in the national
rankings—but more important, it put us back in the state finals
with a chance to avenge last year's loss to Trenton Catholic. At
least, that's the way it looked on paper, but Trenton Catholic
ended up losing in an upset to Cardinal McCarrick in the other
semifinal game, the South Jersey final.

For the second year in a row, our guys boarded a team bus on
a Saturday morning for the trip to the Ritacco Center in Toms
River—only this time we made double sure the driver knew
exactly where he was going. Show up late one year for the state
championship, it's just a screwup, a onetime thing. Show up late

a second year, you're a Mickey Mouse program. You teach your guys to carry themselves like the 1927 New York Yankees when really you're like the 1962 New York Mets.

This time we left an hour or so earlier, just to be on the safe side. And this time we came out on top, even though we weren't as sharp as I would have liked. Clearly, our guys had peaked in that semifinal game against St. Patrick. That ladder we'd been climbing all season? That game against St. Pat's was the top, and everything fell the right way for us so that we were at the top of our game, but we still had a couple games to play.

We kept teetering on the top of that ladder, but just barely. We got past a strong Newark Central team in the semifinal game of the Tournament of Champions the following Friday, even though we weren't nearly as good as we'd been against St. Pat's at Rutgers a week earlier. We were tired, flat. And then we staggered past a feisty Plainfield squad in the Tournament of Champions final on Monday—once again not looking anything like the world-beating team we'd put on the floor against St. Patrick. As we gathered in a team huddle after the game, I thought back to the triple over-time loss the year before and the momentum shift that seemed to kick in just after that. I thought of the great good fortune we had to add two stud players like Kyle Anderson and Myles Mack, the championship habits we'd been able to call upon as we integrated our two new players with our returning players . . . and it all added up to this right here.

11.

2011–2012: THE SURVIVORS

**TODAY I WILL DO WHAT OTHERS WON'T, SO TOMORROW
I CAN ACCOMPLISH WHAT OTHERS CAN'T.**
—Jerry Rice

**IT'S WHAT YOU LEARN AFTER YOU
KNOW IT ALL THAT COUNTS.**
—John Wooden

Coach long enough and you start to notice a framework to each season. Literally, a framework. Every year there'll be some matchup early on that repeats itself late. Or there'll be some carryover from one season to the next, some echo or answer— almost like we're following a script. In 2010–2011, it was the run-in with Michael Kidd-Gilchrist and his St. Patrick teammates in that preseason camp at Linden High School, which set the stage for our North Jersey final. After that, it looked for a while like the state final that followed would be a rematch of the year before— only Trenton Catholic couldn't get past Cardinal McCarrick, so we started in on a new story.

These big-time games against our big-time rivals frame our seasons, and I've come to think it's what we put inside the frame that gives the true picture of how things were. Like this year, we struggled in that preseason scrimmage against Gill St. Bernard's, which we ended up losing. Back of my mind, I had a feeling we'd see Gill St. Bernard's again. At the time the score didn't really matter one way or the other, but it started to matter as we moved through the tournament field; it started to matter that Gill had already seen us when we weren't at our best.

Why did it matter? Well, it mattered because I never liked to give an opponent a reason to feel confident going into a game against us. It mattered because the Gill St. Bernard's coach, Mergin Sina, now had a book on us, even though a lot of that information was slightly off or out-of-date. I like to be the coach with a book on my opponent. I like to know as much as I can about the team we're about to play, and I like it even more when the opposing coach knows next to nothing about us.

But like I said, it was only a back-of-my-mind sort of worry. A lot of things had to break just right for us to meet up with Gill St. Bernard's in the finals, but as the tournament got going that's just what happened. It's like the matchup was inevitable. After that one-sided game against Oratory, with Kyle Anderson showing the basketball world what he could do, we beat Dwight Englewood in the North Jersey semifinal by another big score. Meanwhile, on the other side of the bracket, Gill St. Bernard's was running through its half of the draw, beating St. Patrick and Cardinal Mc-Carrick, setting up a possible showdown in the state final.

Probably, I was the only guy at St. Anthony thinking back to that preseason scrimmage, which came about by pure chance. Probably, I was the only guy regretting that game—not that we'd lost, but that we'd set it up in the first place. Normally, I don't like to play a meaningless game against a team we might meet later on in a meaningful game, even if it's just a scrimmage. I repeat myself, I know, but it's an important point. There's a lot you can reveal about the way you play, your tendencies, your strengths . . . even if you make an effort to hold some things back. Here we'd made no such effort, and it was starting to worry me, until I reminded myself that the St. Anthony team we were running out on the floor for the tournament looked nothing like the St. Anthony team we had run out at the start of the season. Back in December, we'd had a whole different cast of characters, a whole different look and feel to our team. We had Jimmy Hall before he'd been suspended. We had Tim Coleman before his season-ending injury. We had Rashad Andrews, who was serving an early-season suspension but still figured in our plans. Jerome Frink had been out with the flu, and a lot of his minutes went to Kentrell Brooks, who likely wouldn't see a whole lot of time in the final unless the game went lopsided, one way or the other. And we were without a big effort from our two terrific junior guards, Josh Brown and Hallice Cooke, who had yet to play consistently at an impact level but who'd each been coming on strong.

Still, I was getting ahead of myself with these worries, because we first had to get past a resourceful Hudson Catholic team in our North Jersey final, while Gill St. Bernard's had to face an always dangerous Trenton Catholic squad. Turned out we had an easier time of it, with a 53–30 victory to push our record to 29-0 and earn a spot in the state final. Gill St. Bernard's had a tougher time of it, going down 16–2 to Trenton Catholic at the end of the first quarter, but somehow they battled back to tie the game at the end of regulation and came out on top by a single point in overtime.

And so there we were, back at yet another state final—again at the RAC. The way it worked out, our guys handled Gill St. Bernard's pretty well. Jaren Sina, the coach's son, had a killer outside shot, and he was able to get his points, but we didn't give these guys anything down low. They had a six-seven big man named Dominic Hoffman, on his way to Bucknell, and our guys essentially took away his inside game. The Gill guards kept looking for an entry pass that just wasn't there. We came at them with a balanced, purposeful game plan—and we stuck to it, especially in the second quarter when we just buried them, 19–4, putting us up 28–8 at the half.

We eventually pushed the lead to 34–8 at the start of the third—a deep, deep hole for any team. But I wouldn't let my guys see me celebrate just yet. Wouldn't let my own thoughts get out in front of the game clock, but I knew there was no way Gill St. Bernard's could climb out of that hole. Rest of the game was all about preserving our lead and keeping our guys fresh for those Tournament of Champions games after the state final.

After the game, I started telling reporters that this group was the best defensive team I'd ever coached. This was true enough, but I said it mostly to motivate my guys. All season long, we'd been a team without a defining personality. Yeah, we had one of the top players in the country in Kyle Anderson, so in some respects Kyle defined our style of play, but that didn't get close to describing how we played as a team. Kyle was a big part of what we'd been able to accomplish—going 30-0 to that point, on our way to the school's twenty-seventh state championship—but he was only a part. We had big, game-stamping contributions from five or six different guys over the course of the season, and it was tough to predict where those contributions would come from, one game to the next.

One reason I had such a tough time assessing our team was that our lineup had been in a constant state of flux. The cast of characters kept changing—and there were stretches in there, with all the personnel problems we were having, when some of my players really did seem like characters. (Like a bunch of clowns, really.) But then, as I looked back at how our guys had played, the numbers they'd been putting up, the stops they'd been accumulating, I started to realize that this was a special, special group on the defensive end. We'd taken teams out of their game all season long.

You have to realize, I'd also been telling reporters and folks who followed St. Anthony basketball that we were a perfectly imperfect team. I'm afraid I rubbed the shine off that phrase over the course of the season, but the sentiment behind it was fresh each time I said it. Our record might have been flawless, but we were flawed. There were holes in our game that our opponents had yet to find a way to exploit. That didn't mean we wouldn't come up against a team that could figure us out—just that nobody had done so yet.

On defense, that's where we excelled. Just look at the stats: through this state final game against Gill St. Bernard's, which we won by a score of 67–39, we'd given up an average of just 35.6 points per game. That's a historically low number, especially when you look at all the big-time teams we'd played this year, against all those big-time players. And in four state tournament games, we'd only given up 30.7 points per game against the best teams in the state, winning by an average margin of about forty points.

In this, we were led by Josh Brown, who had kind of willed

himself into becoming an outstanding perimeter defender. He'd shown flashes of his defensive abilities the year before, as a sophomore in a limited role, but he was on and off during the current season. He'd shown he could be a force with the ball too. He's lightning quick to the basket, with a solid outside shot and a steady handle, but it was his ability to read his opponents and stay one step ahead on defense that set him apart.

Trouble is, we'd never know which version of Josh Brown we'd get. These past few games, he'd been mostly excellent, but there'd be some games where he was hardly a factor. Even more troubling, there'd be some practices where his head seemed to be someplace else, and around the time I had to suspend him for that one game against Long Island Lutheran I started to think there was a deeper problem. Really, I'd become so concerned with Josh's erratic performance, his unpredictable energy levels, his occasional inability to focus, I started to think he was hanging with the wrong crowd away from the gym. Making poor choices. Maybe smoking weed. Really, I didn't know what to think.

Soon as I confronted Josh with my concerns, he was up front about what the problem was: he wasn't eating. Not enough, anyway. And not any of the right foods, in the right balance, at the right time of day. Wasn't exactly his fault. Wasn't anybody's fault, really. But it was still a problem. This was a kid who was being raised by his father, who was almost never home. His father worked two jobs. So it fell to Josh to take care of his own food, and he wasn't doing such a smart job of it. He ate take-out Chinese a couple nights a week. The rest of the time, he ate leftovers, or not at all—and during the school day he was usually running on an empty stomach.

It's tough enough for a kid to get through school without a healthy breakfast or a balanced lunch, but to then make it through a practice—one of *my* practices . . . well, it's no wonder Josh was flagging.

Turned out there was an easy fix. We put Josh on a program where he was able to get a good hot breakfast at St. Anthony's every morning and another hot meal at lunch. Together with my assistant coaches, we tried to monitor how he was feeling before he took the floor, and there was a complete turnaround. And I don't think it was just the undernourishment piece that turned Josh's game around, although obviously that was key. No, I think the biggest reason Josh was able to lift his game was because we showed him we believed in him. We showed him we cared. And he responded by playing the best basketball of his high school career. Keep in mind, he'd already played at a high level from time to time—high enough to sign a letter of intent *as a junior* to play for Temple University. But now it looked like he'd be able to keep playing at that high level consistently. Now he would have an opportunity to thrive—and he did. On the defensive end, down the stretch, he was our most valuable player, and here against Gill St. Bernard's, a team known for its ball movement and three-point shooting, he did as much as anyone in a St. Anthony uniform to set the tone and stamp the game and make it our own.

The turnaround with Josh got me thinking that this was a team of survivors, so that's another angle I started to mention when I talked to reporters about our season. I mentioned it to my players as well, tried to use it as another motivator. I kept telling them we were here because of them, because they'd each found a way to survive a season of turmoil and uncertainty. I made it a point not to mention the fact that we were undefeated on the season, because I never wanted that string of victories to get in the way of what we were trying to accomplish one game to the next. That stage of the season, when a single hiccup could end our year, no victory was as important as the next victory. As far as I know, the players didn't talk about it either. It just kind of hung in the air, that streak, hovering over our season.

It was for others to talk about. It was for us to play ball.

And here we were, still playing. We'd seen a bunch of players go, but the ones who remained had kept us in the fight. As individuals, a lot of our guys had managed to overcome some obstacle or other. Kyle Anderson had found a way to make the best of a bad situation when he learned that Paterson Catholic was closing its doors. And here he was. Josh Brown had found a way to get past my doubts about his off-court behavior and get his body to perform at an optimum level and lift his game right along with it. And here he was. Tariq Carey had transferred from a program where he wasn't encouraged to play to his strengths and he had survived a bunch of midseason struggles with me to become an important player for us off the bench. And here he was. Jerome Frink had powered past a couple nagging injuries and a brief bout with the flu to emerge as a dominant big man, coming into his own as a player at just the right moment, while he was still being recruited by a number of college coaches. And here he was.

But it was as a group that these kids really dug in and came together. This alone was surprising, because as a group they looked nothing like the team I thought I'd be coaching this year. Remember, we'd graduated four players from our undefeated national championship team of the year before, but then we went and lost another seven players who figured on making a contribution to this year's squad. Seven! As a coach, you try to prepare for these kinds of disappointments, but that's a big, big number. There's no way to really prepare for that kind of turnover in personnel. We'd lost these players to injuries, suspensions, and preseason or midseason transfers—all of which meant there was now an opportunity for seven other players to step up and fill those roles.

Somehow we'd found those seven players.

Somehow we'd helped those players find their way into the mix.

And now we'd go off into battle with this new and improved group. The survivors. The last guys still standing.

No question, defense wins championships—and here our swarming, suffocating style of defense had taken us to another state title. Now it only had to see us through a couple Tournament of Champions games to put a cap on our season—but this was no small thing. As I've written, these games became tougher and tougher each year because we'd be coming off a big adrenaline-high in winning the state championship. That was always our goal, what we played for. The other teams in the field were facing down the same deal, of course, so what you usually wound up getting was a group of talented teams staggering to the finish line. Doing what they could to keep on keeping on. It was almost like taking a victory lap when you were already tapped and being told you still had to beat all these other runners taking the same victory lap. In theory, these Tournament of Champions games were an exciting add-on to close out the season, but it was hard to keep our kids focused and playing at an all-out level.

And so we staggered on.

We beat Atlantic City in the tournament semifinal by another big score, 72–42, which set us up for a final-round showdown against Plainfield—another frame to our season. We'd already faced Plainfield back in February, when Jimmy Hall was still with us, and we'd managed to beat them in their gym by a dozen points, but they were a tough draw. Frankly, I would have much preferred to go up against St. Joseph's, Plainfield's semifinal opponent, if only because they hadn't seen us before; we didn't have any real history. But we don't get to choose our opponents, so we prepared for a real grudge match. Plainfield had been the best public school team in the state for back-to-back seasons. After beating them in the Tournament of Champions final the previous year, I'd pronounced them the favorites to win it all this year, because they'd have their entire team back. We were losing four key players, and at that time it didn't appear that any of our younger players could step up and fill those roles.

But here we were, back in the finals, a rematch of last year, and I wanted to eat my words. That regular-season game in Plainfield, the final score didn't reflect how we dominated. We missed a ton of easy shots and should have won by a much bigger score, and I mention this here not to thump us up but to show that our guys had every reason to feel confident going into this game. They'd outplayed Plainfield on both ends of the floor, so they were liking our chances.

Me, I liked our chances as well . . . but I still worried. Always, I worried. And as it shook out, I had good reason. Plainfield coach Jeff Lubreski had figured us out.

He'd seen us last year, to end his season.

He'd seen us this year on his home court.

And he'd seen enough.

Our guys came out listless, made a couple stupid fouls early on. Josh Brown got into foul trouble in the opening minutes, so he had to sit. This was a problem, because he'd been guarding

Plainfield's best guard, Sekour Harris, and now, with Josh out, the game opened up for Coach Lubreski. Plainfield began playing at a high tempo and getting a bunch of open looks, while our guys were scrambling.

Soon, Jerome Frink and Hallice Cooke got into foul trouble of their own, so I had to sit them as well.

As the first half wound down, I saw that we'd committed ten team fouls, putting Plainfield in the double bonus—meaning that every one-and-one became a two-shot foul—while our guys had yet to take a single free throw.

We were tied at the end of the first half, 25–25, and we were lucky the game was still close. Plus, Plainfield's big man, Yale-bound Justin Spears, went down with an ankle injury, and that was potentially a real game-changer, on both sides of the ball. As a coach, particularly at the high school level, you never like it when an opponent is unable to play you at full strength—at least, *I* never like it, although I've met a number of coaches who'll take a win any way they can. Me, I like to beat a team at its best, so I hated to see this young man go down.

As it happened, Spears left the game in the first quarter but came back in the second half. He was hobbled, but his mere presence on the floor seemed to give his teammates a boost—and now that I look back on it, I wonder how the game might have played out if he hadn't gotten hurt.

I decided to play it cool in my halftime talk. As always, I wanted to keep calm and let my kids know I had every confidence in them, only inside I was churning with doubts. Inside, I thought we'd wasted sixteen minutes, a chance to put some points on the board. After two quarters, we were dead even, and it meant Plainfield now only had to shut us down for sixteen minutes more. But I wouldn't let my guys see my concern, so I said, "We'll be fine.

We just got into foul trouble, that's all. Let's keep them off the line and play our game."

And that was our game plan—the only way to play it. It had been our strategy going in, and it would be our strategy going forward, so long as I could keep my key guys on the floor and they could get into some kind of rhythm. Happily, that's just what happened as we started the third quarter. We started hitting some big shots and pushed it to an eight-point lead.

Kyle wasn't having a strong shooting game, but his all-around game was outstanding. He finished with four steals, four assists, five blocks, and six big rebounds, but he couldn't get some of his shots to fall. As it was, he still managed to score fourteen points and keep us in the game, but his teammates helped him out on the offensive end.

Tariq Carey wound up playing his best half of basketball for us, hit some monumental shots, finished with a season-high eighteen points, but it was Jerome Frink who really came up big. There was a stretch, late third quarter into the fourth, when it seemed like this kid just couldn't miss, and he ended up with twenty-six points, shooting 13-23 from the floor. Curiously, amazingly, twenty-one of Jerome's shots came from inside ten feet, and yet he didn't draw a single foul. Plainfield kept going to the line and hitting their free throws, and we just couldn't get a call, even with Jerome playing such a physical game underneath our own basket.

Still, we had a dominant ten-minute run to put us up by fourteen with about three minutes to go when the wheels nearly fell off our perfect season. All of a sudden, we struggled. All of a sudden, we couldn't hit the open man. We couldn't hit our shots. We couldn't get out of our own way. We were finally going to the line, but it's like we didn't want these easy points—we kept missing our free throws. Turned it over in a couple crucial spots. And in that same "all of a sudden" span, Plainfield started hitting a bunch of threes, and when they hit a final three with about ten seconds to go in regulation, it felt to me like the game was slipping away from us. They'd pulled within three.

The clock was with us. The momentum was against us. And the crowd . . . well, the crowd always pulls for the underdog. No, Plainfield wasn't an underdog in any kind of traditional sense, but we were the defending champs. We were nursing a perfect season. Plainfield had been down big and had scrambled back in the closing minutes. Plus, they were a big public school, with its own rich basketball tradition. It was a neutral-site game, but Plainfield had way more students and alumni and boosters than St. Anthony, so the Izod Center fans were now pulling for them . . . big time.

At this point, late, we were in the double bonus, because Plainfield had to commit a lot of fouls to stop the clock and get back in the game. We shot a lot of free throws, and we missed a lot of free throws.

We inbounded to Hallice Cooke, who was fouled immediately. He had a chance to put the game out of reach, but he only managed to hit one of his free throws, so Plainfield still had a pulse; they could have pushed the ball the length of the floor, drained a quick three, and then hoped like crazy for a quick turnover . . . but we kept them from getting a good look and that was that.

You never know.

That's the thing about this game, this season, this team. We'd just come off an absolutely brilliant stretch, playing some tremendous team defense. And here the emphasis was on our *team* defense, because a lot of our guys were not individually talented as defenders. This is not a knock on any of my players, because they came together and played great, but they did so as a unit. They were fundamentally sound and complemented each other well. Over time our school's best defensive teams have been teams that were able to defend full-court and pressure their opponents and force turnovers. They were quick, running teams, characterized by quick, running players. But this team was not like that. This team played more of a half-court defense, more of a team defense, and we really didn't force a lot of turnovers.

We just denied, denied, denied. All game long. We had a lot of guys with long arms, so we were able to use our length to deflect or disrupt passes. To challenge shots. We made it hard for the other team to get comfortable. And then, on the back of that, we were always able to out-rebound our opponents, so we defended in a different way. We attacked the boards. We clogged the lanes. We stood our ground.

All through the tournament, and in the Atlantic City game, our defense was lights out, so it made sense to think that was how this game would go—but, hey, when the prognosticators talk about how a game might go, they don't really have a clue until the game gets going. And here I was guilty of the same thing. Coaches are the same as anyone else, the way we play the game in our heads before we play it on the floor. That's what I'd started to do here. I looked back to our regular-season game in Plainfield, when we held them to thirty-one points, on a shorter floor. You'd think, in the Tournament of Champions final, on a much bigger stage, on a much bigger floor, that number might even go down a little bit, but Plainfield went out and doubled their point total.

Yeah, we won, but we gave up sixty-two points—the most we'd allowed an opponent during our two-year undefeated string.

It's why you play the games. You can talk about them, and prepare for them, and train for them . . . but until the opening tap, you never know.

You just never know.

POSTGAME

What Winning Has Meant

BE STRONG IN BODY, CLEAN IN MIND, LOFTY IN IDEALS.
—*James Naismith*

MY FATHER GAVE ME THE GREATEST GIFT ANYONE
COULD GIVE ANOTHER PERSON. HE BELIEVED IN ME.
—*Jim Valvano*

In forty years as head coach at St. Anthony, I've had the great good fortune to coach seven different teams that have managed to go undefeated over the course of an entire season, on their way to state titles. I've spent the past couple hundred pages sharing the stories of those seasons, together with the story of my life in and around basketball. I could have just as easily focused on seven different teams from seasons when we fell just short, or seasons when our players were still learning how to win, and there would have been a whole other batch of player profiles and game strategies to consider. After all, there are as many lessons to be taken from loss and struggle as there are from winning. But I've chosen to shine a light on these seven teams because in many ways they represent the best of our winning tradition at the school.

For the record, I want to point out that four of these seven teams were named national champions—five, if you count last year's team, the 2011–2012 squad, which finished 32-0 and extended our unbeaten streak to 65-0, earning us the top spot in a couple national polls.

Each of these seven teams has added to the lore of our program and made the kind of mark on our community that has only raised the expectations for our team in succeeding seasons.

Each of these seven teams will be remembered in the halls of our school, in the streets of Jersey City, and among our extended St. Anthony community for a great many years to come.

But also for the record, let me be clear: these undefeated teams didn't work any harder or deserve anything more or better than any of the other teams I've been blessed to coach. All they did, really, was put themselves in position to win—practice after practice, possession after possession, game after game—which is what all my players have tried to do. It's just that with these seven special groups, it worked out. (Even with that *frustratingly* special group of 2004 seniors, it worked out.) Over and over, again and again, it worked out. In a whole lot of ways, big and small, it's because of these seven undefeated teams that each and every player who's played for me at St. Anthony has had a model of excellence to inspire him to put in his very best effort.

Think about this for a second: *all* of our four-year players have won a ring. Each and every one. I don't set this out to brag or to blow smoke my own way, but it's one of my proudest, most enduring accomplishments as a coach, and so I share it here: every single player who started in our program as a freshman (either on the freshman team, the junior varsity, or the varsity) and continued playing with us all through high school has graduated with at least one state title. Heck, *most* of my guys have two rings. Some—not too many, but some—have three. And a couple even have four. Four championship rings! That's saying something— not about me, but about the culture of winning that has attached itself to our school. Only *I* didn't put it there. No individual player put it there.

But there it is.

People ask me all the time how much longer I'll continue to coach, and I don't have an answer. I have some ideas, but I can't know for sure because it comes down to health and a whole mess of other factors beyond my control. Right now, I'm feeling great and things are lined up in my life in such a way that I don't even think about hanging it up. Really, it's the furthest thing from my mind, and that's because I get more out of coaching now than ever before—probably because I can put more into it.

Here's what I mean by that: I retired from my career in probation in 2001, and from my job with the Jersey City Parks Department in 2008, so now my time is my own. Now I've found the sweet spot. Now I can coach without distraction. It used to be I'd get to the gym and my head wasn't always right for practice. Something at work had maybe set me off, or I was agitated by some detail or other, and I wasn't able to focus. Days like that, practice could sometimes be a chore, but that doesn't happen anymore. Now I get to fill my days doing what I love, without having to run all over the place chasing a paycheck, and that's been a real game-changer for me because, let's face it, there's a clear difference between work and play, and coaching for me is clearly play. It's like that old line about a bad day on the golf course . . . well, a bad day coaching is better than a good day of working, I'll say that.

I'll also say this: the folks at St. Anthony, they have it down by now. The cooperation at school, from the administration and our board of trustees, has just been tremendous. They support what we're doing with the basketball program because they've realized after all these years how much what we do on the court supports what they're doing in the classroom. It all ties in.

The school itself is in good shape. I'd like to say we're in tremendous shape, but it's only tremendous by comparison to how it's been in recent years. Everything is relative. We're still desperate for money. We're still forced to stretch, to make a little look like a lot. We still sweat the holes in our budget. But we're still here, and that's the main thing. St. Al's, St. Michael's, St. Mary's, St. Anthony . . . if you had lined up all the Catholic schools in our area a decade ago and tried to predict which would be the first to have to shut its doors because of declining enrollments or funds, a lot of people would have pointed at us. But the other three have all closed in recent years, and that's been a trend throughout the region. In Philadelphia, in New York City, Catholic schools are closing like crazy, but we're hanging in, hanging on. As I write this, we're in the black for the year, after the kind of impressive early-summer push that almost always follows a successful season for the Friars, and we're in the silent phase of a capital campaign that we all hope will give us some sustainability, some cost certainty in the years ahead. Traditionally, we carry about a $1.2 million shortfall in our budget each year, but the idea is to get our endowment up so we can maybe bring that annual deficit down to $700,000 or so, which is a much more manageable number.

The immediate future for St. Anthony High School looks okay. Wouldn't say it's bright, but we're okay. Academically, we're doing great. I've actually got a couple of my players being recruited by the Ivies, which I take as a measure of our success in the classroom. It's a credit to these particular kids, absolutely, but it's a reflection of the environment where they've managed to thrive. Our principal, Charlie Tortorella, has done a phenomenal job with our curriculum, putting programs in place that help ensure our really bright kids are being pushed and challenged and that our kids who struggle aren't being left behind. And our teachers, in turn, have done a phenomenal job of carrying out Charlie's vision.

I've got more resources to work with than ever before. Used to be I had to buy basketballs and reversible practice jerseys out of my own pocket, but now there's a budget for that kind of thing—thanks, at first, to Sister Alan—and for the past twenty years or so we've been sponsored by Reebok, so they've been good about outfitting our kids and making sure they take the floor looking like a real team.

A lot has changed since I started coaching—not just in my own life or in the halls of our school. For one thing, the game itself has changed. Probably the biggest difference has been in the way kids now specialize in just one sport from a very early age, the way basketball has become more of a year-round game. Back when I was a kid, we played everything, and even up until the time I started coaching I had a lot of guys on my team who also played for our baseball team. In the last ten years, however, I've only had a handful of kids who played baseball. There's just no time for them to develop at any kind of high level—not if they want to keep pace in either sport. The upside to this is that kids are facing better and better competition, at a younger and younger age. When I was growing up, we rarely got a chance to play against the best ballplayers in the city. We just played the other kids in the neighborhood, but now kids can test themselves right away. Now there are all these camps and tournaments and clinics. Now kids coming into high school have been exposed to more coaching, more input from adults who've been around the game.

The downside, though, is that young players don't always take the time to work on their individual games. Basketball skills are developed by repetition—the day-in, day-out stuff we used to do without even thinking about it. Like the way I developed my left hand as a kid. Like the way Terry Dehere, who didn't even start a game for St. Anthony as a junior, went out and worked so hard all spring and summer before his senior year and turned himself into an entirely different basketball player—one who'd eventually take his game all the way to the NBA, all on the back of hard work.

You don't see that anymore, I'm afraid. And it's not because kids today aren't into it the way we were into it. Not at all. Today's top high school players are dedicated, they work hard, but they don't have the single-minded laser-focus we used to see, and even when we do see it, they're kept so busy with their relentless schedule of games and tournaments, there's no time for them to do anything away from their structured sessions with their teams. They're *always* in season, which means they're being cheated out of that all-important downtime—that loose, lazy, unstructured time when you're alone with a hoop and a basketball, free to do your own thing.

I'm afraid we haven't left any time on the table for today's young players to come into their own, and this worries me, at least a little bit. On an individual basis, you can almost always make the case that each new layer of structured development—personal trainer, nutritionist, shot doctor—is in this or that kid's best interest. Yeah, today's player is bigger, faster, stronger than ever before. The game has become much more physical, and so we surround these kids with all these different specialists, to make sure they can find a way to compete. That's great. But it's the bigger picture that has me concerned. It's the ferrying back and forth, the constant game pressure. There's no letup. There's no time for a young phenom to wander off to the playground, just him and a ball, just to work on his left hand.

It's our job at St. Anthony to make sure our kids don't burn out, and happily that job doesn't just fall to me. We've been blessed over the years with any number of caring, knowledgeable assistant coaches who take it upon themselves to guide these young players through some of these difficult paces. If I come across an assistant coach who really cares about the kids but who's somehow lacking in some technical area, if there's an aspect of coaching he needs to improve, I'll coach the coaches, because it's the caring part you can't really teach. If it happens the other way around, if a guy knows his Xs and Os but can't really be bothered with any of this other stuff, then he's of no use to us. Same way it takes a village to raise a child, it takes a community of coaches and educators and role models to raise a champion, and that's what we're all about. We're out to teach these kids to win, on the court and in life.

Another big thing I've noticed the past bunch of years is that high school students seem to know less and less about stuff that seems to matter more and more. This is not a knock on our school or on any specific group of kids from any one part of the country. No, it's across the board. It's a generational thing, I think. It's part of the fallout we're seeing from our technological age. The flow of information running to and from these kids is just staggering. They're plugged in 24/7. They're wired and good to go, but underneath all of that instant messaging and texting and Tweeting there's not a whole lot being said. The simple art of conversation is somehow being lost—and so, with this in mind, we try to use our road trips to advantage. We get these kids in the car, headed to an away game or a camp or a tournament, it's an opportunity to get them thinking about something new. Last thing in the world I want is for them to put their headphones on, put their hoods up, and go to sleep.

We talk about music, politics, business . . . whatever pops up on the radio. On one trip, I made my guys listen to the oldies station on Sirius, and it turned into a lesson on the British Invasion and what the Beatles meant to doo-wop and Motown and '50s rock 'n' roll. These kids had all heard of the Beatles, of course, but they were never really asked to consider their impact on popular music, so we talked about it. Another time we talked about a World War II general I'd just read about. And just this past year, on our annual trip to the Hall of Fame in Springfield, Massachusetts, I made the team watch a documentary on Oscar Robertson, which was all about his high school career at Crispus Attucks, a segregated school in Indianapolis. Most of these kids had heard of Oscar Robertson, but none of them knew his background. None of them had seen footage from his playing days. And none of them knew about the racism he and his teammates faced on their way to winning the first state championship in the country by an all-black high school.

It was a powerful piece, and some of the kids were really moved by it. Some of them wanted to keep the conversation going, so we talked about Pete Maravich, another player they'd all heard about and never seen play, and the all-white team he played for at Louisiana State University. We talked about Bear Bryant, who was somehow considered a pioneer for integrating the University of Alabama; in reality, after his team got completely destroyed by the University of Southern California's Sam "Bam" Cunningham, he was just trying to compete.

Always, you can tell by the questions they ask (and the questions they don't ask) which kids are into it, which ones have an active mind, which ones are willing to be exposed to new ideas. Usually, there's some correlation to how they're doing in school— meaning that the kids who are active and engaged during one of my "lectures" in the car on the way to a tournament are the same kids who are active and engaged in the classroom.

Probably the best lesson we have to teach these kids is self-discipline. Without it, they're nowhere. They've got to learn to grind through a thing if it's not going well. Whatever it is, they've got to slog through it. You know, I love it that these kids move on to some big-time college programs after finishing their St. Anthony careers. I love it that some of them make it all the way to the NBA. But I don't care if they don't play another minute of organized basketball after they graduate, as long as they take away the work ethic we've tried to instill in them. As long as they're organized, diligent, focused. As long as they can recognize an area where they're weak and try to turn it into a strength. That's what I've seen as my main job these past forty years—preparing these kids to set and meet their goals.

But there's one thing I can't teach them. Never even bothered to try. And that's an enthusiasm for the game. They've got to love it, and that love for the game has got to come from within. You can go through the motions on a basketball court, same as you can go through the motions in anything else, but you've got to love, love, love the game. You've got to eat, drink, and sleep the game. If you just like it okay, if you can take it or leave it . . . well, then you're not going to be successful. It asks too much of you, takes too much out of you. And what the game itself doesn't take, I'll be there with my hand out, taking a little bit more besides. My assistant coaches, they'll be there with their hands out too. We're pretty demanding of our players, and over the years the kids who've managed to dig deep and give their all have been the ones who are passionate about the game.

They're here because they want to be here, because they can't imagine themselves anyplace else.

It's just like any worthwhile pursuit. You want to be a doctor, you've got to love it, because if you don't love it, if you're not good in science, if you can't find your way around a lab, you better be prepared to put in twice as much work as the guy sitting next to you in class.

The only way to be successful is to outwork the other guy.

Truth is, the seven undefeated teams profiled in these pages have lifted our entire program and helped to stamp my time at St. Anthony. But it's one thing for this group to have given every other group a boost, a leg up. It still falls to all of my other players, all of my other teams, to climb the rest of the way. Consistently, and over time, they have done just that. Our school record books are filled with a bunch of long winning streaks that maybe didn't stretch across a full season, and even with a few losing streaks I'd sooner forget. We've won a bunch of state championships—twenty-five, and counting. And perhaps most important, we've sent nearly two hundred players to continue their basketball careers at collegiate programs across the country—most of them on full scholarships, most of them carrying the hopes and dreams of their families, often as the first in their household to graduate high school and attend college.

And so, while it may seem that this book is a celebration of these seven undefeated teams, my hope is that it comes to stand for something more than that. Something bigger. Something *else*. My hope is that by revisiting these unblemished, undefeated seasons, we can celebrate the entire St. Anthony community and the hundreds of young men who've run the floor for the Friars with purpose and preparation.

They are champions all—and they inspire me every time I step into the gym.

ACKNOWLEDGMENTS

I wouldn't be in a position to write this book without the talents and extra efforts of all the players I've coached over the years—even the ones who might have cost me a few gray hairs and a couple of sleepless nights. I'm also indebted to all of the coaches and assistant coaches who've made my job easier, especially Ben Gamble, and to the faculty and board of trustees of St. Anthony High School, who have helped provide a winning environment for our basketball program—basically, for giving me something to write about in the first place. At home, I'm grateful to my family, most especially to my wife, Chris, for supporting me in every endeavor, including the writing of this book. The book wouldn't have happened at all without a push from Mel Berger of William Morris Endeavor, and his colleague Jim Ornstein, who put it in my head that this was a project worth pursuing. They also put me in touch with my co-writer, Daniel Paisner, who helped me to gather my thoughts and present them on paper in a page-turning way. I thank them all. Finally, I must thank Sean Desmond and his talented team of associates at the Crown Publishing Group, particularly his assistant editor, Stephanie Knapp, for believing in my story and working so tirelessly and creatively to bring it to wide attention.

INDEX